To Lauren
Peace & Love

"I knew that no matter how big or fancy the house
we lived in was, we were still the same old malnourished,
Medicaid card-toting, free lunch-eating, hand-me-down-
wearing foster children we always had been."

One Woman's Incredible
Journey From Foster Child to
World Championship Boxer

Being

TOO
FIERCE

Lisa P. Cohen
with Tansy Howard Blumer

ISBN: 978-0-578-17131-9

Printed in the United States of America
Signature Book Printing
www.sbpbooks.com

Editor:
Tansy Howard Blumer, Washington, DC 20008
(tansy@starpower.net)

Book and cover design:
C. Baker Johnson, C. Baker Johnson, LLC, Bluemont, Virginia 20135
(baker@cbakerjohnson.com)

Front and back cover photos of Too Fierce:
Fredde Lieberman, Lieberman Photography, Silver Spring, Maryland
(www.freddefoto.com)

This book is dedicated to the children growing up in foster care as well as the ones who have aged out. Some of you have had good experiences and some far worse than mine; either way remember that family can be whoever you choose to invite into your life. Just be fierce enough to take a chance.

Table of Contents

Preface

An announcer's voice is calling out, *SHE'S DOWN!* Just after I throw that final left hook and Kathy goes down, the ref shields her with his body and calls a halt to the bout, and I let my legs give in and just drop to my knees on the canvas in a double-slow-motion kind of way. It feels natural — my arms fully extended forward and my forehead touching the mat. As I stay there holding that bow, I'm thanking God with everything I have. Time stops while I don't even move, and soon I stop hearing the crowd and start seeing myself better than ever before.

I begin to rise up slowly from the canvas, first my head and then one knee at a time. A new heaviness in my body makes each movement take longer than normal but the higher I get, the lighter I feel. I'm starting to float again. Now the clouds in my head are clearing but I still have to cover my messed-up left eye to see things best.

I start tuning in on the audience clapping and yelling. My heartbeat is pounding out of my chest and new energy is surging through my body. I sprint to a corner of the ring, leap onto the third rope and bounce twice, gloves to the sky and give out a victory shout. I'm into it now, and pretty soon I've done the same routine in all corners of the ring.

I trot back to the center where my trainer Reddz is waiting with his cocky smile of sureness stuck just so. He starts the business of coaching by pulling out my mouthpiece and blotting my face, neck and arms with a clean white towel. He cuts the tape from around the laces of my gloves, snatching each one off with a yank, and then starts peeling off my sweat-soaked hand-wraps. The adrenaline is pumping like mad and I can't even feel those blows I took in nine rounds. My hands are trembling like crazy.

As I start to come out of my trance, the ring announcer — in the most perfect baritone voice I ever heard — says, "The new I-F-B-A Junior Featherweight Champion, Lisa "Too Fierce" Foster! The ref is raising my right arm high and Reddz grabs my left and raises it the same. As the promoter places that precious huge white and gold, stone-incrusted leather belt around my waist, a dozen flashbacks start to cycle through my mind and I'm hearing voices from my past.

My first trainer Gene's voice is saying; "Don't leave it in the hands of them judges!" and then my brother Mark's voice is saying again and again, "Lisa, dance like Ali! Dance like Ali!" But then I'm hearing that mean bitch Mama Graves reminding me over and over, "Nobody don't want you," and after her, a chorus of those fakers at the gym back in DC just waiting for me to give up as they mutter under their phony grins, "She ain't shit." I guess hearing those last ugly voices is why I collapsed right there on the spot when Kathy finally went down. I always knew I could do it. I always knew they were wrong, and now that I finally won, the feeling was too overwhelming for me to stay on my feet.

In that amazing moment I feel a distinct shift and things seem like they have started working more smoothly. Sort of like I am the world with a bent axis which gets straightened out with a slight nudge so now I'm spinning just right. Whatever that correction is, it turns out to feel even better than winning the title. I can't put my finger on it but it gives me the idea that things will be different for me now.

Coming into that fight I heard a rumor that I was a 13-to-1 underdog. My opponent Kathy "Shake 'em Down" Williams dominated as a champion in the junior featherweight class, with over 25 amateur bouts and a 13-and-2 professional record. A tough police officer from Thunder Bay, Canada, and according to all the experts, she was a real shoo-in for the title. No wonder they thought she'd beat me; my record consisted of only 2 amateur bouts with one loss. I had to challenge all contenders and champions to even get a crack at the championship, so my pro record coming into the bout didn't look like much with a record of only 4 wins, 2 losses and a draw. I can see how people might think I'm a 'tomato can' with just enough boxing skills to get by, and an easy stepping-stone for the up-and-coming title holders and media darlings in my division. I guess it's why a woman named Cassandra, a new, very green fight commentator froze when she climbed into the ring to interview me right after I beat Kathy. She knew exactly what she was going to say when Kathy won, but she hadn't prepared herself to share a mike with an unknown like me. I was ready to pour out my feelings into that mike — I wanted to speak out loud and proud like Ali — to say something to make the doubters sit up and pay attention to me. But Cassandra was completely speechless and never asked me a thing.

The thing those managers and promoters and odds makers never took into account was my 13-and-0 record in another tough game — the Washington, DC foster care system. They didn't know that 'Too Fierce' was one determined young black woman who overcame abuse, neglect and downright evil-ass people my entire childhood. I became a successful contender in that foster care world first and what I learned along the way would help me make it in the boxing world too. It would be a lie to say that winning wasn't a big deal for me or that the opportunity to perform in such a huge arena was enough without the winning. No, winning was the *only* deal for me and all my chips were on the table that night when I went nine successful rounds with the cop from Thunder Bay.

That mysterious shift I mentioned — the straightened-out axis that gets the world spinning right — is a feeling that has repeated all my life as a sign of a change occurring in me. Those moments always seem to end up being extraordinary, so I am always expecting something to change afterwards — maybe something about how I look, or how I think, or maybe my health — but never knowing just what. The feeling of anticipation but not knowing what it's for is in itself quite overwhelming. Kind of like a kid finding herself in an empty amusement park with free access to all the rides, candy and food she can handle but all she does is stagger around with a huge smile plastered on her face and some serious intent. I felt like that little kid when I stood in the ring on May 15, 2002 while that enormous championship belt was being fastened around my waist. I had been chasing it with everything I had since 1996 and now it was mine! At last that underdog label was torn away and replaced with the *World Champion* label. That night those patrons at the Treasure Chest Casino Resort in Kenner, Louisiana should have skipped the slots and table games and put their money on Too Fierce with her 13 to 1 odds.

People expecting me to lose never bothered me when I was chasing the championship; if I did lose, I didn't let myself feel real disappointment or let-down. After all, I was there to fight, so either way the experience was going to be good. But, man, when I did win, that instant influx of fans, and the greater respect from boxing promoters, managers and critics was worth all the waiting and hoping and all the work that went into the training and fighting. The impressions I had of that night of winning my first championship carried me for three surreal days until on the third morning I woke up with all the blemishes, aches and swelling from the fight feeling much better and proclaimed to myself that I was really and truly the undisputed champ. I thought with a big grin on my face; *Yes, it's really here, I'm touching the championship belt and it's mine!*

After that amazing fight, memories of the first time I ever saw a championship belt in real life came rushing back. I was back in Atlantic City, scheduled to fight Mary Shaida, an up-and-coming contender from California. My first two pro fights had been in meager venues, but this one was at the upscale Tropicana Casino Resort and I was impressed. There was an all-female card consisting of women coming from the US, Canada and Europe who were defending and competing for vacant titles in three weight classes. I was there to start fighting my way up the ladder. When I arrived at the hotel with Gene, my trainer at the time, I was looking all around and admiring the fancy billboards and posters which announced the show with beautiful photographs of the main eventers. We were on our way to get some food when I saw, coming towards us on the up escalator, Kathy "Wildcat" Collins followed by her entourage. I noticed right away that she was carrying her championship belt and I just stared at it in awe. It was bright white leather with shiny red stones sparkling in the lights. While I stared at it, I was thinking; *That's so fly! I'm gonna get me a belt of my own!*

Just seeing how Kathy proudly owned that belt gave me goose bumps! When I back-stepped to get a better look at her, our eyes met. Then we both stopped in our tracks. It seemed like she sensed that I was a boxer too, and I caught how she automatically went into a little defensive mode, pulling that prize belt a bit closer to her body. I flashed her a big smile, offered a gentle fist bump, and said a warm "How you doin'?" She relaxed a bit and smiled back while we bumped fists and exchanged *good lucks*, ending with a mutual, "See you at the weigh-in."

As Kathy walked away, I sneaked another quick look as she slung that beautiful belt over one shoulder. Then I whispered to Gene how one day I was going to win me one of those. Gene said "Yeah" but then he pushed me to hurry up before the line at the café started to snake out the door. I started to walk but then stopped and said to Gene in a really serious voice, "I'm gonna to be ready, Gene. And I'm not gonna stop training even if I don't have a fight coming up. I just gotta be ready for a championship."

"That's what you s'posed to do, Fat Head," he said, laughing.

"And while they sleep on my skills that phone will start ringing," I said, dead serious. By now, we were standing in the buffet line choosing our food and Gene started complaining about my plate not having enough food on it. "How you think you gonna fight with no fuel in your body? Eat!" he ordered.

I plopped another serving of pasta on my plate, rolled my eyes and pooched my lips the way I do when I'm showing some attitude, then said, "Okay, I'll take some more food then. But you gotta know I'm serious about what I'm saying, Gene."

Then Gene got his own attitude on and raising his voice a bit said, "Yeah, I know, now *EAT!*"

I have always had enough unleashed anger to be a good fighter. My brother Mark used to be an in-and-out-of-jail type of guy and is one of those people who loves to fight. He and I have the same taste for fighting, but he likes to engage in unplanned, disorganized street violence. As for me, I like the planned, scientific kind of violence that happens in a boxing ring. Some may say that I went through more than my share of trainers in the seven years I studied the sweet science of boxing. But this was nothing new to me; before I was finally old enough to enter the Independent Living program of the DC Foster Care system, I had lived with more than my share of foster families, only two of which seemed to care about me like a family member. The rest seemed only in the business of fostering for the money and the saintly reputation that comes with the title of foster parent.

Unmanageable and hardheaded are just two ways a few people described me when I was boxing. And to that they usually added that I asked way too many questions. Well, with boxing it was my ass on the line, so I did what I felt I needed to do to survive. It's not an exaggeration to use that word — *survive*. A boxer has to piss or get off the pot. So piss I did, like a horse on a big ol' rock because I knew I had to learn quickly. In the boxing game, if you can't perform quickly and well, everybody disappears and you are on your own again.

But when I was a child, many of the black folk — teachers or my foster parents — described me harshly as: "Too dark-skinned;" "Can't read;" "Country pickaninny", "Nothin' but the devil in her." Hearing this, I got used to being on my own and feeling I needed to keep my guard up most of the time. As things turned out, spending much of my early life without the stability of a loving family and being bounced around from one foster situation to another turned out to be good preparation for getting beat up in the ring and surviving even stronger.

In boxing there's someone in charge in your corner trying to keep you out of harm's way. That someone works with you every day to get your body hard as steel and holds your corner while you take a minute to get your wits back after a blow. But when I was growing up in foster care, it seemed like most of the time nobody was there to cover my back. Usually all I had was drifters passing through just long enough to give me bits and pieces of life's vital information. I had to put those bits and pieces together myself because when I was a child I didn't dare ask any questions.

I took to boxing because it felt so familiar and comfortable. The honesty of the sport is what really sold me on it. It's not like those passive-aggressive sports where opponents 'accidentally' put you out of commission while you try to slam a little black disk into a net or carry a funny-shaped pigskin ball across a goal line. To me, nothing seems more honest and true than climbing into a ring and going toe-to-toe with another woman of the same approximate weight and experience.

An old Pug once taught me, "You can *play* basketball, football, tennis and all the rest, but you *can't* play boxing." He stammered those words through his partially paralyzed lips and peeped at me through his permanently drooped eye while I listened intently, trying to absorb every drop of his experience and wisdom. It was comforting having guys like him around the gym. They defined the traditional old school of hard knocks for me. In those days, Midtown Youth Academy where I learned to box was the school of hard knocks, and those guys were its philosophers-in-residence.

Eugene Hughes — Gene — was my first boxing trainer. He had been an amateur coach of young boys and men in the DC area for more than 20 years. His grassroots boxing and youth center was a safe haven for many of the underprivileged and at-risk boys and girls in the then-poverty-stricken neighborhood of Columbia Heights in DC. Every day after school, those kids flooded in and out of Midtown Youth Academy to do their homework, play video games, use the computer, or get in a few rounds of boxing even if they weren't serious about competing. For many, boxing was a way of staying sharp for whatever might come their way within the small space in which they traveled.

Sometimes in the summer, Gene left the front door open until midnight to make his young charges welcome and keep them from becoming delinquents or victims of dangerous activity right there on the 14th and W Street corner. Once a US Army tank was stationed diagonally across the street from the gym. I wondered if it was because the drug scene was so bad there or if there was some sort of national threat that nobody was talking about. But nobody even bothered to ask about that tank. In fact, it seemed to me that I was the only one bothered by it while everyone else kept on with business as usual.

Gene began boxing as an adolescent in DC after he was rescued from the streets by his long-time trainer, Sonny Boy, who spotted him in one of Gene's many neighborhood brawls. Gene was no bigger than 110 pounds all the way up through the high school years, but he took on all comers, big or small. When I met him, he was in his early to mid-sixties. His 5'6" build was accented with a slight shadowing of former muscle definition and some puckers of loose skin left from recent weight loss. He was born with one leg much shorter than the other and camouflaged his limp with a slow, confident pimp walk bolstered by a cane carved with two looping elephant heads on the top and African designs from its neck down. His true age couldn't be gleaned from his smooth pecan-colored skin, but clues to his many years had been embedded in his face by those familiar expressions he used over and over again.

Gene is the first trainer to take me seriously as a potential fighter. Although I was to go on and train with other trainers in my boxing career, he was the one who first gave me the confidence I needed to mix it up in a violent sport. He still presides — although now from a wheelchair — at the Midtown Gym in DC. If the many framed pictures of me on his wall are any indication, I think he is proud of my career and of his role in making me a professional fighter.

Eleven years after my confidence-building victory for the world title, I was in creative writing classes at the University of the District of Columbia, working on a long-delayed college education. I was bursting with stories from my life and started cranking out drafts and taking them to class to read. I had not anticipated the emotion and the laughter that my stories elicited from classmates. They were already a bit awe-struck by my aloof persona and the way I dressed up for class while they wore the familiar jean-based student garb. But now they were hearing my stories and waiting eagerly for my next turn to present another. Clearly, there were no foster children in the group and foster care problems were new to most of these students.

While they were enjoying hearing my stories, I was finding that telling them satisfied a deep-seated need to talk about what my life had been. This book has taken me several years to write, but has provided me with a satisfying way to dispel some of the ghosts of the past and move into the next phase of my life. In that phase, I will continue to look for ways to make people hear what goes on in the foster care system, and maybe even have a part in bringing about some badly needed changes.

Chapter One

HOME SWEET INSTITUTION

Case#: T 513.207.6

```
    The Ponder family became known to the Department
of Human Services in December, 1963. This referral
was due to extreme marital discord and possible
battering of the children. It was also reported
that Mr. Ponder had a drinking problem and he would
take out his hostility by beating the children.
It was alleged that Mr. Ponder had burnt two of his
children. The investigation seemed to indicate the
burns were accidental and the case was closed in
July 1964.
    The case was reopened in August, 1966 when Mrs.
Ponder was hospitalized at St. Elizabeth's Hospital
for psychiatric observation. The children were
without adequate care and supervision. There were
four admissions to Junior Village when Mrs. Ponder
was hospitalized at St. Elizabeth's Hospital. The
children were again placed at Junior Village when
Lisa was born.
    Lisa was committed to the Department of Human
Services as a neglected child on December 11, 1969.
A Section I Complaint (extensive danger to life
and health) had been filed on September 18, 1969,
as a result of alleged abuse, inadequate care, and
failure of the mother to provide supervision...
```

My being born in April of 1968 in Washington, DC only weeks after the worst riots in the nation's history says a lot about how my childhood would unfold. I arrived on the 15th — only eleven days after Dr. King's assassination —

while the overwhelming sense of black anger and pain still lingered heavily in the air. The hundreds of torched buildings and thousands of shattered windows and mounds of soot and trash filling many city streets suddenly called attention to the simmering ghettos that had long been ignored.

I was born in Freemen's Hospital, but unlike most babies, I didn't go home with my mother. Instead, I was taken away to be cared for at Saint Ann's Infant and Maternity Home, an institution for abused, neglected, and abandoned children and pregnant and parenting teenage women. In the meantime, my troubled mother paid another of her frequent visits to Saint Elizabeth's Mental Hospital as a patient. During her absence my four brothers — Jeffrey age 1, Mark age 3, Anthony age 7 and Winston age 8 — were staying at Junior Village, the place where Anthony and Winston had been housed since 1963. That hellhole on the southwest side of the city was at the time one of the last-standing orphanages in the country.

My father was Minor Ponder. I know nothing about him other than what my brothers have told me. I have no recollection of ever meeting him in person and have only seen a single photograph of him; in his Army uniform. He and my mother remained in their troubled on-again off-again marriage long enough to be the biological parents of all five of us. Mark adored him and told fairytale-like stories about him fighting in the Korean War and getting stranded in the jungle where he survived by eating birds' nests and bugs. It all sounded very confusing and gross to me, but when I saw the pride Mark took in telling about our father, I felt proud of him right along with Mark.

Winston, on the other hand, told a different kind of story which focused on our parents' rocky relationship. He started by acknowledging our mother's problems: "You know our mother is sick and that is why she do the things she do." Then he continued with his version of our parents' marital problems. "Daddy is a truck driver who has to drive all night sometimes. But when he comes home, our mother don't understand and puts him out of the house. One time he came home and gave her a roll of money right after he got paid. It was wrapped with a rubber band. When she found out he had been drinking before he came home, she got so mad with him that she took the whole roll of money and flushed it down the toilet as soon as he walked out the door."

"They used to fight a lot," Winston would say, following up with a frightening example. "One day when our mother got real mad at our father, she waited until he was good-and-sleep, then hit him in the head with a high heel shoe. He had to go to the hospital because the heel had a steel rod running through it and it got stuck right in his head. Euww… blood was everywhere." But Winfred was always careful to add in his protective way, "Remember, our mother is real sick and can't help the way she is."

I really didn't understand what Winfred meant, because whenever I heard the word sick, I thought of the common cold or flu. One day I asked him, "Then why don't she just take some medicine and get better?" He laughed and said, "Not that kind of sick. She sick in her head."

"Oh," I answered with a regular voice, still not understanding.

The city wasn't the only thing that took a beating in those days. My family was a disaster area too. After being cared for as an infant at Saint Ann's, I was eventually returned to my mother and brothers to live in her tiny two-bedroom apartment a few blocks from Howard University. By then, my brothers were being cycled regularly between her home and Junior Village. While black tensions seethed in the city, the anger and tension which had long been present in the Ponder household continued to boil after I arrived. Soon the family came unglued for good and we would never again live together as a family.

By the time I was born, an organization called For the Love of Children (FLOC) had been in business for three years. Founded to save the underprivileged, abused and neglected children being warehoused in Junior Village, it was FLOC's highest priority to shut the place down. The organization remained dedicated to the idea that whatever alternative solution they might find, surely DC could do a lot better than housing its needy children in such an appalling, overcrowded place. Finally, in 1973, Junior Village became just an embarrassing memory when it shut down for good. It had been considered by many to be "a breeding ground for future criminals," and based on all the horror stories I heard from my brothers who were shuffled in and out of that place over the years, I think that is not too far from the truth. Lucky for me, I was too young to have any memory of that sorry-ass institution.

The ward for older children was where my six-year-old brother Mark learned to fight and to stay on his guard day and night, fists clenched, sharp-eyed, his body coiled and ready to spring like an angry rattlesnake at all times.

The infants like me and my brother Jeff were plopped into another ward, packed three and four into standard-sized cribs separated by gender and watched over by overworked black caregivers who had only enough time to peek into the rows of cribs to make sure the crying was not due to illness or injury.

A former social worker once told me, "I couldn't stand going over there. It was right across from the water treatment plant, so before you even got to the place, the stench from the plant would hit you in the face. When I'd drive up, the first thing that would come to mind was *concentration camp* because of all the tents set up in the yard surrounded by fences." She continued, "See, the place was only designed to house three-hundred children at a time, but before it was all over there was more like nine-hundred. That's why they had to add those tents, otherwise there would have been children literally left out in the cold." Hearing that, I had a hard time accepting that I was in that mix as a baby. I tried to imagine what my older brothers had gone through there. Mark had once told me, "Man, I can remember just like it was yesterday how I would just be sitting down watching TV, not bothering nobody. And this boy who was just a little bit bigger than me would ball his fist up and punch me in the same eye every time he walked past me. I used to just sit there and cry but nobody ever said anything. That shit used to hurt bad, too, man! But one day I got real mad and just waited for him to come over there, and right on time he did… Man, Lisa, I beat him up so bad that I scared myself. And you know what, the people who worked there didn't even say nothing. As a matter of fact, they used to set up fights between the kids for their own entertainment. I guess that's why I started fighting so much. I said to myself, *I ain't never gonna let nobody hurt me again.* After that, nobody else even wanted to fight me."

When I think of that story, it kind of explains why Mark got into so much trouble in school, wound up in reform school and then went to jail so many times. Every time he felt threatened at Junior Village he reacted emotionally like a traumatized war veteran reliving old battles. But he was only six.

Though I have never had any kind of real conversation about this with my second oldest brother, Anthony, it has always been plain to see that he took a mental beating through it all. Whenever I've asked him anything about Junior

Village, he drags out a comment like, "Yeah, I remember staying at Junior Village." The blank darkness in his eyes lets me know that I might as well not even try to go any further. Then I wonder; *Were my brother's experiences at Junior Village so traumatic that he has completely blocked them out?* I tell myself that Junior Village could be part of the reason Anthony has somewhat opted out of society both socially and mentally. Maybe it is why he does just enough to make it in life.

Winston, on the other hand, has freely talked about being there. Without giving any real detail, he tells me, "When Anthony was nine and I was ten, we used to go over to where Mark used to sleep and visit him sometimes. We couldn't see you and Jeffery because y'all were real little. There was a lot of little babies in there. And it was loud. Sometimes I tried to go in there anyway to make sure y'all were alright."

It should be comforting to know that there was a big brother coming to check on me no matter where I was, but after hearing how chaotic and understaffed Junior Village was, I can only thank God that we all came out of there alive. And for the millionth time I ask myself; *why in the hell would our own mother allow us to be subjected to such a horrible place as Junior Village? Why didn't she fight to keep us with her no matter how hard things got?*

I was to stay warehoused at Junior Village until I was 18 months old. It was then that the Parkers — Raymond and Ida — came into our lives. They were to be the first of many foster parents in my life. How lucky it was for me at that tender age the Parkers were loving and generous people and not evil like some of the other ones I was to live with as I tried to grow up.

Chapter Two

COUNTRY FOLK

Case #: T 513.276.6

Lisa's stay at Junior Village was marked by steady progress and growth. Earlier observations in the family record mention Lisa's nearly total lack of affect, very withdrawn behavior, almost autistic in nature... At the time of her release to a foster home, cottage counselors described her as a very sweet child, affectionate and outgoing. She has reasonable vocabulary for her age.

Lisa has only one health problem of concern. She has been to DC General Hospital Crippled Children's Clinic for correction of her bow-legged condition. Presently she has been [wearing] night splints to hold her feet in position.

On 3-18-70, Lisa was placed in the Raymond Parker foster home in Columbia, Maryland with her four siblings.

The Parkers had come to Junior Village to get a baby or two to raise as their own but left with all five of us Ponder children. Jeff and I were already bonded from being in the infants' ward together, but I met my three older brothers for the first time when we were all bundled into the Parkers' long, white wood panel-sided station wagon on our way to a whole new life with them in Maryland. Like all other potential foster parents, the Parkers were given the grand shopping tour of the noisy Junior Village nursery and slowly moved around the room smiling at each little face they were able to make eye contact with. According to Ida Parker, as soon as she laid eyes on me, she made up her mind that she was taking me home, and without a second thought, Mr. Parker agreed. As they began to realize that I had four brothers at Junior Village, I imagine their conversation went something like this:

> *Ida:* "It would be a crying shame to break these chirren up. Besides,
>   what's gonna happen to the rest of-um? They just gonna stay here?"
> *Raymond:* "Naw, we ain't doin' that! That wouldn't sit right
>   with God.
> *Ida and Raymond together:* "We gonna take 'um all if it's ok
>   with y'all."

Once the decision was made, we were quickly gathered together to go with our new foster parents. As far as any personal belongings we might have to take with us to our new home, there were none. We were to leave with just the clothes on our backs, or in the case of Jeff and me, the diapers on our butts. No children at Junior Village owned anything. The clothes and shoes we wore were shared among other children of the same size and gender and would be needed for other children still to come. The few toys in the place were distributed throughout the wards and only the luckiest or most aggressive children got to play with the dirty, over-handled pieces of plastic that could only vaguely be recognized as objects such as naked and bald-headed white doll babies missing an eye or random limbs. I wouldn't know, but my older brothers insist those toys were worth fighting over on a daily basis because they were all there was to play with in that chaotic hellhole.

Raymond and Ida Parker were sincere about what they had just signed up for. They were in their mid-forties and had long been looking forward to starting a family of their own. Even though their true place of residence was in rural Emporia, Virginia, they realized there were too many legal details they had to wrap up in order to take care of five foster children in DC before they could return home to settle down. The only way they figured it would all work out was by staying close to the DC area. Though they had relatives living in Southeast DC whom they visited quite frequently, they considered it too much like the unsavory environment we had been subject to our whole lives and decided to move temporarily to the suburbs in Columbia, Maryland. They thought it would be a perfect place to raise children and far enough from DC that it would be difficult for my two oldest brothers to consider wandering off to visit our birth mother as they had when Mama

Parker visited her Aunt Mary while in DC. They never got very far but it was still a concern for the Parkers.

Our new foster parents weren't anything like the parents Winston and Anthony were used to. The boys had gone from a neglectful environment which left them with the freedom to do whatever they pleased, and now found themselves under constant parental supervision which they thought cramped their style. The small Columbia community was quiet, clean and predominately white. The Parkers fit in well; they were considered "good country people," and most of all, they were the non-threatening sort of black people.

Finally my three oldest brothers were going to a stable school while Jeffrey and I were in our new home getting as much attention as possible from our foster mother. She was the down-home traditional type who took care of everything in the house and did all the cooking, cleaning, and taking care of the five of us while Daddy Parker did 'what men did.' Almost as soon as we were moved to Maryland, he found a job as a janitor in a nearby office building. On nights and some weekends he drove a taxi. Mama Parker said that was the way it should be, and Daddy agreed. More than once, I heard her say, "The woman takes care of the house and the man brings home the money."

Daddy Parker liked to joke around with me even when I was just a toddler. He would grin and say, "Go on in there and help your mama with the cooking! You know how to cook, don't you?" Then he'd laugh, reach down, hoist me on his shoulders and carry me to where Mama Parker was cooking. Our new parents were simple people with a simple lifestyle and had only good quality, necessary things in their house. It was plain to see that family meant more to them than anything material.

The move to Columbia gave Daddy Parker time to build out their double-wide trailer in rural Virginia. He turned it into a solid brick house that would accommodate us all in comfort. In the meantime, we kids started a series of mandatory visitations with our birth mother that was always supervised by a FLOC caseworker. During these visitations, we were present during court hearings about our progress and the status of our living arrangements. As soon as these hearings ended, our birth mother took us out for short lunches at a hot dog stand or sandwich shop near the DC courthouse. During these visits, the caseworker usually took a snapshot of the six of us and afterwards delivered us kids back to the Parkers.

Visitations with our birth mother — both the formal ones in court and the randomly requested visits she made to keep some degree of control over our emotions — became much less frequent when Mama and Daddy Parker moved our whole family down to their upgraded home three hours away in rural Virginia. By then, we had lived for nearly two years in Maryland and had been calling the Parkers 'Mama and Daddy' for a long time. I was stuck to them like glue. No matter what Winston said, they were the only parents I knew. He liked to remind me of our biological parents — usually when it was time to take our semiannual trips back to DC to family court. He would say things like, "We're going to see our real mother today." Then he spoke in a slow baby talk voice as if each word needed to sink into my head separately. "Do – you – know – who – our – r-e-a-l – mother – is? She – gonna – be – so – h-a-p-p-y – to – see – y-o-u – . You – gonna – be – h-a-p-p-y – to – see – her – too. R-i-i-ght?"

As he slowly formed those words, trying to get me to be as happy as he was, I would pull away and find one of the Parkers to cling to. Winston always made it his job to keep two things fresh in his siblings' minds and often re-peated two favorite refrains, "We have a real mother and father" and "I'm the oldest." But Winston's stories of our real mother and father began to lose their luster as I became more aware of who my birth mother was. The longer I was with the Parkers, those court visits — filled with her disapproving, harsh looks and her mean comments about how the Parkers weren't taking proper care of our appearance — served only to make me dislike her more and more. It must have been clear to her that the luxury of being the 'real' mother with no responsibilities had begun to fade for her, along with her parental rights. Her way of dealing with whatever feelings she had about losing her power over us was to badmouth the Parkers whenever she could while keeping safely out of the hearing of our social worker.

My total disregard for our birth mother showed itself every time I was in her presence during scheduled visitations or on annual court dates. I felt a sense of uncomfortable distrust and a growing fear every time I was in a room with her. Despite her calm, reserved demeanor and soft-spoken voice, I still felt unsafe and vulnerable. Her voice, though quiet, seemed to me to be as tightly wound as the large bows she tied around her collar on the puffy-sleeved, white blouses she always wore. Her plain dark skirts and opaque flesh-tone stockings with tie-up nurse-style shoes made her look like she was on the church deaconess board and ready to flip into hallelujah mode at any moment. She always carried a Bible in her purse and pulled it out to pray without warning. I learned quickly that, when the Bible came out — almost as if she were pulling out a weapon — we five children were expected to bow our heads in fellowship or be scolded. I'd follow my brothers' lead and remain quiet but I never dared close my eyes; I had to keep an eye on her every move. This scene was repeated many times when we sat in the small waiting room outside the courtroom doors before going in to see the judge. I hated being closed in that tiny windowless space with her. Every time she laid eyes on me, she would tug on my clothing and say; "Ugh, look what they got you wearing. It don't look right. *Unngh*, what she tryin' to do to your hair? I don't like it."

She never shouted and rarely spoke above a whisper but her facial expressions said it all. The scrunch of her nose and her twisted lips screamed disapproval. That small room had only two or three chairs so we all had to share and that gave me a good reason to stay clinging to one of my brothers. I always did this until Winston walked over and picked me up. He'd talk and play with me while slowly heading in the direction of our birth mother. Then he'd deliver me to her and say; "Stay over here by Mommy. Don't you want to visit Mommy?"

Feeling betrayed, I'd sit there and pout without saying a word. Her touch seemed cool and unwilling to me and made me understand that she probably didn't want to be there either. Before long, I'd wiggle my way back down onto the floor and situate myself back next to Jeffrey or Mark. I could sense that they, too, were dying to open the door and escape. Judgmental and dissatisfied was all I knew of her. I had found stability with my new foster parents, and our attachment grew so solid that whenever they weren't around, I cried and desperately sought them out. These visits with my birthmother did nothing to change that. The father I had never met was still at-large and as time went on, no one even asked of his whereabouts. He didn't mean a thing to me; I was satisfied with my life as a Parker just the way it was.

No question about it, Emporia, Virginia was not the suburban dream that Columbia, Maryland had been. As the Parkers' station wagon slowly moved over the dirt roads of the little town on the way to our new home, we saw people lounging on wooden porches waving long, hardy hellos. As the road dust was still landing softly in our wake, we pulled up to the yard and parked on the gravel that crackled beneath the tires. Daddy Parker had done such a good job with the conversion from the old double-wide trailer that there were no visible signs that it had ever been a trailer. There were no gates to unlatch or fences to maneuver around; just our brand new-looking brick rambler with an extended addition on the back and a large screened-in back porch with cement steps. There was even a working soda machine parked against one wall. Mama Parker planned to make a little side money from the neighbors who would be knocking on the door to buy penny candy, Little Debbie snack cakes and mini pies and then wash them down with ice cold sodas from the machine.

The house was located on the very end of a row of tidy yards and neatly kept trailers without fences. Our lot seemed huge, stretching as it did beyond a straight tree line that extended far down to the final end of the row of houses and led to a large wooded area. Everything about the place seemed to me to be just right for the seven of us.

I was four years old and eager to begin Head Start in the coming school year. My two oldest brothers Winston and Anthony were to enter the junior high while Jeffrey, Mark and I would go to the elementary school together. The Parkers made it clear to us that they wanted us to do well in school. In fact, this was as important to them as making sure that we attended church every Sunday.

It didn't take much time before I loved our long backyard and ran and played with my brothers in the lush green grass. As I passed the wall of honeysuckle bushes, I always grabbed some blossoms and popped the ends off, sucking out the sweetness. Or, if they seemed ripe, I often pulled off a plumb or some juicy berries as I ran by. Mama Parker often sat outside by the porch, snapping off the ends of fresh string beans, shucking lima beans and husking corn while watching us play. We played at that end of the house so much that in time there was no grass left, just a patch of light brown dirt that blew around in little dust clouds when the wind gusted. I sat and played in this dirt for hours, often using a stick to draw pictures in it, or making little mountains I called houses. When I got really into it, I rubbed the dust on my skin like talcum powder and licked it off while no one was looking. I was usually covered in dirt, but Mama Parker never got mad about this. She'd just call to me and say, "Don't get that dirt in your hair!" But I did anyway and she patiently washed it out. Sometimes she even dragged out the big tin tub filled with bathwater and foaming bubble bath dribbling over the sides and let me soak in the tub outdoors.

Mark taught Jeffrey and me how to do cartwheel flips. These were a part of his James Brown imitation which ended in the splits position. That is until he decided to do a flip off the concrete landing onto the dirt and broke his arm. The Parkers piled us all into the car and took us to the emergency room and we all sat in the waiting room while Mark got the cast on his arm. From that day on, cartwheels were forbidden.

Daddy Parker started a new building project as soon as we moved in. He and some older male relatives offloaded building materials and started building what ended up being a pigpen and chicken coop along the edge of the yard at the opposite end of the house. The chicken coop looked like a little playhouse to me and I became fascinated by it. The wire that outlined the coop reminded me of all the fenced-in yards I had seen back in DC.

Daddy Parker wore his loose dark blue coverall uniform from his job so he always looked more like a maintenance man than a farmer, but it was clear that he knew what he was doing in both roles. He soaked down the pigpen and filled the long, deep trough with clear water. Then he lined up and stacked bags of grain in a small area on one side of the yard. He covered the burlap sacks with pieces of thick clear plastic to protect them from the elements and animals. In a matter of two days he managed to fill both the pigpen and chicken coop to capacity with newly acquired livestock. The new animal ruckus in back of the house livened up the place — a country version of sirens wailing on city streets. I had never seen farm animals up close before so when the chickens and pigs arrived, I was both excited and scared. Daddy Parker took on all the farming chores like slopping the pigs and feeding the chickens and kept our new zoo neat and orderly.

Mama Parker took pride in keeping our new house clean and organized. The Parkers were true family people whose house was filled every day of the week with the smell of freshly cooked food, lively music, and loud talking and laughing. Mama Parker always laughed and called me 'Daddy's girl' because I loved being around him whenever I could. He'd let me sit at the head of the bed on his pillow and do my very own version of plaiting his hair while he rested and then fell asleep. When he woke up to get ready for work the next morning, he'd have to spend extra time combing the knots out of his short bush. Mama Parker thought this was hilarious and laughed happily when he allowed me to do it whenever I asked.

"Y'all come on in here and sit down, I have something very important to say," Mama Parker announced one day in an unfamiliar somber voice. I felt my stomach tighten. The living room was usually a happy place where the record player constantly spun the entire Motown collection as well as soulful songs by Gladys Knight and The Pips and James Brown. That evening it was dead quiet as Mama Parker continued, "Today I got a phone call telling me that ya'll's father died." Immediately, my two older brothers began to cry. "I just want y'all to know that y'all are going to be a'right," Mama Parker said soothingly. Then she consoled Winston and Anthony as she embraced them with hugs.

The idea of ever meeting my natural father meant nothing to me. Though I had a clear understanding that Minor Ponder was out there somewhere, the only daddy I had ever known was Raymond Parker. So, when the devastating news broke that my father had died, to me, it meant Daddy Parker. "Daddy is died?" I asked, hoping I was wrong. "Yeah," Mama answered as she picked me up and began to rock me on her knee. I cried for a while and finally stopped as I found comfort in Mama's rocking back and forth while I sucked my thumb. But the pain had begun to shoot through my heart. "He's not going to come back?" I asked, hoping that dying in people was different than what I had seen among the chickens and pigs in our backyard.

There was no playing outside in the yard that day. We all sat quietly watching TV until it was time for dinner and Mama Parker made her way back to the stove to tend to the food. "Okay now. Go on in the bathroom and wash your hands for dinner," she said softly as she did every day. But this time she didn't have to holler outside for the older boys who would be playing somewhere down the road. Anthony helped me wash my hands and just as we sat down, the front door flung open. I heard keys jingling and suddenly Daddy Parker entered the kitchen. My eyes widened at the sight of him and joyous laughter spewed from deep inside me.

"Ha Haaaa – haaaa – haaaaa haaaa – haaaaa haaaa – haaaaa haaaa – haaaaa!" I rejoiced as I looked around at everybody and called out, "Daddy ain't died, he right there!" I jumped out of my chair and ran to him and reached up to him. He picked me up and laughed with a surprised look on his face. "What's wrong with this girl, Savanna?" He said, calling Mama by her middle name. Before she could speak, I shouted, "Mama tricked us! She tricked us good! Mama said you was dead but you not! Ha – ha – haaa – ha – ha!"

I was so happy that I didn't even want to eat, I just wanted to be wherever he was. As he laughed at my antics he turned to Mama and asked again, "What's going on, Savanna?"

As he sat me down in front of my plate of food, Mama explained, "No Lisa, I didn't trick ya'll. Your real daddy back in DC died today."

"Oh! My daddy in DC died!" I repeated. Then I shouted happily, "Well, that's a'right 'cause my daddy here ain't died."

Winston snapped at me. "It ain't alright! That was our real father!"

Mama spoke quickly, "Winston, she don't mean nothing against ya'll's father. She just don't know him. She don't mean no harm. She don't even know what she's saying because she ain't nothing but four years old."

My other brothers shook their heads in agreement and Winfred calmed down and said, "I know. She don't know no better."

Soon we were due for another court visit, and a visit with our birth mother. This time the Parkers drove us to DC and the caseworker picked us up and took us to the court building. Our birth mother talked to Winston most of the time and asked him all kinds of questions about the Parkers' house, the schools we went to and how we were being treated. It didn't matter what Winston said because her words and tone were always disapproving. As usual, she plucked at our clothes and trashed the Parkers. "What she got on ya'll, don't look right. Now they got ya'll all the way down there in Virginia. Ump… umh-huh. I know what they trying to do and they're not gonna get away with it either," she said darkly as she busied herself adjusting our clothing to show us that if she were the Parkers, she would do things a whole lot better than they did.

This time I spoke up and asked, "Who ain't gonna get away with what?" And as usual, she dismissed me and my question by saying, "You are too young and won't understand," and I quietly began wishing we could be back home right away. I wasn't used to being treated that way and I didn't like her for it. We ate lunch in the courthouse cafeteria that afternoon and afterward the caseworker told us to say good-bye because we had to hurry back to meet the Parkers. Life back on the Parker farm was good; it was exactly where I wanted to be.

The day my oldest brother Winston disappeared changed our lives. He didn't come home from school. In a panic, Mama called all the relatives she could think of while daddy got into the car and canvassed the whole community. He drove everywhere, checking the places he knew the boys Winston's age hung out in after school. When he located Cheeseburger, Bo-Bo and the rest of the older boys, Daddy Parker yelled out, "Hey! Is Winston with y'all?"

"Huynh? Naw, Sir. He ain't wit' us," one of the boys answered while the others snapped to attention. Cheeseburger, one of Winston's best friends shouted back, "I ain't seen him at school neither, so I was about to come over to y'all's house."

"Awright! If ya'll see him, tell him I said come on home," Daddy Parker said as he hustled back toward the open car door and got in. "Yes, Suh," the boys answered together, then watched him drive away.

By the time Daddy returned home, it was dark outside and Mamma had called the police. Down that unpaved road where we lived, there were no street lights and everyone turned on their porch lights when it got dark. Otherwise it would be so pitch black that you couldn't see your own hands.

Emporia at that time was one of those small towns where grownups kept an eye on everybody else's children. They scolded us if we got caught doing something wrong, and offered us something good to eat if they thought we were hungry. They even took us home to our parents if they saw us doing something unsettling. The Parkers knew everybody in town and knew that if somebody spotted Winston, they would let them know right away. But there were no phone calls of that sort; just the many that came in asking if he had shown up yet.

The Parkers tried their best not to let it show, but we kids could feel their growing panic as they waited for news about Winston. Daddy didn't even go to work the next day, but instead set out early that morning to check the bus depot and the schoolyards as children were being dropped off. He checked back down at the police station to see if they had him, but still nothing.

Mama kept saying that she didn't understand why he would leave without letting her know where he was because he always asked permission before even leaving the house. "Now that boy ain't never left this house without me knowing. He was suppose't go to straight to school an' come right back home. I had to call DC and let them know that he done gone missing. Oh, Lawd, now they worried to death like me," she said unhappily before retreating to her bedroom.

Late the next afternoon began the domino effect that would end with the dismantling of the Parkers' happy home and family. For us, it would be the end of a stable, nurturing environment. There's no telling how things might have turned out for us as adults if things had not fallen apart at the Parkers' house, but I'm pretty damn sure my childhood would have read much better if that incident had never happened.

The phone call Mama was waiting for finally came in. The good news was that my brother was safe and sound, but the bad news was that he had run away and turned up at the door of our birth mother's apartment back in DC. He had hitchhiked the whole way. The caller was a caseworker from the DC Department of Child and Family Services on behalf of my brother Winston and our birth mother, Doretha Ponder. As the caseworker tried to speak, Mama Parker could hear our birth mother in the background demanding that we be bought back to DC. Then she could hear Doretha saying to Winston, "Go on Winston, tell them what you told me." This was the loudest anyone had ever heard her speak. Without missing a rehearsed beat Winston recited, "The Parkers beat us."

The caseworker interviewed him while holding the phone so Mama Parker could hear what was being said. "Who beat you? And who else did they beat?" Then Doretha interrupted, "He ran away from down there in Virginia back here to me because he said those people down there be beating on them."

As Doretha ranted on, saying all the things she disapproved of about the Parkers, the caseworker closed the door to keep Doretha out of the conversation and continued the phone call with Mama Parker. "As you heard, Mrs. Parker, Winston is accusing you and your husband of using corporal punishment to discipline him and the other children in your home." Still in total disbelief, Mama Parker slumped into one of the kitchen chairs as she listened closely. Then she asked, "Who did you say this is? Are you sure you have the right family?"

As the caseworker repeated her statement, Mama pulled herself together and tried to reason with her. "I don't know how all this came about but what Winston is saying is not the truth. Then she said, "Winston's birth mother put him up to this. He was doing fine until that last visit with her and now he is in DC lying to y'all about us beating our chirren." Mama had begun to sob. "I can't believe Winston would tell you that. I know his mother is putting him up to it. She is sick and needs some help! I swear to God me and Ray ain't never laid a hand on these chirren. We treat 'em as our own."

"Well Mrs. Parker," the caseworker replied, "We here at CAFS have no other choice but to terminate your foster home. Please prepare the remaining children in your home for removal."

Just like that, the first domino had fallen. On September 27, 1974 we left the Parkers thinking that we were going to DC for another routine court visit.

Chapter Three

By the time our social worker, Mr. Keeney, pulled up and parked in front of a big red house perched high on the corner of 9th and Webster Streets, he must have been jumping for joy inside. The three-and-a-half-hour road trip we had just finished, including several bathroom stops and a sit-down lunch with four lively foster children unknowingly being transferred from one loving and familiar home to one completely unknown to them, must have been a first even for him, a laid-back white guy.

It was Anthony who finally cleared the air by asking about Winston. Mr. Keeney seemed concerned and then answered, "I think he's staying with your birth mother." We hadn't seen Winston for at least a week and Mama Parker, clearly upset, had told all of us that he had run away to go back to DC to live with our real mother. Then came that day when we four were packed into Mr. Keeney's car to go to DC for what we believed was a routine court visit and saw that Mama and Daddy Parker were weeping as we said the usual temporary goodbyes. I had never seen them so sad before. As she hugged me tight, I told Mama to stop crying because we would be coming right back. Of course, I had no idea what was coming or how long it would be until I would see the Parkers again.

The first fifteen minutes in the car was fun. Jeff and I played clapping games like *Miss Mary Mack* and *Pat-a-Cake* and then started gnawing on the green apples Mama Parker had picked from the tree in the yard and packed in a snack bag for us. But soon the motion and the boredom got to us and our heads nodded forward as we drifted off to sleep. When Mr. Keeney stopped at a rest stop for the first time, my brothers began pestering him with, "Are we almost there yet?" Each time he heard the question, he gave the approximate number of miles left in the trip and turned up the light rock station on the radio. The Q&A was repeated endlessly until we came within reach of DC. Since we had been there many times with the Parkers for our family court appointments and for visitations with our birth mother, we recognized familiar landmarks and knew when we were getting close to the city. My brothers waited until we crossed the 14th Street Bridge and then excitedly called out once more, "Are we almost there now?" Relieved, Mr. Keeney cheerfully sang out, "Yes, we're almost there!" As soon as those words passed his lips, our chorus of four burst into laughter and song:

"We're al-l-l-l-most there! We're al-l-l-l-most there! We're al-l-l-l-most there! We're al-l-l-l-most there! We're al-l-l-l-most there! We're al-l-l-l-most there!"

Occasionally Mr. Keeney softly asked us to lower our voices but never demanded silence. So we just kept singing until the car came to a complete stop and we piled out like a crowd of circus clowns from a miniature car. After Mr. Keeney locked the car doors, we stood waiting to see which way our social worker would go. When he turned from the sidewalk and began climbing the steps of a large house, the four of us raced right past him and began pressing the doorbell. "Okay now, that's enough," he said in the same patient tone he always used.

After much doorbell ringing, an unfamiliar face appeared in the small window of the front door and peered out at us. Then the door sprang open and standing before us was a woman of average height with dark brown skin. Her small beady eyes were dark with yellowish whites and small areas of skin around her eyes looked darkly bruised as if by an injury. She wasn't ugly, but she was not at all pretty either. She was dressed in a well-fitting pantsuit but wore house slippers instead of shoes. She had on lipstick and wore an obvious wig, like the shiny, stiff, synthetic ones the old ladies wore to church in Emporia. She took her time before speaking and then said in a surprised tone, "What in the wor-l-d, is this?" She followed up with a fake smile to cover up her disgust. Mr. Keeney moved forward and spoke up. "Hi, I'm Howard Keeney from FLOC and I have with me the Ponder children. We would have been here sooner but we had to make several stops along the way."

Keeping her lips in a forced, tight half smile, she pushed the outer storm door open further and escorted us in. We Ponders bunched close together and walked in behind Mr. Keeney. Once inside we stood frozen, in awe of the unaccustomed luxury of the place. Our eyes and mouths were wide open as we marveled over what we were seeing and crooned softly, "O-O-O-O-o-o-oh." In the entryway, hanging from what seemed like a mile-high ceiling, was a large brightly lit chandelier filled with glass prisms that resembled icicles dripping from an ice cold street lamp. We stood awestruck, our feet sunken into a plush carpet that reached into every corner of the rooms within view of the foyer. Along the wide-open corridor sat round-end tables with cream-colored marble swirl tops that displayed lamps which perfectly matched the enormous chandelier. On top of a skinny, rather stilted-looking table fitted into an alcove next to the four-stair landing perched a pearl-looking antique style telephone trimmed with gold accents. We continued to stare, open-mouthed, until the woman stiffly instructed us saying, "Now, you all come on in here and sit down."

She led us into the living room to a pristine antique-style couch where Mark, Jeff and I sat closely bunched together, while Anthony angled himself on the corner of one end. To us, it seemed that all the furniture in that room would be suitable for a castle. Even the firewood sitting on the stand next to the fireplace by the brass fire tools seemed to have been perfectly cut to fit into a special niche. There was one oversize chair that didn't match the furniture set, but perfectly followed the rust and yellow print color scheme. The lid to the in-cabinet record player was propped up, exposing a neat stack of large records in their original jackets. As we rubbernecked from where we sat, we gave ourselves a visual tour of that room and then as far as we could see into the room directly across the foyer. There a long dark wooden table was placed along with six matching chairs with shiny plastic covers protecting the off-white cloth seats and seatbacks. In the exact center of the table, sitting on a white lace doily was an elaborate Liberace-style candelabrum with a long, unused white candle in each holder. We had never seen anything like the inside of this house before except on TV, and we whispered excitedly and pointed at each new fascinating thing. Still planted on that couch, we maneuvered our bodies around while the two adults talked together in low tones. Mr. Keeney said he had to use the phone to call his office, and the two adults left the room together.

We watched them walk to the antique-style phone in the foyer and saw Mr. Keeney gently pick up the gilded handset with one hand and place his finger into the holes of the rotary dial as he entered the numbers. In astonishment, Jeff looked at Mark and blurted, "Hey, it works!"

The woman shot Jeff a stern look but then quickly turned away. While the adults were busy, we became a little more relaxed and changed our whispers into low voice tones and giggles. Then Mark stood up and walked over to examine one of the matching lamps. Moving slowly, he then carefully lifted one of the smaller hanging prisms from the lamp, held it out in front of him, and hurried back toward the couch saying, "Look, earrings for Lisa, earrings for Lisa!" He held the prism close to my ear and waited for affirmation from the adults out in the foyer. Mr. Keeney's eyes opened wide as he realized what Mark was holding and while continuing to talk on the phone, frantically gestured with one hand for him to put it back. Mark flashed all his teeth at both adults and continued to admire his discovery. Suddenly, like rolling thunder the woman bore all of her 160 pounds across the thick carpet, barreled back into the living room and snatched the glittering prism from Mark's hand so hard and fast it seemed she must have taken his fingers with it. As she stormed back over to the table and reattached the bauble, all the proper citified enunciation left her speech and became a down-and-dirty southern drawl as she said in a low, growling voice, "These ain't no durn earrings!"

Rolling her neck and moving her head from side to side she then put us all on notice. "Let me tell y'all something right now. This is my house and y'all ain't to touch nothing in my house unless I tell you. This house don't belong to FLOC, it belongs to me so don't touch nothing in it."

Her eyes and lips got all tight and creased around the edges, and the sight of it made me huddle even closer to my brothers. Then she looked us each up and down and repeated the law, "I don't know where in the world y'all came from but you don't touch nothing in my house. Do you understand?" Frozen stiff in fear, we didn't utter a word, so she repeated, "I said, do – you – under – stand me?"

Mark looked her straight in the eye and quietly answered yes, but that was not enough for her, so she added in a fierce tone, "I'm talking to each and every one of you. Do – you – understand?" Like soldiers in a row, we answered a meek yes one after another.

"Yes, Ma'am!" She growled. "When you answer me you say, Yes, Ma'am. Do you understand?"

"Yes Ma'am," we all sang out. My lips had been quivering a bit from the moment I stepped into the house and now I started to cry in earnest. She gave me a hard stare and I lowered my eyes toward Jeffrey. Mark whispered gently, "Stop crying."

Mr. Keeney's phone call was finally over and I was more than ready to climb back into his car and go back home to the Parkers. But as he reentered the living room, he said, "Well, Mrs. Graves, everything has been taken care of. Should we begin the introductions?"

She answered yes in her fake pleasant voice like nothing had ever happened. Even her body language changed back to a more acceptable welcoming stance and she continued speaking in that fake refined way, to match our social worker's style. Then she said, "Let me go get Gavin and Herman down here." After she walked out the door and disappeared around the corner Mr. Keeney informed us that this was to be our new foster home. This was a shock. But we didn't make a sound.

When our new foster mother came back into the room, she stood next to the big chair and ran her eyes over each of us. Seconds later a beautiful light-skinned version of the young Michael Jackson entered, out of breath. He walked over to her and said, "Yes, Ma'am?" He was Gavin, her beloved, well-trained foster child. She smiled at him as she introduced us and it was very clear to us that she was very proud of him.

After we met Gavin, a husky dark brown Chubby Checker clone walked into the living room. His snatch back hairdo was heavily permed like James Brown's, but was carefully tapered around the nape of his neck. Clearly, he was our new foster father.

A week had gone by and I still wasn't used to living in my new foster home. Nothing seemed real to me, and I was totally confused. I ached to see the Parkers again and missed Winston. I was wrapped in sadness and no matter how hard I tried I couldn't pretend to be happy and often cried and that infuriated my new foster mother. Her disapproval of my crying for the only parents I had ever known offended her so much that she said, "You better shut up all that noise in my house; you don't have no reason to be crying. Those people didn't take good care of y'all and now they done gone on 'bout their business. Shoot! They ain't think a bit more about you than the man in the moon."

I understood the meaning and intent of what she was saying and right away something made me just stop crying. I wiped my face and eyes with my hands and stared up at her as a chill climbed up my back and made the hairs on my neck stand up. I had never experienced such meanness before and the feeling made me feel helpless. I wanted to say something mean back to her. I wanted to tell Mama and Daddy Parker on her. I prayed they would come take us all back home so this bad dream would be over.

I no longer cried for my lost parents in front of her. I didn't want to hear what she had to say about them as I was afraid she could possibly be telling the truth. During the next few weeks I quietly mourned my loss for short periods of time while lying in bed at night. We soon learned to call the Graves, *Mama* and *Daddy*. As for our new foster brother, he was just *Gavin*.

It hadn't taken long after our arrival at the Graves house for me to develop a new kind of nervousness that seemed to stay with me until the day I left four years later. I had been shown nothing but love by the Parkers and wasn't used to being judged or expected to follow such a disciplined regimen as Mama Graves imposed on me right from the beginning. It seemed she was making up new rules for us as we went along. Even worse, during that first week there, I had found myself being weaned away from the comfortable companionship of my brothers. It wasn't a slow, gentle weaning. It was more like being ripped away. Louise Graves believed that girls didn't play with boys and that became clearer to me each time I asked, "Where JJ, Mark, and Anthony?" She didn't answer, just pointed to the screened-in porch where I was expected to play by myself.

I often paced the length of that porch in tears, hoping that one of my brothers would appear from around the corner while rushing in to use the bathroom or something. That almost never happened, and eventually I just stopped checking for glimpses of them. It was summertime and there was no school, so I was left with a lot of empty time on my hands. The only evidence that my brothers were still around came at mealtimes. Mama Graves served family meals like clockwork, and those set times were the highlight of my day because my brothers were there with me. There wasn't much talking at the table, and Mama Graves took advantage of these times to drill some table manners into our "country hind parts." She taught us her way of saying grace — her

greatly favored light-skinned foster child Gavin always reciting the words —
and sternly ordered us not to chew with our mouths open, put our elbows on
the table, or dare to call a napkin "a piece of paper."

Mama Graves always seemed to be disgusted with us. But when Daddy
Graves came home each day from his job as a chauffeur for a Garfinckel's
executive, her attitude seemed to change. She'd lighten her tone and lower
her volume to a normal speaking voice. She always became more jovial
around him and she often gave me the idea that everything about us Ponders
was a joke to her. She and Gavin would snicker about things we couldn't understand and Daddy Graves sometimes laughed along with them — not to be
mean, but to lessen the embarrassment which he seemed to feel about their
leaving us out of their in-jokes. My brothers didn't always sense that exclu-
sivity, but I did. It didn't fool me for one second. After all, I was the one left
in the house within hearing distance of all those times when she laughed and
talked on the phone about how 'country' and 'uncivilized' we were. I can still
hear her loud, mocking laughter.

"Gurl…they almost made me sick enough to get up and vomit! Those
chirren remind me of pigs eating out of a trough!" As I sat on the kitchen
steps, I heard the return laughter blaring from the other end of the phone.

Since there had been pigs on the Parkers' farm, I knew very well how
nasty a pig trough was. Even at the age of five I could recognize an insult
and often fished for the words in my head in order to silently deliver one back.
The only one I could ever think of was a muttered, "you ugly" followed by
my rolling eyes. Oblivious to my presence, Mama complained every day to
her sister Judy and to her two best buddies who were also FLOC foster mothers. They compared their own twisted stories of the hopeless handfuls they
were kind enough to take into their beautiful homes as they vowed to change
our ways even if it meant beating the devil out of us.

Nighttime was the scariest time. Having a room of my own wasn't a good
thing for me at that age. I yearned for some company, especially at night. The
boys slept on the third floor while I was left alone on the empty-feeling second
floor. The Graves's bedroom adjoined mine, but the connecting door stayed
locked and blocked by the nightstand between the twin beds in my room. I
often cried myself to sleep in those first weeks as I tried to sort out the things
I heard and saw in this unfriendly house. I dreamed of falling and being

chased by snakes of all sizes and these dreams often triggered what Mama Graves called "the devil." I remembered the dreams but only learned of these episodes from Mama Graves's phone conversations the next day. As I sat on the kitchen steps or the side porch, I listened quietly as my foster mother whooped it up about how sick and crazy I was — just like my mother. "All this foolish screaming and fighting she doin' ain't nothin' but the devil in her. It don't make no sense," she would exclaim in her most dramatic tone.

"Yeah, she had the nerve to wake me and Herman up, scared me so bad I thought somebody broke into the house. I had to go in there and untangle her out of the window blinds."

This comment was followed by loud, cruel laughter; "Hahahahaha... Yeah, fightin' the blinds, gurrrl! I'll tell you, it ain't nothing but the devil trying to come out in the night. Gurrrl, can you believe I got this demon in my house? Hahahaha..."

At first I wasn't sure she was talking about me, but she gave it away when the question of my whereabouts came up, and she gave me the evil eye while answering into the phone, "Right here staring in my face!"

Often she inflicted further pain by saying to me, "You better get out of my mouth and stay out of my business, little girl with your grown-self." This word 'grown' quickly became her favorite insult. When she discovered how careful I was with my household chores — especially the vacuuming — she riffed on the word by giving me the hurtful nickname of "Grownie," a name that echoes painfully in my ears all these years later. I knew I was supposed to be intimidated by her talk, but because she made such ugly faces and changed her voice so dramatically, to me it was like watching a strange kind of TV show. I would listen and then half laugh, catching myself in time to avoid a quick slap. And often I waited eagerly for the funniest show of all. That was when she would be talking in her coarse everyday voice with one person on the line and then would flip to call-waiting, answering in an exaggerated operatic soprano tone; "HELLOUUUUUE?"

Out of all the holidays celebrated at the Graves home, the one that stands out in my mind the most is Halloween, especially the first one. Unlike Christmas, Thanksgiving, Easter and even the 4th of July, Mama Graves didn't believe in or support Halloween at all. I remember her saying to us: "I'm a church-goin' woman who don't celebrate no durn devil's holiday so don't even think about askin' me to go trick-or-treating because the answer is NO!" She said this while tearing open two large bags of assorted candies, one chocolate and the other hard candy, and poured them into separate bowls. She continued her lecture while placing the bowls near the front door, "If it wasn't for all those demon-possessed hoodlums running around out there laying-in-wait to tear up my house, I would just turn my lights off and go to bed on Halloween. Shoot! I know exactly how they do. If you don't open your door and give their begging-butts some candy, they throw eggs at your house and put dog dung on your front steps."

I amused myself while imagining her slowly lifting her slippered foot out of a hot steaming pile of dog mess. When she'd talk like that it seemed like she was speaking from experience because a loathing expression came on her face and her tone changed to a throaty gurgle. I visually placed a hairy wart on the tip of her nose and black witch's hat on her head, which went perfectly with her green ankle-length velour robe that zipped straight up the front and had long flaring sleeves. It all went together. Even the way she acted when she answered the door after a group of kids would yell, "TRICK-OR-TREAT!" I could hear how it all played out while lying in my bed as the clock approached eight o'clock. She sounded just like a wicked witch trying desperately to change her voice to nice. I could picture her striking up a jovial persona as she tried to show the small visitors that she cared a lick about them. "Ooooh! Look at all the nice costumes. You are a pretty little girl. What are you? A ballerina?" She would dribble out these fake niceties as she slowly divided out the number of pieces she would give each kid the same way she did for us before sending us to bed without Halloween.

"1-2 and 3 for you, 1-2-3 for you and 1-2 and 3 treats for you." Then, as they turned to leave, she'd say in a dead-serious-coated-with-fake-pleasant way before closing the door, "Now I gave you those treats so don't do no tricks on me!"

That first Halloween, I sneaked out of bed to catch a glimpse of the kids in their costumes while Mama was busy counting and her back was turned. I loved seeing the Casper, Batman and Clown costumes their mothers took the time to go out and buy just for them. I thought, Dag… *they so lucky. They have nice mamas that let them have fun. Ugggh! I hate her! We can't ever do nothin'. They got all that candy in their bags and all we got was two little pieces. That's not fair either! I'm gonna get me some more of that candy.*

That night, I could no longer control my desire to get more of that candy. I jumped back into bed when I knew it was nearing the 9 o'clock closing time. She was muttering to herself, "All that ain't got won't get if they ain't here by fifteen minutes because at 9 o'clock I'm turning off my porch light and every other light in here, and I'm takin' myself to bed and if they don't like that, too bad for them. I bett' not see one thing wrong with my house in the morning."

I lay there in my bed trying to figure out how I was going to get downstairs to the candy bowl. The last time I had peeped down, I saw there was more than half a bowl of assorted mini chocolates and Tootsie Rolls left and I was determined to get some. Furious at Mama Graves for being so mean I talked myself into the petty larceny. I knew that when I got to school the next day that most of my classmates would have some of their candy with them and would be talking about all they had collected in their neighborhoods. I would have nothing to say, and the unfairness of that pumped me up to the point of daring. I walked lightly across my bedroom carefully avoiding the places where the floor creaked. I didn't put on my house slippers, robe or anything – just stood at the top of the stairs and waited for the right time to make my move. It was way too quiet in the kitchen and I could imagine her sitting at the table watching television as the time ticked away to her deadline. Then came my chance; *Riiii-n-g*, the telephone rang and she quickly answered. "Hey Gurl! Yeah I'm still up handing out candy…"

I knew she would be talking for a while, so I tiptoed slowly down the steps at first and then sped up to the bottom of the steps. As I made my way down the last step and across the area rug between the door and the steps, I could see the bowls on the shelf by the door, higher up than I thought. I wasn't going to be able to pick out the ones I wanted the most so I decided to just reach both hands in and grab as many as I could, turn around and jet back up the steps to the safety of my bed.

Mama Graves was getting more engrossed in her conversation with Aunt Judy and I felt home free. I made it over to the bowl, reached both hands in and pulled out at least three pieces of candy in each of my small six-year-old hands, spun around and immediately froze. Daddy Graves was standing there with his usual unlit cigar clinched between his teeth. I couldn't say a word and felt frozen to the spot. Then he spoke in a kindly whisper, a slight smile showing through the cigar clinch, "You better hurry up and get back up those stairs before your Mama see you."

Squeezing the candy as tight as I could to make sure I didn't drop a single piece, I sprinted past him up the steps, and jumped into my bed. I pushed both hands under my pillow, letting go of the candy and pulling the covers over my head. I lay still, face down in my pillow, for several minutes, feeling as if I was in shock from almost being hit by a car or something worse except I would rather have been hit by a car than to have come face-to-face with Mama Graves. All I could do was lie there waiting to see what was going to happen to me. I didn't know if I should cry or laugh and I certainly didn't have a taste for the candy anymore. Finally, I heard Mama hang up the phone and announce that Halloween was officially over in the Graves house. I listened as hard as I could to see if Daddy Graves responded to her. Nothing. He was the same as he always was, very quiet. Mama had turned the television set off in the kitchen and now I could hear her short quick steps coming up the stairs. I lay still in my bed and feigned sleep just in case she decided to look into my room. I kept my face pressed into the pillow and didn't move until I heard her bedroom door click. At that sound I realized I was in the clear and began to giggle softly to myself. I moved aside the pillow to reveal my prizes. Touching each one I counted, *1-2-3-4-5-6-7. Yeah, I got me seven pieces of candy!*

I delicately opened a piece the same way I did when I was in church being careful not to be heard and took small bites savoring the taste like a chocolate connoisseur while I sorted out what had just happened, *Daddy didn't even get mad at me. He didn't even tell Mama! I didn't even get in trouble by him.* This kindness by Daddy Graves was one of the rare times that I was to feel protected while living in that home.

I wondered if my brother Winston was happier living with "our real mother" than he was when he lived with us. I remembered how he always talked about us all being back together like a real family. But now he was nowhere around. According to Winston and "our real mother," getting us returned to DC was supposed to be the beginning of the reuniting of the Ponder family.

The second part of this scheme was put into motion one warm fall afternoon when Winston showed up on the Graves's front porch ringing the doorbell. Winston had just turned fourteen and considered himself the man of the family since our biological father had died. He politely introduced himself to Mama Graves.

"Hi, I'm Winston. Anthony, Mark, Jeff and Lisa are my brothers and little sister. Can I visit with them, please?"

She looked at him, startled after finding out who he was and told him to wait out front. She turned and walked back into the house closing the door behind her. Clearly caught off guard and unnerved by my brother's unexpected arrival, she nevertheless called out, *"Anthony! Mark! Come on up here for a minute."*

The boys had been playing and watching cartoons and quickly ran up the basement stairs and she said, "Your brother is out there on the porch talking 'bout he wants to visit. Go on out there and see him for a few minutes."

When I overheard that Winston was standing on the front porch, a long lost smile returned to my face. Mama Graves quickly fixed that and got me straight. "I don't know what you grinning about because you ain't going out there. Jeffrey either." Trying to regain her power, she added, "In just a few minutes, Anthony and Mark will have to get their butts back in here."

I watched her every move as she paced around the kitchen nervously talking nonstop. When their allotted time was up, she walked over, snatched open the front door and issued an order; "Okay. That's enough, now you two come on back in here!" Then she stepped outside and discovered that Mark was sitting there by himself. "Woooo! What in the world?" she shouted. Then, "Where is Anthony?"

Mark answered, "They went to the store. Said they'd be right back." Then Mama shouted at Mark as if he was to blame, "What'd you say? Come in the house!"

When it dawned on her that the boys had run away, I saw surprise and fear in Mark's eyes as she snatched the receiver from the wall phone and dialed as fast as the rotary phone would allow. She was calling the FLOC office. I could see that she was nervous and for the first time since coming to that house, I could see unsettled fear in her face and hear it in her voice. When she was finished telling on Winston, she hung up and shouted at Mark,

"Anthony can't come back in my house! Your brother Winston came over here and took him back to your sick Mama's house with him, so Anthony is not welcome back into my house."

Now Anthony was gone, and after hearing Mama Graves's little speech I was pretty sure we would never see him or Winston again. That thought just added to my already overflowing sadness. I vowed to hold on to my last two brothers as tightly as I could.

Only a few weeks later both Winston and Anthony showed up unannounced at the front door of the Graves's home. This time, Mama refused my brothers any contact with the three of us. She wasn't falling for that phony polite approach this time.

"I don't care if your brothers and sister are here or not, y'all can't come to my house just any time you decide."

I was sitting in what had become Mama's designated place for me, the three-step landing leading into the kitchen and could turn around and see straight through to the front door where my brothers stood. They had stopped the polite act. Winston shouted, "You better let us see our brothers and sister you ugly ass bitch!"

Mark had managed to make his way to the front door and onto the porch, but Jeffery and I dared not move, given Mama's warning. As she stood in front of the door while the three boys met, I could feel the tension. Soon Mama and Mark walked back into the house. He was crying and mad when he told me, "I was supposed to go with them. They came back to get *me* this time." I didn't like seeing Mark so upset, but felt secretly happy that he didn't get to go. Jeff and I needed him here.

Chapter Four

THE HAIR JUSTIFIES THE MEANS

"Sit in *the chair!*" That was always one of those demands I dreaded hearing from Mama Graves. She shouted that in a loud voice that rang throughout the kitchen, and my legs would weaken while I slowly moved toward the tor-ture chair next to the gas stove. The thought of those two hours of guaranteed verbal and physical assault slowed my movements to baby steps. "You better hurry up and get over here before I change my mind," she would growl. Then she always added a threat which was never enough to make me come more quickly; "You can go to that ole FLOC Christmas party for pitiful kids looking like a little pickaninny for all I care."

The one thing I knew about Mama was that she would never pass up the chance to break into *bourgee* mode, her lame attempt to impress the social workers. That party was a chance to slap on her shiny over-brushed going-out wig and plop on top of that a big hat cocked way to the side. Each year the party was a chance to show off the glad rags she bought exclusively from Garfinckel's, where, as she always said grandly, "the white folk shop." It was also a chance to complete her personal Christmas makeover by using that af-fected falsetto voice she used when answering the phone. I wondered if the social workers knew she was faking, and if they talked behind her back the way she talked behind theirs. When she talked to them or other foster parents, I stared intently at the faces of her listeners hoping to catch any little sigh or eye-rolling that would prove they knew she was a big phony.

Church was the only other time she'd dress up and leave the house, so I knew this yearly occasion was important to her. Just before we left home, she always gave us the evil eye, lowered her voice and growled, "Be nice." Once we got to the party, she would completely adjust her attitude, and like a confident mother duck, she paraded us fosterlings around in front of every-one to make them believe she was the best foster mother in the system. She never, ever touched us affectionately at home, but in front of such an impor-tant audience, she made it a point to hold our hands tightly and act proud of our progress and growth while accepting as her own whatever compliments came our way.

Mama made sure that we looked worthy of her when we went to the party. In my case, my first party dress was red velvet with a white collar, white patent leather shoes and a tiny matching purse with a mirror inside. My brothers wore their three-piece church suits and black dress shoes. They were lucky; they went to the men's barbershop where they got close haircuts that left their scalps shining through. I envied them this exotic outing and wished I could avoid the at-home hair torture Mama saved for me. But Mark hated the boys' hair ritual. He was sensitive about people seeing the scars our birth mother had inflicted on his scalp with the nozzle of a hose she beat him with while in one of her rages. It was common knowledge among us kids that the DC foster authorities came and took us away from her after she did that to Mark.

As I grew, the color and style of the velvet dresses changed, but I always had to wear a pair of hateful tights with a crotch that stopped at mid-thigh. Mama Graves always got them too small because she never bothered to find a size better suited to my long legs. Those, along with my long arms, seemed an annoyance for her and not a reason to look for a better fit. She often shouted in frustration; "Ain't nothin' fit you right witchu long limbs!" One year, she put red ribbons in my hair. I thought they looked pretty until I heard the kids laughing about those stiff, shiny, mismatched, cheap-looking bows — pinned into my hair with black bobby pins — and realized that she was re-using bows from Christmas wrappings. One mean girl made sure I under-stood that when she said, "Is your hair the present?" Puzzled and a bit intim-idated, I answered no, and she skipped away shouting gleefully for everyone to hear, "Then why you wearing those Christmas bows?"

I began to believe that what happened in the chair was necessary in order to achieve the desired end results. I cringed from the overly tightened twists from the marble-like barrette balls, and from the sizzle of my burning flesh caused by "accidental" taps on my ear or neck with the smoking steel prongs of a straightening comb. Those burns almost always drew tears, but there was never an apology from my foster mother. She just barked; "Keep your nappy head still before I give you something to cry about!" The strength of my reflexive flinches and forward lurches depended on how long the hot comb had touched my skin or how sharply the after burn lasted. Right on schedule she'd respond to my defensive moves by saying, "Gurrl, if you make me burn myself, Ima gon' tear you up!"

These words were usually accompanied by a painful clunk on the top of my head unless I was quick enough to duck forward in time to catch instead the greasy handle of her favorite hard bristle brush in a washboard-like trip down my spine. I had no control over the first part of this well-rehearsed routine, but I became an expert double dodger of the second part and often managed to avoid contact altogether. Oddly, if she missed, she never tried a second hit and that was a relief. As I got better at defending myself, I enjoyed the pleasure of outwitting her and developed a dramatic eye-rolling sigh accompanied by raised brows which infuriated her. Mama Graves's comeback temper tantrum usually consisted of an assortment of insults about my "bad hair" blasted at the back of my head in puffs of warm breath. To my memories of these scenes of togetherness were added the smoke of the hot comb and the smell of the Dax hair grease that dripped onto my scalp, scalded me, and then stiffened up like candle wax as it cooled. I can still hear her time-tested zingers that went with this painful ritual. "When you and your country brothers came in my house, y'all looked like the African children in one of those *National Geographic* magazines. Ha-Ha-Ha, Woo! I had to pinch up that little mess on your head because it wasn't no longer than this!" To emphasize her point, she'd snap her fingers loudly, then continue her loud commentary; "Don't make no sense, you sitting up here acting like I'm killing you! Those other foster parents ain't do nothing for you and neither did your own mama."

I know I had seen a *National Geographic* somewhere by then, but I had no way of making sense of what I saw. I remember wondering; *Where are those women with naked titties and mud smeared on their bodies in strange designs or tangled in their nappy hair? And why is Mama telling me I was like them and then accusing our first foster parents of making us look like them?* The thing I didn't wonder about at all was the fact that Mama felt nothing but scorn for those people in the photographs, and by association, for me, my brothers and the Parkers.

I always heard every word Mama Graves said but once I had figured out how to duck and dodge her moves like a prize fighter, that talk no longer fazed me one bit because instead of listening, I would be basking in the glow of my juke moves on her. I used to hear my brothers brag that the Redskins players made touchdowns after dodging tacklers and never being touched. Like those players, I was spiking my ball long after my successful moves to outwit Mama.

I hate to say it, but Mama Graves was right about the means justifying the end result with my hair. After she finished the final touches of greasing and brushing my baby hair flat around my hairline, she always called after me as I ran up the long flight of stairs, "Don't touch it, 'cuz I'm not doing it again!" As I ran, I could feel the warm stiff curls slapping the back of my neck. It was exciting to imagine how it all looked, but my first mission always was to relieve a long-held pee before peeking at my hair in the bathroom mirror above the sink. To see my hair in the mirror, I had to jump up repeatedly while holding onto the sink and being careful not to pull the sink away from the wall, a crime too terrifying to imagine. After a quick hand washing and a few taps on the towel, I walked to my room grinning from ear-to-ear at the glorious sight of myself I had just seen.

Why, I have way more hair than I ever knew! I thought. *If the girls at school who called me bald-headed could see my hair now they'd be jealous of my curls and get all up in my face!* I'd proudly swing my curls like Cindy on the *Brady Bunch*. I tried not to touch them but couldn't resist and gently put my fingers through the loops in a few of the curls, carefully keeping them intact. Then I'd stretch my tightly coiled bangs down my face just to see if they were long enough to touch the tip of my nose. After that, I rolled those bangs back up with my two fingers all the way to the top of my forehead. I just *knew* I was cute.

After I turned eight, Mama left my hair alone. Winnie, an attractive eighteen-year-old girl who lived only a few blocks from our house then became my personal stylist. Winnie was very gentle while making each part in my hair and often complimented me sweetly for not being "tender-headed." In our community, if your hair is nappy and you are tender-headed, it isn't easy to achieve a good hairdo; black girls just have to learn to sit there and take the pain associated with having acceptable hair. I thought Winnie was pretty because she had a big Afro blowout like a dandelion gone to seed, and she wore stylish bellbottoms that fit her like one of *Charlie's Angels*. I loved her jeans and her fingernails which were long and perfect and I often asked her if they were real so she would let me tug on them gently to check.

After my hair session with Winnie, Mama always spread some dollars out in her hand like a fan in payment for her services. I thought it was a lot of money, but it was probably only five dollars. She used to talk to her friends about Winnie in a low voice, much lower than the one she used when talking about me. She gossiped that Winnie was marrying too young at 18. But in those days, a lot of black girls were getting married at that age.

The last time I wore a 1980's Shari Belafonte haircut with the "V" shape-up down the neck was right after my fight with Rose Johnson at the Tropicana Resort and Casino in Atlantic City. I loved how easy the Shari do was to keep up, especially after I had failed to wrestle my hair into dreads. They may look natural, but they are anything but; the high maintenance dreads require was way too much for me to handle. All the twisting and waxing in the world couldn't tame the cotton ball texture of my hair which unraveled on the ends no matter how tightly I tied them down at night. In those days, while trying to be a champion boxer and also keeping up with my two little children, I just didn't have time for all that fussing with hair. So, a Shari cut it was. I had loved seeing her in all the fashion magazines with that do and thought I could sport her low cut in an equally feminine way. The only other famous black woman I can recall who was brave enough to carry such a short cut was Grace Jones. But Grace's cut was much more androgynous — even downright masculine — with its high top and temple taper.

I didn't know that the Shari do just wasn't me until I saw the video from the Rose Johnson fight. I had been boxing for eighteen months and putting everything I had into strengthening and sculpting my body and perfecting my jab. The majority draw decision of that fight prompted me to review the tape over and over again looking for ways to improve my boxing technique and make ref's decisions start going my way. But while I was watching the tape over and over, I could see that the Shari hairdo — along with the look of my big boxing trunks, sports bra and bulging biceps — had completely transformed me into a version of Grace Jones, *not* Shari! Watching that fight video, my eyes stayed riveted on that devastating hairdo. Up to that point I had considered it a compliment when guys at the gym said, "Girl, you fight just like a dude." Now I saw that comment as having a lot to do with how I looked. It was like going to the fanciest party of the year and finding out afterwards that all night you had a huge chunk of collard greens lodged in the gap between your two front teeth.

So now I knew that my hair was terrible and I had to do something right away if I wanted to look and carry myself like a champion. *Maybe cornrows or braiding*, I thought. It had been two years since I had been to a head shop, and up to then I had no intention of asking for more of the pain that was handed out in those places. Just thinking about going to one brought back powerful memories of the torture inflicted by Mama Graves in the chair. I knew that although every once in a while I had lucked out and stumbled upon a decent shop with good stylists, most times there should have been a warning sign on the door saying, SIT AT YOUR OWN RISK.

Hair braiding shops come a dime a dozen in the DC metro area and range anywhere from a small unit with two chairs on the second floor of a storefront to a full service salon with up to twenty chairs. A good day is getting into a chair early and being finished within five to seven hours without having to take prescription painkillers. A bad day is finally getting into a chair at eleven o'clock in the morning and staggering out at eight at night with your head feeling like it is on fire and your face pulled so tight that your eyes feel like mere slits in a tight mask. Nothing works for the pain except a prescription painkiller, and I learned I'd better have something with me to take the edge off right away. There were variations among these experiences, but there was always that one awful truth; two months later, the process would have to start all over again.

For my new braided hairdo I chose a 15-chair shop that had some ads in the *Takoma Park Gazette*. Claudette, a thickset well-dressed African woman

— the shop's owner — greeted me at the receptionist desk with a cheerful hello. Behind her I could see ten braiders working intently on customers' heads. The place had a newly-renovated smell and lightly-used immaculate workstations — a relief from the worn and burning-hair-smelling shops I had experienced in the past. I had come in with the idea of getting something quick — cornrows maybe — but knew they would not last nearly as long as individual braids or a Senegalese twist. As Claudette showed me the swatches that indicated length and width, she explained, "The longer and thinner the twist, the more it will cost." I asked how long it would take and she told me that my braider was fast and could complete the style within 6 to 7 hours. Seven hours was a day at the gym for a boxer!

As I sat waiting for my braider to arrive, I listened to the African music blaring from the CD player mounted on the stand behind the greeting desk and tried to get into the general spirit of the place despite knowing it would be a day in *the chair*. Soon a twenty-something African girl entered the shop talking loudly and rapidly in French on her cell phone. Claudette introduced us and I received a heavily-accented hello from Folie as she pushed my head forward and went straight to work. Because of past experience of having my edges ripped out by overeager operators, I made it clear to her where on my head I wanted her to start and asked her not to pull my hair too tight. It seemed as if she only half-heard me so I pulled away and in a slightly slower, clearly annunciated way, repeated myself.

It didn't take any time at all for the flashbacks of Mama's treatment to loom up behind my tightly closed eyes and strangely, although I wasn't being hit, burned or ripped, quiet tears freely seeped from the corners of my eyes at the long-ago memory of *the chair*. I wasn't that little girl any more but I still couldn't understand why it needed to hurt so much for a black woman to look acceptable in her community.

The hypnotic background beat of the African recording that filled the place was soon muted by the rhythmic clickety-clacking of the braider's bright purple acrylic nails next to my ears as they weaved the long strands of synthetic hair into my own. I clinched my butt cheeks together to better grip the red leather chair and keep myself from running out the front door, and then I reached into my pocket for a pain pill. It was going to be a long day. To add insult to injury, Folie had the nerve to talk on her cell phone in French while working on my head. *Was she talking about me? Laughing about me like Mama Graves so often did to her friend on the other end of the phone?* Aside from my paranoia, it did seem that every time she answered that phone, the clickety-clacking of her nails slowed way down and time began to stand still. I just wanted the torment to be over. I tried to sleep in the hope that she would be finished by the time I woke up, but each time I nodded off I was jerked awake by her ungentle efforts to reposition my head.

Eventually, I heard the snap of the cigarette lighter as Folie prepared to burn the ends of the twists and pinch them secure. Relief spread through my body. The end was finally near. When the air around me was filled with the smell of singed synthetic hair extensions, Folie grabbed the spray bottle and misted my head all over in a useless attempt to soothe the throbbing pain of my over-stretched scalp. Her final touch was the swivel of my well-warmed chair back toward the mirror as she proudly showed me her latest work of art. Despite experiencing 6 ½ hours of misery along with a parade of sad memories, I was pleased with the results, but that didn't stop me from jumping out of that chair as fast as I could. In my haste, I threw a wad of money over the counter without waiting for a receipt. Folie's cash tip fluttered into her hand after I tossed it in her direction while dashing out the door.

My biggest worry now was that the painkiller would wear off before I got home to lie down. It had been a day of torture, with many more of those to come, but I knew that my look was now closer to the image I wanted to project in my climb to a world boxing championship and the jewel-encrusted leather champion's belt I so coveted.

Chapter Five

Throughout my boxing career I can honestly say that I never received an ass-whipping or a beat-down. Not even in my last fight at the Lincoln Theater when I got KO'd by Trish Hill. She caught me with a devastating, looping hard shot out of nowhere that sent me reeling back into the ropes, prompting the referee to call a halt to the bout. Thank God for referees because we boxers often don't know when to give in. It is a fact that no matter how I lost a fight, receiving the "L" on my record hurt me much more than any of the blows I received in the ring. And truly, the ass-whippings I received as a child hurt me far worse than the blows or losses I received as an adult.

When I was sparring or in a real bout, there was never an instance where I wanted to be in the ring with a person that I clearly outclassed or could take easy advantage of. The whole purpose for using strict weight classes and a ranking system in boxing is to match competitors as evenly and fairly as possible, assuming everyone involved is dealing aboveboard. So, when I think back to the times when I was clearly outmatched, in the wrong weight class, and things simply weren't in my favor I always think of Mama. I didn't stand a chance when she started physically abusing me. By the age of eight, I had already taken more than my share of backhands across the face, belt lashings and whippings at her hands.

I have no memory before the age of five of ever being hit by anyone in the world. I was the little girl who loved to laugh and learn, blessed with my foster parents, the Parkers, and four brothers who protected and loved me. I didn't know what pain, fear or worry meant. But when Louise Graves came into my life in 1973, that all changed with one burning slap across my face. It shocked me, but still I didn't understand that it was just an appetizer for what was to come. By 1975 I was well-versed in her secret, silent world of whippings. It was an exclusive society that I dared not mention to anyone. Or else! She made sure of that the first time she declared, *"What goes on in my house, stays in my house!"* I knew it meant I better not say a word to any-body — not even my brothers — about the whippings I was getting regularly from her.

After my first year at the Graves house, I started to ask God why, if all those things Mama said about me were true, was I even born? Getting a slap or a hit with the hairbrush was one thing. I always seemed to bounce back and forgive Mama like a little innocent puppy. And because she was always preaching and telling me she was making sure we had it better than we ever had it before, I thought I wanted to stay with her.

But finally Mama's growing violence against me brought me to my senses. After one bad whipping, I jammed my thumb in my mouth to keep from yelling too loud and being heard, and then picked up a brand new sheet of notebook paper. I frantically wrote the number one with a period after it and then wrote, *that bitch, I will pay her back for hurting me.* Since I couldn't really write or spell, the statement must have looked like some ancient code.

That was the beginning of my revenge list. I stared at that paper and wanted to add exactly what it was I wanted to do to Mama Graves but couldn't think of anything except give her a whipping when I got grown enough to do it. Maybe I would lift her up by one arm and dangle her in the air like she did to me. When I finished I folded that paper up into a tiny square and shoved it as far under my mattress as my arm could reach. That simple act somehow gave me a great feeling of relief.

There would be many times to come when I would feel I had reason to pull that raggedy piece of paper from under the mattress, but there were also times when things were okay and I didn't think about my list. The okay times were when I was at church with Grandma Arrington, the elderly boarder who later came to live at the Graves's and made life so much better for me, or at school on a field trip day. But a year is a long time, and by the end of my first year the paper was filled top to bottom on the front and half of the back. It was smudged and wearing thin from erasures, and there were some soft blurry spots where tears had dropped on it. It's funny, but just knowing I had something to do after somebody did or said something mean to me gave me a feeling of absolute power. It was like having my own super hero to take care of my unfinished business.

As I passed from foster home to foster home after leaving the Graves household, I somehow knew that only the important things should go on my revenge list. My body seemed to sense when it was time to write. When the feeling came over me, I felt that my body was shaking on the inside but barely able to move on the outside. My eyes welled up with tears and my heart beat fast as if I had just run a mile full-out. But it seemed to me that every stroke of my pencil was a bit of revenge. While I wrote, I cursed out and tattled on my abuser, often with a mirror as my witness. At each stroke of the pencil and each muttered threat, I was reducing a bit of the desire for revenge that was bubbling up within me. When this ritual was over, I always felt I had come out as a champion. My brand of revenge made me feel alive despite the terrible things that I felt I needed to avenge. And perhaps most important, the revenge list made me feel that I was not crazy like Mama said our real mother was. Writing stuff down gave me proof that after the bruises healed and the tears dried up, I didn't have to keep things straight in my head; I had my list.

At seven I was long and thin. According to Mama Graves, my body type was not to her taste. She'd say in her mean voice, "You not big as a minute and shaped funny — with your butt high up on your back." But it was not only her dislike of my body that brought the harsh words and sudden movements that made me flinch. It seemed that the mere sight of me made her angry. Oddly, despite her distaste for the sight of me, she insisted that I stay sitting somewhere close by so she could keep an eye on my every move. I chose the top step of the landing leading from the kitchen. Sometimes I made it out onto the screened-in side porch, and if I was really lucky I could sit out on the patio in one of the heavy steel chairs that matched the umbrella set in concrete. By then, the memories of the past — living with the Parkers and having my brothers always close by — were starting to fade behind the ugly present.

There was never a way to prepare for Mama's whippings, especially when they occurred right after school, usually on Fridays when we had gone on one of the exciting field trips I looked forward to each week. I was going to FLOC Learning Center then — a small private educational facility in a

Catholic church located on 14th and V streets—which was exclusively for children within the foster system who had behavior issues and/or various learning disabilities. The eighteen students who attended the school were taught by a staff of eight teachers, with a different teacher for each subject area. To encourage us to cooperate and learn, there was a point system which allowed us to go to the school store and spend our saved-up points on candy, jacks, little dolls, and other trinkets. Mark always managed to get his points taken away before he could use them. When this happened, he'd say to me, "Whad'ju get at the store?" I'd say; "Pretzels." And he'd say; "Well, gimme some," because he never had any points.

The center was where I got positive attention from adults, talked and played with other children, laughed and had fun. I always looked forward to going to school in the morning and hated to leave each day. I even enjoyed the routine of catching the bus to and from school with Mark despite his serious and unsmiling sense of responsibility towards me. I had been sent to the school because I was very far behind in arithmetic and reading. Jeff didn't have to go to FLOC, but Mark went because he was always in trouble. If there was ever a fight among the big kids, the street phrase they used was "GED AU ME" (get off me) and there were always kids like Mark having to be restrained from serious fighting. But they didn't get suspended because at FLOC the counselors were expected to handle the problems and move on.

Most adults didn't really talk to kids like me in those days, but at this school they did. Previously, I had been told to say to teachers, "Yes, Ma'am, Yes, Sir," but at this school the teachers told us to use their first names. In reading group, they waited patiently for us to sound out each and every word. And then they helped us correct our mistakes. It was individual attention — important stuff, especially for a kid like me.

I guess it was a slave mentality thing that the black people I came in contact with outside school in those days often criticized the white teachers at FLOC and told me, "Those white people don't care nothin' about you." What they didn't realize or accept is that white people were mainly the people who were nice to me! There was a white teacher named Don who taught me Language Arts. He was the first person aside from the Parkers who ever said to me, "Lisa, you are very pretty." In a funny way, it was an important validation for a confused little girl with low self-esteem.

When the specialists figured out I had learning problems, Mama Graves lost no time telling me I was "borderline retarded." She said, "You suck your thumb, and you don't know anything. They say you won't even graduate from high school!" But somehow I knew instinctively that I was better than what her cruel words described.

I had been in the first grade at the FLOC learning center for almost a year and knew everyone by name and considered them all to be my friends. My two best friends were Laverne and Betitte, but Kevin and Lorenzo were also in my class and we often played together. Field trip day was Friday when we kids got to hang out together at a place within the DC area chosen by the teachers. Our trip always ended with the usual van ride back to the school, and one day our crew of five decided to exchange telephone numbers by writing them into our hands with an ink pen and promising to call each other when we got home. I loved the idea but knew that there was no chance that I'd get to use Mama's phone for any reason and didn't even bother giving my number to the other kids. But I did get Lorenzo's number and wrote it on my hand as clearly as I could, along with his name in bold letters. The numbers faded quickly, but the name was still clear when I got home that afternoon. I was still excited by the day's activities, and as I walked into the house, the happiness in my step and the smile on my face caught Mama Graves completely off guard. Suspicious of my happiness, she yelled, "S-T-O-P! STOP RIGHT THERE! Don't be running up in here like you ain't got a bit of sense. You better calm down right now."

I stood frozen in my tracks while Mama squinted her eyes and bent all the way over, scowling directly into my face. Shaken by her aggressive approach, I threw my hand up to block what I thought was certain to be a slap across the face. And that's when she saw the letters — L-O-R-E-N-Z-O — and immediately ordered in a loud voice, "What in the world is that on your hand? Hold it out!" I was hesitant and slowly held it out with a half-cupped palm hoping she would not notice what it said. "Hold. It. Out!" she shouted. As I slowly opened my hand, I could feel a cold chill going up my spine.

"Lorenzo?! Lorenzo?! Who is Lorenzo?" Her face twisted into a menacing mask. "Oh no, don't cry now! You weren't crying when you wrote that boy's name in your hand, you little Jezebel. You know what you gonna get, so put your bag down and go out there and get me my three switches."

By then the tears were flowing, but no sound was coming out of my mouth. Slowly, I put my book bag down in the corner by the step. Then I crept out the open kitchen door with my face partially buried in my shirt. My steps got smaller and slower and my breathing heavier as I opened the screen door and headed down the porch steps onto the patio. The "switch-tree" was back behind the house in the narrow pathway where Girl, the family German shepherd, paced back and forth, attached to a long rusty chain. Girl was harmless, but she was big, and the smell of the dog shit she trampled over as she went back and forth on the narrow pathway was overwhelming.

As I moved slowly along the path trying not to step in any of the dog shit, I leaned forward and grabbed the first switch I could from the bottom of the tree's main limb and bent it down until it peeled away. It was twice the length of my arm — just the way Mama liked them. Now I had to find two more of equal size. I knew that if I didn't get them right the first time she would get even angrier and make me go back and repeat the whole process. I moved a little closer to the tree where it pressed into the links of the fence. Sticking my thin little fingers through the chain link, I snapped the next one clean and held it in my other hand along with the first switch. The third one had to be that perfectly bendable one growing through the links of the fence. I grabbed it and quickly broke it away. As I stepped back toward the house, Girl ran to the other end of the path out of my way. Holding all three switches in my hands — tears streaming down my cheeks — I stood on the grass and ran my hand down each one, stripping the leaves off each just the way Mama had taught me, with one long swipe.

I heard Mama's voice from the house; "It don't take that long to get no doggone switches! If you don't hurry up and get your butt in here, you gonna wish you did! Get in here now and go your butt downstairs and wait for me to get down there." The more she shouted these orders, the more I shook. Finally, I handed her the three switches and sobbed: "I – didn't – even – do – nothing!" And then I stomped down each stair loudly, repeating those sad words of protest. It was a routine I had endured many times, but each new time was as terrifying as the first time Mama stood behind me nudging me down the steps and then straight back to where the washing machine, big tub sink and heavy washboard were located.

I stood in front of the sink waiting to hear her footsteps on the stairs and stared at the small blazing flame of the hot water heater in the corner of the room. Finally, I heard the slow careful plonk of the heels of her house slippers hitting each step. As she circled around the corner back to where I waited, I watched her coming toward me in that ugly long velour housecoat she always wore. She grabbed the three switches and began plaiting them together, wrapping a green rubber band around each end. Then she held them between her clenched knees and plaited them together tightly. As I stood trembling, she took the second green rubber band loosely dangling from her wrist and wrapped and twisted it as tight as she could to hold the flimsy end of the switch together. After three or four flicks of her wrist to check her weapon for precision, it was time for her to attack me.

For starters, she barked at me, "Didn't I tell you about being grown! Take off those clothes of mine, I don't beat no clothes! Take'em off right now!"

"Please, Please! I ain't do nothing, what did I do?" I was full-out pleading with her now but she ignored me. As I dropped the last piece of "her" clothing to the floor and stood naked before her, I felt the first burning lash land on my lower back and part of my butt.

"H—H—H-H-h-h-h-h-h-h-h-u-u-u-a-a!" As I heard my own blood-curdling scream emerge from deep within my throat, I tried to move away from her. "You betta not run. If you make me come after you, you gonna get it worse!" Her dark claw of a hand reached out and grabbed me between my armpit and shoulder blade and anchored me between her legs, whipping me continuously. I screamed and hollered.

"*H—H—H-H-h-h-h-h-h-h-h-u-u-u-a-a. H—H—H-H-h-h-h-h-h-h-h-u-u-u-a-a.* Please stop, I won't do it again. Oh God! Please!" Everything hurt as I struggled to get out of the leg lock.

"You think you are so grown but I'm here to let you know that I'm the only grown women living here." I gasped for air and coughed until I began to heave and gag, and my screams began to stick in my throat. My mouth was wide open and I was yelling from the pit of my stomach, but no sound rose out.

"Gurl, if you throw up on my floor I'm gonna make you clean every bit of it up. Now shut up! Can't nobody hear you down here no way so I don't care how loud you cry."

During this eternity, there were times when I thought she was trying to kill me. But it didn't matter that I was going to die; I wanted to. Then she suddenly grew exhausted and sweaty, and I realized she was done. As she released her grip, I slunk down to the floor. Then she gave her final order, "Now put your clothes on and get you butt up there on those steps. I betta not hear a peep out of you when you get up here." As she disappeared up the stairs, I lay there for a moment on the dirty, concrete floor whimpering and hiccupping.

As I inched toward my clothes, I could feel the long red whelps rising on my skin. I was feverish and sweat-drenched, and my legs wobbled when I finally rose. Wet, watery snot dripped from the end of my nose and rolled down my lip as I sniffled and tried to wipe it away with my elbow and a damp sock I picked up from the floor. As I tried to brush off the white dusty grit of the floor, I looked at the nasty red lesions that covered my body. The sight of them sent me into breathless panic while an unfamiliar and sorrowful moan emerged from my throat as I lightly touched the small drops of blood drying on my skin and eyelashes. As I pulled myself up the basement stairs I could hear the familiar rattle of dishes as Mama fluttered around in the kitchen preparing dinner as if nothing had happened. Once in the kitchen, I walked past the short landing and headed up the stairs.

"Where you going?" she said in a low steady voice. I was cautious in my answer, fearing more violence, "Upstairs to use the bathroom." When she didn't order me to stop, I continued up to the toilet where I sat for a long time, studying the long whelps exposed above my pulled-down jeans. "I HATE YOU!" I blurted in the direction of the kitchen but not loud enough for Mama Graves to hear. Soon, I left the bathroom, went immediately to the mirror in my bedroom and leaned in close to see if there were any obvious wounds on my face. As usual, Mama had skillfully managed to avoid putting marks on my face. It was a relief, but still, there was a part of me wishing she had given me a black eye so someone would figure out what my loving foster mother was doing to me.

I hate her, I hate her and she's a cold bitch, I thought over and over. At seven, I had already heard the word "bitch" many times. I saw it written on the playground in chalk and also heard it in a nasty cheer the neighborhood girls used to chant in the public school yard.

Chorus: *Titty Bump—Titty Bump—Titty Bump*
First girl: *I said a – Oooh!*
Look at my boo –ty…
Chorus: *I said a – Oooh!*
Look at my boo –ty…
First girl: *Oooh!*
Ain't it fine…
Oooh!
Look at my tit-ties…
Chorus: *Oooh!*
First Girl to next girl: *Bitch, they will blow your mind.*
Chorus: *Titty Bump—Titty Bump—Titty Bump*

I used to laugh at the boldness those girls showed while rhythmically reciting these words and prancing around like Diana Ross. And I was fascinated at how they kept right on chanting loudly even while adults passed or stood by watching and shaking their heads. I knew that the word bitch was as bad as an insult could get because when one girl posed the challenge to the next girl, pointing at her and saying, "Bitch, I'll blow you mind," the other girl always came out harder and much more aggressively in reaction.

Bitch is what I'm going to name you since you to call me 'Grownie.' So, you're a bitch! I talked into the vanity mirror as if Mama were standing face to face with me. While repeating my vengeful new name for her I could feel my nerves start to settle. Finally my face was dry of tears and the trembling in my hands slowing down. Now with clearer vision I could examine the shredded patches of high red blistering on my skin. But, as I lifted up my T-shirt to take a closer look at my wounds, I lost it all over again. *You mean, ugly bitch!*

Finally composed again, I sat straight and felt the anger in my face while my temples throbbed with pain. I quickly smoothed my bed to conceal my 'bad behavior' from Mama's critical eyes while I still held onto the anger. Calm once again, I walked toward the door and checked the mirror, purposely maintaining my angry look. I walked back down the stairs and plopped down on the familiar third step, frozen in anger with my arms folded tight in front of me.

I passed out of FLOC Learning Center with improved skills and confidence and started the second grade at Clark Elementary School in my neighborhood. Before going to FLOC, I had attended first grade at Clark for a few months and had been teased every day by the other kids in my class. The teasing from the girls had usually emphasized my short, unstylish hair and my limited, plain, ill-fitting wardrobe. Even when I wore a dress, a little group of girls often approached me, laughing, and boldly asked a question they already knew the answer to: "Are you a girl or a boy?" Embarrassed, withdrawn, and extremely shy, I found it impossible to make friends at Clark and believed all of Mama's repeated insults, often telling myself; *Nobody is ever going to like me.* During those few months in first grade, I remained socially isolated, and comforted myself by sucking my thumb, a habit which infuriated Mama.

But now that I was reentering Clark as a second-grader, I was excited that I'd be walking to school with Jeff and would possibly be able to see and play with him at recess. In fact, I was happy to go back to that school because the FLOC Learning Center experience had brought me out of my shell quite a bit and I had finally dropped the habit of sucking my thumb in public. Adjusting to the new school and new ways of doing things seemed natural to me after the positive experience at FLOC, and I was beginning to build some confidence. But I didn't know that Mama Graves had already poisoned the well at Clark. She had talked to my teacher, described my family background, and emphasized that I was a problem *foster child*. Just knowing that I was a foster child gave my light-skinned and ignorant teacher a license to treat me poorly. If there was a reading group seated around her semi-circular desk in the front of the class, she made a point of excluding me because I couldn't read very well. She would announce this painful fact to the class and then add sternly, "Put your head down on the desk until we are finished." I wasn't the only child she treated this way. I noticed that the other "problems" were also foster children or were very dark-skinned.

One day, a sassy little girl came up to me as I entered the classroom and said, "Are you a girl or a boy? Hah Hah Hah Haah!" I rolled my eyes as hard as I could so she could see. She continued, "I *said*, are you a girl or a boy?" I answered her sharply, "You see my dress, so you know I'm a girl!" Still not satisfied, she purposely bumped her shoulder against mine. "O-O-w-a!" I yelled and immediately pushed her to the floor. The teacher saw this and automatically said to me, "Oh, you gonna get it now!" Then, with the class eagerly watching the show, she wrote a note, pinned it to the front of my dress and said, "Give that to your mother as soon as you get home. You're not gonna come to my class acting like a fool. Now go sit your butt in that chair until 3:00."

I knew I was going to be in trouble when I got home but stayed optimistic, hoping that the note would tell exactly what happened. As we walked home slowly that afternoon, I explained to Jeff what had happened. "That girl hit me first so I pushed her back. She ain't even get in trouble though." Jeff tried to ease my worry by saying hopefully, "Well, if she started it then you won't get in trouble so don't worry about it, Lisa."

When I handed Mama the note I could tell by the expression on her face that what she had read wasn't in my favor so I tried to explain what happened. Apparently, the note suggested that I had been in an all-out brawl. "I knew this would happen!" she shouted. "You ain't been in a real school for five minutes and you up there fighting already. You don't make no sense, gurl. But that's ok, 'cause I got something for you tomorrow." Tearful, I tried to explain my version of the story, "But I wasn't fighting, the girl was messing with me then she bumped me and I pushed her back."

"Just shut your mouth and go change into your play clothes," she ordered, pointing up to my room. Relieved that she hadn't sent me out to get some switches, I thought she believed my version of the events and the issue was over. It wasn't.

The next day at school I sat at my desk just after lunch waiting for my teacher's afternoon instructions. The woman never really said much to me so I was surprised when she called me up to the front of the class, "Lisa, come here for a minute." I pushed back from my desk and walked toward her as she moved to the door. Once there, she pushed it open and motioned for me to walk under her arm to the hallway. That's when I saw Mama wearing her favorite green polyester pantsuit and her signature tam cocked to the side, and standing in the hallway with her hands on her hips, a mean smile on her face. Her oversized patent leather triangle purse was thrown over her shoulder and she looked as if she was going to a tea party. Then she spat out these words to me, "I told you I was going to get you. You thought I was playing, didn't you?"

"Noo-o-o..."

"Now I'm going to embarrass you 'cause you embarrassed me. Get in that class where I'ma tear you up." As she said this, her voice was low and determined. The teacher stood there, hanging on every word, clearly getting some pleasure out of my situation. By now I was shaking all over.

As we three entered the classroom, the teacher told the class to remain quiet and stay in their seats. Then Mama reached into her purse and pulled out what looked like one of Daddy Graves's old black leather belts with a large brass buckle on one end. At that moment, I noticed that my teacher walked over and stood in front of the classroom door, blocking the window which otherwise might have provided a view from the hallway of what was about to happen to me.

So Mama had decided to change the game and give me a public beating. She had always told me that there were people out there just waiting to tell her what I did wrong and now she was going to prove it. Knowing what was about to occur, I was overcome with embarrassment. She held the belt buckle and then wrapped the belt several times around her hand until only the part with holes in it was exposed, making it short enough for her to control without hitting herself. Not knowing what to do or how to act, I stood facing her and waited for the first lash. When it landed I let out a shrill scream, H-H-h-h-h-h-h-h-a-a-a-a-a…

"You better shut up that noise right now!" She growled through clenched teeth as she grabbed me by the collar and pulled me close to her chest. As the stinging burn from the first blow died down, so did my scream. Then with a quick release of one of her hands she began to give me steady snapping-blows with the belt across my legs, arms and body. My classmates watched from their desks with eyes wide with shock. Finally, I sank towards the floor, my dead weight hanging as my foster mother held all sixty-five pounds of me by one arm and continued hitting downwards at me, making sure not to hit my face.

When she was done, she let go of me and barked, "Stand up and get yourself together!" My slow rise from the floor made her angry and she repeated herself. "I said get up — ain't nobody killed you yet. Get your butt up now!" Her regular voice returning, she added a final threat, "Now go sit in your chair and don't make me have to come up here no more."

"Yes ma'am." I whimpered. Then I sat down at my desk and buried my face between my folded arms, touching the cool wooden desk with my hot forehead.

There was complete silence in the classroom, even when my teacher left to walk Mama out into the hallway for a friendly farewell chat. When she returned, she got on with the lesson as if the public lashing had never happened. Eventually, I opened my eyes and raised my head and began rubbing the thick red whelps on the backs of my hands and on my arm. Then I pulled down my sleeve as far as it could reach to hide the damage Mama had so publicly inflicted on me.

The little girl sitting next to me looked at me with sadness in her eyes and said with real concern, *"Da-a-ag... You ok? That looks like it hurts bad. Dag. Do it still hurt?"* Of course I shook my head no.

I knew that after a few days, the whelps would have vanished and the only outward signs of my public humiliation would be the thin white lines that appeared after the dark crumbles of scabs were shed. Over time, all visual evidence of her cruelty would go underground, leaving only emotional evidence layered firmly in my soul.

After three full years of being in Mama Graves's home, my eight-year-old self had evolved from a nervous, scared little girl to a more worldly wise, cool and collected character. Like a fighter, time and hard training had taught me toughness. I no longer flinched at her raised hands and sudden outbursts. And her loud, cutting voice no longer terrified me. The first test of my new persona came when one day in reaction to a now-forgotten misstep of mine, she shouted her usual order, "Get out there and get me my three switches," and I simply did not react as she expected or wanted. My defenses had become sharper now, and this clearly made her uncomfortable. No longer was I willing to frantically scurry behind the house to fetch my own punishment tool. Instead, I was determined to walk tall and deliberately onto the porch and straight out the door. This time, I turned the corner slowly and stood patiently while Girl scurried to the other end of the path to get out of my way. Then I slowly tore town three leafy switches and stripped the leaves off before proceeding effortlessly and coolly back into the kitchen. "Here," I said, angling the bundle in Mama's direction.

She glared sharply at me and snatched them from my hand without a word. As soon as I felt the sticks leaving my hand to hers, I turned away and moved purposefully through the doorway and down the basement stairs.

Knowing she liked to keep me waiting before a whipping, I took time removing my clothes and hanging them carefully across the iron basin. Then I leaned the arch of my neck back against the cool washing machine and rested there, idly running my hands through a bucket of brown wooden clothespins. When I heard her coming down the steps, I stood in the middle of the floor in front of the sink as usual. Then, while she plaited and stabilized her whip with rubber bands, I looked around the room without expression. This unnerved her and she reacted defensively, "I'm sick and tired of you. You think you gonna drive me crazy but you not. You got the devil in you, gurl, and I swear-fo God that I'm gonna beat it out of you!"

I looked at her coolly as she bucked toward me and raised her hand, waiting for my usual desperate retreat. But, this time I didn't flinch, and her eyes widened as if she had just seen a ghost. Then she wrapped her hard, jittery hand around the upper part of my arm and began striking me with the switch she held in the other hand. The sting of the lash and burn of the lift after each hit made my body simmer with heat. I clenched my teeth and lips, and with tears running down my face, I kept my feet planted to the floor, determined to unsettle her.

"O-OH! You think you bad now? O-OHH ! You so bad that you ain't gonna cry?"

With each swing as she tore into me, she repeated her taunt, "You ain't gonna cry? You bad now? You ain't gonna cry? You think you big and bad now?" I tightly clinched every muscle of my body, but allowed my cheeks to puff out, letting rapid streams of air push through my nose. Throughout, I kept silent. I hung my head toward the floor to let the tears, sweat and snot flow freely, but still I did not make a sound.

Growing almost frightened, Mama let go of my arm and growled in a low voice, "You got the devil in you, gurl!" Then she backed away quickly and disappeared up the stairs, leaving me to celebrate my first victory over her.

Chapter Six

PSYCH

```
Case #513.276.6
```

> Early on, Lisa was diagnosed as having rejection dysphoria which meant she was unable to deal with love and rejection. In October 1976, she began therapy with Dr. Livingood.

Back in those days, the stigma of mental illness played like dark comedy in the black community. The terms *sick, crazy,* and *nervous breakdown* were warning labels stuck to anyone who dared to enter a psychiatrist's office. The two most overused Yo-Mama insults of the day were, "Yo Mama wears combat boots," and "Yo Mama stays at Saint E's." This last one referred to the Saint Elizabeth's Mental Hospital located on the southeast side of DC. That putdown was usually served up with aggressive eye rolling and the familiar rapid finger circling around one ear which implied that your mother was nuts. All of us kids at school had heard of the mental hospital from some place or another, so cracking that joke was good as gold and always sparked laughter from even the quietest kids on the playground. For some people, it was a personal insult that often hit so close to home that it could instantly incite a schoolyard brawl. Almost worse than that one was *going to a psychiatrist.* As a damning label it ranked right up there in the #1 spot with *pissing the bed.* If anyone ever found out that you had either of those problems, you might as well transfer to another school right then and there because your life would become unbearable all the way through. While humor had its part in playing off the seriousness of mental issues that plagued the community as a whole, many of us suffered in silence and denial and covered up any unexplained emotional deficiencies in order to appear as normal as possible. This is why I never discussed with anybody the subject of where I had to be every Wednesday promptly at 3:15.

After Mama had filed numerous complaints to FLOC about my behavior, I was given a series of psychological evaluations at Howard University Hospital. Despite my foster mother's attempts to get me diagnosed otherwise, the results came back as *normal with an average IQ for her age and a reasonable vocabulary* even though I spoke very little at home. Nevertheless, Mama continued to push her own diagnosis of me and reminded FLOC of my "bad behavior" which included "nervousness" and "mannerisms" which to her mind skewed the bell curve in favor of insanity. As she often reminded me, my skittishness made me "just like your sick mother." My thumb-sucking habit had not been extinguished by Mama's hot sauce and tie-down method and I still had a small swollen lump on the back of my left thumb from the habit. That, and my fingernails which I constantly bit to the quick, made her certain that she was more knowledgeable about me than any of those doctors at Howard. Her reports to the agency apparently carried more weight than those of the professionals and I was placed in the category of "Special Needs Child." With this new label came a substantial benefit for Mama Graves — a boost to her monthly stipend for taking care of me.

As much as I disagree with Mama's assessment of me and would argue that I was perfectly normal just as the tests had shown, I admit that she was right-on about my deep-seated issues. But these were the issues I developed while living with her! Even at the age of eight, I was certain of that. She had worked the system well and was now receiving a larger-than-usual stipend for taking care of me. But she had not anticipated FLOC's procedural process of placing children into therapy if there were any questions of mental health. Ironically, when it came to raising black children, therapy went against everything Mama believed. Like most black people back then, she didn't believe that there was any such thing as therapy. She called psychiatry "white folks' foolishness" and often ranted about such a useless waste of time.

She often said, "Psychiatry don't work on no black children. It's something white folk made up for their children because they don't know how to handle them. White children talk back to their mamas and daddies and call them asses and everything else to their faces." Then she'd launch into an imitation of a whiney white woman voice, "Now Johnny, if you get up off the floor and behave yourself, I'll buy you an ice cream cone."

After that, she'd shift back to her regular ranting voice and continue, while banging pots and pans and slamming cabinet doors as she prepared dinner, "I see those bad white kids falling out all over the floor at the store when they can't have something they want. Umph Umph Umph... It don't make a bit a sense. Ooowee... Just let a child of mine fall out on the floor with me anywhere. I would tear them up right then and there and embarrass them like they trying to embarrass me."

At first I didn't know what she was talking about when I heard this part of the rant. I just figured she was disgusted by something she had witnessed while out shopping earlier that day. After all, this seemed to be her normal way of dealing with the experience of coming in contact with white people. She'd smile and nod in their faces and then come home and vent until the vessel overflowing with hatred emptied out.

When she learned that as a consequence of her comments to the social workers at FLOC, I would be going to Children's Hospital once a week for therapy, she was livid. This time the white people rant was all because of me. "Those people down there at FLOC act like they know what's best for y'all! They don't care a thing about y'all and think they can run my house. Now they think you need a therapist. You don't need no therapy, you just need the devil beat outta you!"

While in Mama's house, the normal feelings that I had about myself were far outweighed by a series of anxieties which I suffered in silence. Among these was a mountain of secrets I was afraid to even acknowledge. I lay awake for hours at night as I sucked my thumb or chewed on my fingernails asking myself these questions over and over:

Why did Mama and Daddy Parker get rid of us?

What happened to Winston and Anthony?

Why does Mama Graves beat me all the time and hate me
*   so much?*

How come our real mother is so sick?

What did our real father look like?

Why is Gavin always trying to put his tongue in my mouth and his
*   fingers in my private place?*

How come I can't play with my brothers?
Why am I a foster child?
Am I gonna die soon?

I had never seen Mama that mad with the FLOC people before. I sat quietly with my elbows on the table and chin resting in the palms of both hands and let my eyes follow her as she darted from one end of the kitchen to the next. Soon she stopped in her tracks and stood directly over me. Startled, I jerked my back flush against the vinyl padding of the kitchen chair, anticipating one of her spontaneous slaps. But no, this time she waved her bony crooked brown forefinger toward my nose in rhythm with the syllables of the words she now directed at me; "Lisa, let me get one thing straight with you right now."

I looked away from her bobbling finger and made eye contact with her as she glared into my face and spoke, "By now you know that whatever goes on in my house stays in this house, don't you?"

"Yes ma'am."

"Those people down there at FLOC want you to start going to a psychiatrist next week. So now I have to waste my time and take you down there. Those whiteys don't know nothing about nothing. All those busybodies do is pry in other people's bidness."

That next Wednesday, Mama put on one of her dressy pantsuits along with a matching tam and purse and called a cab to take me to my first appointment at the newly built Children's Hospital. At first it felt like we were going to a regular doctor's appointment — like when we went to Dr. Michael's busy pediatric office. But when I saw that huge, shiny new building with its mirrored windows glinting in the sun, I knew it was going to be a different kind of visit. I felt special going into such a beautiful new place where I was to have an appointment just for me. The waiting room was quiet and everything in it was new and colorful. There were bright carpets, the newest toys and books, and even a hanging television set at the perfect level for kids my size. The young woman at the receptionist desk answered the phone with a singsong voice, "PSY-CHI-A-TRY." Hearing that made me snicker to myself; was she trying to sound like an old-fashioned telephone operator?

Mama told me to sit down and wait while she checked us in. I wanted to go straight over to the toys but I knew better than to do anything she hadn't told me to do. Though there were chairs placed together in twos and threes, I chose one that was set off by itself with an end table next to it. When Mama came over to sit down, she shot me a dagger for not choosing to sit with her. I didn't care because I knew that in that place I was at least temporarily safe from her. We sat quietly in the empty room. After just a few minutes, a little woman with a bouncy blond mushroom haircut called out as she walked past the reception desk, "Lisa Ponder!" She looked me straight in the eyes and said, "Are you Lisa Ponder?" I nodded and she continued, "Lisa, I'm Dr. Livingood, your new doctor." Then she turned to Mama and said pleasantly, "And you must be Mrs.Graves."

I saw that subtle trace of intimidation that came over Mama's face whenever she met white people and I took some pleasure in knowing that as Mama was getting more uncomfortable with the situation, I was feeling *more* comfortable. We followed the little woman back to another hallway and into a corner office. It was a small space, with a grownup-size desk pushed into a corner. Aside from that desk, the rest of the office looked like it was designed just for kids. Like the waiting room, there were lots of books, toys, and art supplies. There was a big plate glass window and through it I could see the entry and bus stop at the front of the hospital.

That first meeting with Dr. Livingood didn't really involve me. The two grownups talked while I sat in one of the big chairs with both of my hands wrapped tightly around its wooden arms. My feet swung rapidly as I gazed to the opposite side of the office wanting desperately to play with those toys. A part of Mama's home training was that whenever I went anywhere with her, I was to be quiet and not be fidgety. So I stayed planted right there in that chair until the meeting was over. But, still, I couldn't help being excited while I was so close to toys and books that I had only seen on TV. Another of Mama's rules was never dare speak or look in their direction when grown folks are talking. So from my chair I stared at every book spread on the table and every toy on the shelf. I imagined myself emptying out all those cans of Tinker Toys, Lock Blocks and Lincoln Logs onto the floor and building something huge. As I stared at the forbidden fruit, I thought to myself, *Man, if only I could just go to that little table over there in the corner and draw on one of those papers. I would draw something with the pencil first and then trace over the lines with the markers. Dag! Mama makes me sick! I can't stand her ugly self!* Then I dared take a quick sideways glance at her and roll my eyes in a slick way, so she wouldn't notice.

Every now and then Dr. Livingood asked me something that I barely heard through all the distractions in my head. When I did hear her, I snapped to attention, looking toward the sound of her voice, but then quickly glanced over to Mama to see if it was okay for me to answer. She wouldn't respond in any way so I replied, "H-h-h-u-u-u-n? Wha'd you say?" The doctor repeated the question and I answered. This happened several more times until the hour was over and it was time to get back into a cab and go home. On our way out, Dr. Livingood stopped me and explained that I would be coming by myself to see her every week for one hour. Then she said, "How do you feel about that, Lisa?" I tried not to but couldn't help but smile at the thought of going back every week and getting a chance to play with all those toys.

"Fine," I said, not wanting to seem to Mama Graves like I was too eager. She snatched my hand and walked briskly out the door. Dr. Livingood stood in the doorway and watched as we left and I looked back over my shoulder and let out a cheerful, "B-y-e-e-e-e!"

Dr. Livingood waved back and my fast walk turned into a joyful skip. Mama yanked me forward and said, "Come on here, girl, before you make me miss my cab!" Despite Mama's yanking and hurrying, there was no cab waiting outside and she had to spend ten minutes fussing and fuming while trying to hail one on busy Michigan Avenue.

This was the only time Mama was ever to set foot in Dr. Livingood's office. She didn't need to. She had skillfully convinced me that she and my therapist were in cahoots and would be chatting on a regular basis about the contents of my private conversations with the doctor. Doctor/patient confidentiality was not a concept I knew anything about in those days. So I thought about that whippin I had received from Mama in front of my class only months before and remembered how my teacher sided with and protected her instead of me. Remembering my embarrassment and the sting of the belt in Mama Graves's hand, I swore myself to secrecy; *I ain't saying nothing to that doctor 'cause all Ima get is another whippin.* I was to meet with Dr. Livingood on Wednesdays. And during that hour each week, I would be protecting my-self and Mama's secrets with everything I had.

I knew all about catching the Metro buses in DC because Mark and I had been routinely catching them to get to the FLOC Learning Center. But now I would be taking the bus alone and a series of unreasonable worries began to go through my mind:

> *What if the bus breaks down?*
> *What if I get on the wrong bus and it takes me somewhere*
>   *far away and I can't find my way back?*
> *What will I do if someone tries to snatch me away?*

When I started going alone to Children's, I had to get used to the idea that Mark would not be around trying to hold my hand, nagging me to walk faster, and protecting me as he always had. But after the first month or so, I was well-versed in the routine of walking four blocks to Georgia Avenue, catching the bus to Irving Street and then transferring to the second bus which dropped me right in front of that beautiful hospital building. At first I entered through the front entrance, but soon learned a more exciting way to get in. Instead of getting off the bus at the front entrance, I could wait until it went into the un-derground garage and then hop on an escalator to the second landing where there was a ceiling-high mirror which extended the whole length of the wall. I loved that mirror and always spent a few extra moments dancing and posing in front of it until it was time to rush through the double door to the main waiting area where there was a must-stop gift shop.

It was the best store my eyes had ever seen. There were stuffed animals, dolls, toys, games, trinkets, gadgets, snacks and candy. And it wasn't just any old kind of candy. It was all the latest novelty candy shown on TV. My fa-vorite was the Fireball Jaw Breakers for five cents apiece. After walking through the store, checking out all the newest stuff, I would lay twenty-five cents on the counter in whatever form I had scrounged together during the week. The store clerk was always nice to me and didn't act like she thought I would steal things. She just rang up my fireballs and said *goodbye* cheerfully as I hustled out the door to get to the psych office on time.

The Psychiatry receptionist knew me by name and always said the same thing. "Hi, Lisa, do you have your Medicaid card ready for me?"

"Yes," I'd answer while reaching into my book bag, past the fireballs, to grab the little green card. When she was finished with it, I slipped it back into the book bag and drew out one of the beloved red fireballs, tucking it carefully into one cheek. Then I went to one of the big chairs by the *Highlights* magazines and turned to the see-if-you-can-find puzzles to find as many objects I could before the doctor came out to escort me to her office.

Dr. Livingood was always patient with me. Almost every week without fail I entered her office sucking on a fresh new jawbreaker fireball, and she never once asked me to get rid of it. The first time I did this, I thought she would, but when she didn't, I enjoyed that ball of flaming goodness to the fullest, shifting it slowly from one cheek to the other until the heat finally forced me to reach in with my thumb and forefinger and remove it to get some relief from the burning of soft tissues in my mouth. Touching the fireball always coated my fingers with wet, sticky red goo and part of my deliberate delaying tactic included taking a Kleenex from Dr. Livingood's desk, carefully licking my fingers clean, wiping them dry with the Kleenex, and after plopping the candy back into my mouth, starting the process all over again.

As our conversation crawled along because of the frequent jawbreaker breaks, Dr. Livingood observed me patiently without judgment. Although I was well aware that these shenanigans would have enraged Mama, I took full advantage of the delaying tactic because, as nice as the doctor was, suspicion and the possibility of betrayal were always present in my mind. I started to gain confidence because of her unwillingness to correct me over the jaw-breaker ploy, and then I was comfortable enough to get playful with her. She would ask me about my day and how I was feeling, and I would turn these questions right back on her. To her predictable, "How are you today, Lisa?" I would answer by imitating her voice and tone, "I'm fine. Now how are you today, Dr. Livingood?" Then I underlined my daring act with a shot of silly laughter. Without batting an eye, she would reply; "I'm just fine, Lisa. How was school today?"

As much as I might have wanted to comply with Dr. Livingood's attempts to reach out to me, I wasn't about to get caught up with having any kind of real conversation with her. My anxious mind always went back to how Mama had warned me off talking about what went on in her house. But I enjoyed the independence of having appointments with Dr. Livingood and the process of getting there, so after a few weeks of shyness, I did begin to talk to her. I usually chose my words carefully, but there were times when I got on a roll talking about something and slipped up and mentioned something off limits — usually something about home. But I quickly realized these slipups and fell back into silence before it was too late to hide the truth from her.

Chapter Seven

A Grandmother and a Fairy Godmother

I was at school when the old woman moved into the Graves's second floor rental apartment. She must have come that morning because, by the time Jeff and I had returned home from school, she was unpacked and completely settled in. Surprised to see the open door directly across the hall from my bedroom, I stood in my doorway waiting to see who was rattling the pots and pans in the small eat-in kitchen. I could hear 'white-people' music softly mingling with the mysterious rustling and clanging in the lowly lit space and wondered if an actual white person was in the house. As the noises of the pots and pans died down, I could make out a white man's voice on a transistor radio singing to the beat of a snare drum:

> *"Just slip out the back, Jack*
> *Make a new plan, Stan*
> *No need to be coy, Roy*
> *Just set yourself free"*

Although this music sounded way different from the disco and soul music I was used to hearing, soon I was bobbing my head on the downbeat and realizing that I liked this strange new music. Still no one appeared at the apartment door, so I hurried back into the bedroom to change from my school clothes into my play clothes. I had let nearly fifteen minutes slip by and knew that soon Mama would be yelling up the stairs for me to hurry and get down there. I sat on the side porch all that afternoon waiting to hear her say something about that person rattling around the upstairs kitchen. But Mama didn't talk on the phone that afternoon, and it wasn't until dinnertime that she finally came out and announced, "The lady staying in the room upstairs is Ms. Arrington. She will be living here from now on. Now Lisa, I want you to go up there and see if she needs anything when you're finished eating." Surprised and delighted by the request, I hurriedly chewed all the food in my mouth and answered, "Yes ma'am!"

The only times I had ever known of anyone staying in Mama and Daddy's house was when relatives from New York or Virginia came to spend a few days. I always loved having company because when guests were there, Mama focused less on me and acted way nicer than usual. She was already behaving differently toward all of us that night — like she did when we were out in public and she put on the perfect family act. After dinner, Mama even let me help wash the dishes, which I loved to do. While drying and stacking the dinner plates on the kitchen counter for Mama to put into the high cabinet, I looked up and saw a little white-looking woman enter the room. She was small; only a few inches taller than I was.

"Hi, Ms. Arrington!" I called out.

"Hi you," the woman replied and pulled out one of the chairs and sat down.

Mama explained with that familiar fake smile in her voice, "This is Lisa, she's eight years old now and I'm gonna send her up there with you so she can help you out. Okay?"

The woman replied, looking at me, "Why that's fine, that's just fine. All the little girls and boys at my church call me Grandma, so you can call me Grandma too if you want to, Lisa." I looked up and made eye contact with her, answering happily, "Yes ma'am!"

That's when she became a lodger in the Graves household and my Grandma Arrington. All these years later, I wonder if Mama somehow realized she had gone too far in disciplining me and wanted someone else to move in to take some of the pressure off raising me herself. Whatever the reasons, Grandma Arrington's arrival began a new, delightful and humane chapter in my young life. I had been living unhappily in the Graves household for three years, but after Grandma showed up, as long as I was in her small space, I felt safe and valued.

No longer was I forced to stay downstairs each day after school under Mama's total control. Now I was able to go into Grandma's warm kitchen where I was welcome to sit down at the four-chair dinette set which fit perfectly within the small space. I always sat in the same chair and soon Grandma was calling it "Where Lisa Sits." There was always a new smell coming from a pot, pan or the oven, and I joyfully wrapped myself in those delicious smells and Grandma's warm, nurturing presence.

Grandma Arrington was only five feet tall and weighed about 125 pounds. She had very fair skin, and this fact, along with her soft shoulder-length wavy hair which she kept shining and well-managed with a dab of V05 oil conditioner, meant that she was often mistaken for a white woman. I could see that she had been a real beauty in her younger years because she was still beautiful, even though there wasn't a tooth in her head. At first, I didn't believe my eyes when I saw her toothlessness, but she was so calm and self-assured she didn't even try to hide it.

Grandma had a slight southern accent, and her words always came out clear and precise despite the absent teeth. I studied her mouth, thinking that her teeth would grow back in, just like a wound that was healing. But after a while, I stopped noticing her teeth unless she mentioned them. Once in a while she would put in her dentures to see how they felt, but it always came down to her saying in a matter-of-fact way, "I'm not wearing these darn things when they hurting my mouth like this. Lord no! Can't even chew my food with 'em. Besides, my gums are hard enough to grind up everything, even fried pork chops and okra, and I love fried pork chops and okra." Then she would laugh heartily while taking the ill-fitting plates out of her mouth and carefully placing them back into her yellow denture cup.

Grandma often told me about her life and I loved listening to her stories. It seemed to me that she must be the oldest women in the world when she said, "I was born in 1908 in a little country house. Wasn't no doctor who delivered either — it was a midwife."

"Why?" I asked, in awe of her ancient age. "They ain't have hospitals where you lived, Grandma?"

I pictured her childhood home in the middle of a large field with an old outhouse in back, lined on each side with a deep woods and one lonely road in the front leading nowhere. I liked it when she talked because she was always so sure of things and also because although I was only eight, she always made me feel equal and important.

Besides Dr. Livingood, Grandma was the only grownup who would actually sit and have a real conversation with me and care about what I had to say back.

I was intrigued by everything about her. A short cherry wood buffet table pushed flush to the wall next to the kitchen door displayed photographs, a transistor radio, a clock, and her daily dose of medication. One of the black and white pictures displayed there was of a young, beautiful woman with long black flowing hair and a bright smile that looked like a white woman I saw once singing in a musical on television. She saw me staring at it and said, "That is me when I was 36 years old."

"That's you for real, Grandma?" I said with my eyes bulging toward the framed photo.

"Y-e-e-e-a-a-s, that me! And these are my daughters and three grand-babies," she said while pointing to the other pictures lined across the back of the table. I was intrigued when I noticed that one of her granddaughters was Winnie, the girl who braided my hair so gently and was so kind to me.

I had always been made to feel that because of my dark skin, short kinky hair and long, thin frame I was inferior to any person who looked like Grandma at any age. But it wasn't Grandma or people who looked like her, or white people who made me feel inferior. It was black people with skin tones lighter than mine who made it plain to me that I was too dark to be equal to them. Grandma Arrington didn't seem offended by my appearance or even the fact that I didn't have a mother or father as many people who looked down on foster children were. In fact, when I walked with her to the Safeway five blocks up Georgia Avenue, she'd tell people I was her granddaughter, and in doing so made me feel proud to have such a wonderful grandmother.

With Grandma Arrington's arrival, my days of feeling completely alone at the Graves's home were over. Now I was doing everything with Grandma. My clothes and belongings remained in my bedroom just across the hallway from her kitchen but now I was sharing the bedroom she slept in. Everything in her room seemed enormous compared to the furniture in mine. She had two twin beds that stood high off the floor and had matching wooden headboards fit for a princess. Those beds were so high off the floor they came with a three-tier stepladder. Even though the beds and matching chest of drawers, dresser and mirror were old, they still looked nice because of the fresh coat of black paint that made each post look shiny and bright.

Before Grandma Arrington arrived, my bedtime, as decreed by Mama, was 7:30 every night except on weekends when I could go a half hour later.

I hated going to bed that early because it made me feel I was being treated like a baby and because I just couldn't get to sleep that early. During the summer months it was still light outside and I'd be lying in bed staring at the ceiling, not dozing off until long after Grandma came into the room to go to bed sometime after 10 o'clock. I could hear the sound of whatever television program she was watching and try to follow along with it in my mind. Sometimes I'd even tiptoe over and sneak a peek through a crack in the door just before speeding back to the bed and diving under the covers when I heard Grandma getting up from the kitchen table. Then I giggled and laughed under the covers filled with the joy of outsmarting a grown-up.

After a while it felt like I lived with Grandma instead of the Graves family, and that was perfectly fine with me. She even extended my bedtime to 8:30 so that I could watch my favorite show, The Brady Bunch. She always listened to Lawrence Welk and light rock. She would watch me dance and then smile and joke, "Lisa, you gonna go to hell with that dancing."

Soon I stopped going to church with the Graveses and started going to Grandma's church with her. That change was really special for me because Jeff started going with us too. Finally, I was able to talk and interact freely with one of my brothers, and not just during the commute to and from school. Jeff and I loved going to the little storefront Baptist Church with Grandma every Sunday. The congregation was made up of mostly friends and relatives of the pastor and, just like Grandma's kitchen, it was a warm and welcoming place where there was always something good to eat being offered. Jeff and I got very excited when they had bowtie donuts there for us to feast on. There were about 20 people in the church during services. Jeff and I watched the goings-on and laughed together happily. Afterwards, we went to the Safeway with Grandma and helped her carry home the bags of groceries she had bought.

Grandma often cooked for Jeff and me and we loved that. But her pancakes were the worst ever. They were gritty with the cornmeal she used, too thick, and loaded with grease. We covered them with syrup just to be able to swallow them. But, still, it was a pleasure to eat them because Grandma made them for us. Pancakes generally were my favorite things to have for breakfast and when Mama made them, they were so fluffy and light I always wanted more. But Grandma's pancakes were special in another way. Her pancake mix didn't come from a box with a picture of a black woman in a headscarf on the front. She scooped it with a measuring spoon from an airtight flour canister. I loved watching her mix the batter with eggs, a pinch of this and a dash of that into a glass bowl. I often said, "I can help you mix that if your arm gets tired."

"Naw, naw little girl, I got to do this" she would say smiling, proud of what she was creating in her heavy black skillet. The resulting batter was such a thick consistency it had to be spooned from the bowl with a large serving spoon and scraped free from that spoon with a smaller tablespoon. She lightly patted the two cakes with a metal spatula while the sides sizzled in the grease. After flipping them over two and a half times each, she'd lift them out of the pan and place one atop the other and add a scoop of margarine she dug from a big plastic container. After adding a healthy serving of syrup she'd say, "Come on and get this plate while it's hot." Smiling, I'd happily reach out for the heavy plate with both hands and sit back in my chair. By the time I said my grace and took a bite of my perfectly crisped bacon, the pancakes had already soaked all the syrup from my plate. After swallowing a forkful, the only sensation in my mouth was grease. Three or four bites were my limit. After that, I slid forkfuls off into an outstretched napkin lying in my lap. When I was finished I would ball the napkin up and hide the discarded pancakes in my robe pocket until the coast was clear and I could trash it. Repeating the process as often as I did left a big greasy stain in the pocket of my housecoat. Apparently, Grandma never discovered what I was doing with her special pancakes, but Mama sure did. I was terrified the day she called me into the basement to ask me, "Why in the world is this housecoat so filthy?" Luckily, she was quite willing to accept the excuse that I was clumsy and spilled food on it. I didn't want Mama to know that I had a problem with anything about Grandma or her pancakes for fear of her telling Grandma I didn't like her pancakes or even worse, making me eat every meal downstairs with her instead of Grandma. The fact is, Jeff didn't care what he ate as long as he was full. And I didn't care what I ate because Grandma made it and I loved her. So we sat there and happily ate what we could of those horrible pancakes because we were happy to be with her. Best of all, she allowed Jeff and me to play together in her place.

Grandma Arrington brought the best changes I could imagine into my life. Like me, she was usually alone and I made it my business to be her constant companion. On a typical day I would go straight into the tiny kitchen and sit in my chair with the back leaning against the wall. Then Grandma would command, "Go'on now and get your homework." With these words, she would place two large iced Archway cookies in front of me along with a cup of milk or some colorful drink. Often I didn't even have homework, so I pretended that I did. I loved the attention she gave me even when she was being stern in her own special way. Nobody had ever even asked me if I had homework! In fact, Mama always kept it fresh in my mind that we Ponders were not smart and never were going to be. She used the word retarded to describe my brothers and me, and often predicted none of us would never get out of high school. But for Grandma, even when I didn't have any real homework, I would copy several pages of something out of any book I could find. I was still not able to read very well and wished that I could, but one day Grandma shared a secret with me that she herself could not read. "I ain't get no schooling because Mama and Daddy had us working," she said quietly. Up until that point I had believed that all grown-ups could read.

Learning that Grandma couldn't read gave me a chance to do something nice for her. I would say, "Grandma, let me read this book to you." And she would say, "Okay, go ahead." Then I would look at the pictures and tell my own story: "Well, once upon a time, John and Tracy were playing in a field. You see that field right here? Then a snake came out and bit John."

Grandma would laugh heartily and say, "Lisa, I've heard that story before!" Then I would laugh because I knew she knew that I was making the whole thing up because I couldn't read either. And I'd laugh too. This was our little joke together, and although she was laughing, I never felt hurt. Grandma was too wonderful to make me feel embarrassed or ashamed about my problem with reading.

Mama's whippings weren't as frequent with Grandma in the house because I was up there with Grandma most of the time, away from Mama's sight. Often Grandma would say with a smile, "You do that again and I'm going to whip you." And then I'd purposely do it again and she would say, "Com'ere." And she'd tap me gently with something and pretend she was whipping me. I loved that and would do fake crying and then laugh.

Sometimes Grandma would say to me; "You know, Lisa, when I was young, I could pass for white." Then one day, she told me a story: "I was on a train once and the ticket taker came by. He said, 'You don't have to sit back here, Ma'am, you can go up front and sit with the white people.'" Then she said, "I told him, 'No, that's alright.'" Then she summarized the point of the story by adding, "I could but I never would want to pass for white." I looked at her and said, "Oh, I would have!" To not betray your race was a huge thing, and despite my own childish reaction, I understood that this was something Grandma was trying to teach me.

I was nine when we were removed from the Graves home. Nothing had been explained to us kids, but all through that last week a strange energy circulated throughout the house. Oddly, when I stood by the front door beside three groupings of overstuffed plastic trash bags and small brown boxes labeled with masking tape with our names scrawled on them in black marker, I felt myself beginning to miss what I had become used to for the past four years. As usual, Daddy was at work and Mama was at home supervising as the boys loaded up the social worker's hatchback. The last week living there had shown us a different side of our foster mother — a nicer side. It wasn't that she was being extra charming or outwardly kind to any of us; she simply stayed off our cases and kept from reprimanding or giving dirty looks. The usual harsh talk about our birth mother had silenced and months had passed since any whippings had been administered in the house. I guess Mama wanted us to remember her as the woman she portrayed the final week of our stay.

Ms. Bell the social worker spoke with a thick Georgia accent that gave me some comfort and I trusted her. Between talking to Mama and the three of us, she attempted to fill in some of the areas of our confusion. I remember thinking to myself; *What's going on? Where are we going now?* Mama was smiling one of her phony smiles she saved for social workers, except this time she seemed to be directing it to the three of us while my brothers and I climbed into the packed car. Somehow I detected a bit of sadness in her voice when she said to us, "Good-bye. Be good" as we pulled away from the curb.

Soon after we left, I remembered the Christmas gift Mama had taken away from me and put in her closet. *Aw man! She kept it. Why didn't I ask her for it outright?* I thought. Santa had given it to me two years earlier at a FLOC Christmas party. It had been one of the biggest and prettiest wrapped boxes under the Christmas tree. Tied to its huge white bow was a tag on which

Lisa Ponder was written in elegant calligraphy. As I tore away the wrapping paper, I saw pictures on the side of the box depicting two little white girls in fancy dresses seated at a child-size table playing tea party. It was a child's china tea set! I couldn't wait to play with it. It was the perfect present for a little girl like me! When Mama saw it at the party she smiled and watched me show it around joyously. But when we got to the car she interrupted my excited plans for a tea party when she said, "Oh no! Don't think for one minute that I'm going to let you play with that tea set. Look at it all you want now because, that's it. Why in the world would somebody give a child a nice china set? Those crazy white folks. This is going up in my closet until you can take care of things. Otherwise, you'll just tear it up."

"But I won't tear it up..." I had said meekly from the back seat while holding the box tightly. I rested the wide flat box on my lap and kept touching the raised flowers on each piece of china through the tightly stretched clear plastic. I had hoped she would change her mind, but that didn't happen and I never saw it again after she put it away. Now I hated myself for not having the courage to ask for it back when I was leaving her house for good.

Suddenly it dawned on me that I may never see Grandma again and blurted out, "Dag! I didn't even get to say bye to Grandma."

"Grandma? Who is Grandma?" our social worker asked. Mama had awakened me that morning and I had breakfast down in the kitchen with the boys. Grandma's kitchen door had been closed and she hadn't made an appearance all morning. There was no food smell coming from her room and there were no sounds of radio, TV or even Grandma herself humming one of the church hymns she'd sometimes have stuck in her head.

I couldn't help but wonder if she was mad at me or hiding for some reason. Suddenly I realized she was hiding. I became certain that Mama had told her to hide from the social worker. She didn't want it to get back to FLOC that she had a renter in her house while foster children were living there. Hadn't she always warned me, "What happens in my house, stays in my house?" I thought about all the times I had told Dr. Livingood stories about Grandma, and me and Jeff all cozy up in her little kitchen. Grandma had been one of my best subjects to talk about when Dr. Livingood wanted me to talk. I laughed when I talked about the people getting up and shouting in the church aisle. I talked about how I would play by myself on Grandma's back porch and how she occasionally brought me out snacks like prunes with pits still in them and graham crackers. I even told her how I used to hide Grandma's special pancakes in my robe pocket to keep from eating them and how Mama objected to the stain on the robe. I told her how I loved everything that Grandma cooked except for the pancakes, slimy okra, squirrel, and worst of all, deer meat with buck shot still in it. But Dr. Livingood didn't seem interested in whether Mama was cheating by having a renter. She was probably happy to get something, anything at all, out of my carefully controlled mouth. The next week when I visited with Dr. Livingood at my next appointment, I told her how much I missed Grandma Arrington and what I wouldn't give for one of her special pancakes.

Each year, our mandated visit to family court came around as regularly as a federal holiday. The feeling of dread I felt when facing my birth mother on these occasions felt worse each year as my awareness grew. It all came to a head for me in my eighth year. I had such a severe strep throat that doctors decided to remove my tonsils. After the operation, she showed up uninvited at my bedside while I was still groggy from the anesthesia. I was so surprised by her presence that the first words to pop out of my mouth were, "What are you doing here?" Normally, I would have been careful not to offend her or call her attention to me in any way. The look on her face left no doubt that she had indeed been offended, but I had meant each word; the anesthesia merely brought my true reaction to her out of hiding.

"What do you mean what am I doing here…?" she snapped.

I stared at her without speaking, daring her to follow with something like; *because I'm your mother.* But she didn't and I was glad. I had already seen her once that year, and that had been plenty for me. But after speaking so plainly to her, I wondered how she would behave towards me at our next court date. Already that year had been a sad, confusing time for me because I was regularly experiencing Mama's physical and mental abuse and at the same time was enduring a whole new kind of horror; repeated sexual abuse from my 15-year-old foster brother, Gavin.

All I had ever expected to get from my birth mother when she showed up at the courthouse was the same old criticism and disapproval she had been doling out over the years. As she became more embittered towards the legal system she had subjected all five of her children to, it hadn't taken long for her to be fully stripped of her parental rights. That came swiftly after the final act of fierce corporal punishment she inflicted on Jeffrey and me while we were on a home visit at her one-bedroom public housing unit. We two had been trying to polish her shoes for her and clumsily dripped black shoe polish on her bedspread. We tried desperately to clean it off, but only made the stain worse. I often wonder if that blot of shoe polish was — in her twisted mind — worth losing her last shreds of power over us.

The older I got, the more I hated going to that courthouse, sitting in that small room and then having to go out and listen to a bunch of grownups talk to the judge about what they thought would be best for me and my brothers when they really hadn't a clue about what went on in our lives on a daily basis. The only people who actually know these things are foster parents but they weren't required to be in the court building on those days. In fact, it seemed more like an unwritten policy that they wouldn't show up. We were always assigned at the last minute to a court-appointed lawyer. Those brief lawyer interviews just prior to going before the judge seemed artificial and staged to me, but I understood that my only alternatives were to play along with the charade or come off as a problem child. I was a very little eight-year old, but my physical size didn't keep me from being alert to all that was happening around me. I listened closely and many times wanted desperately to defend some of the outright lies that were being read off stapled forms from FLOC to the judge about me or my brothers.

"The foster mother has reported to FLOC that Lisa has been eating the chipped paint off the headboard of the bed she sleeps in," my attorney intoned, reading from a laundry list of concerns that had been received from the agency and handed to her just before the hearing.

Hearing those words, I stood behind the long wooden table and stared expressionless up at the judge and screamed to myself; *That bitch said I ate what?*

I had never heard of anybody eating paint before and couldn't fathom why Mama would accuse me of doing something so random. But I just stood there with a flat affect, revealing nothing of my true emotions.

Near the end of this hearing, the judge did something I'll never forget. She addressed Mark, Jeffery and me individually, asking us a series of questions about ourselves. One question she asked both of my brothers caught my attention; "Is there anything special you'd like to do this year?"

My mind suddenly racing, I thought to myself; *Wow! If she asks me that, what will I say? Maybe, go to Kings Dominion or Busch Gardens. Maybe I'll ask to go to camp 'cause I never get to go when the boys go. Shoot! I never get to do nothing.*

We had been appearing before Judge Sylvia Bacon for years. She was an attractive middle-aged white woman wearing a strange black robe and sitting high up behind a huge wooden desk. She had seemed distant to me in the past; just another two-dimensional figure in a sea of unfamiliar characters in my drama. But today I began to see her in a wholly different light. When she began speaking to me, it was in a kind, gentle voice quite unlike the stern one she used when addressing the adults in the courtroom. And while she spoke, she looked directly into my eyes, making me feel somehow valued in a way I was not accustomed to feeling.

"Hello Lisa. How are you today?" She said to me from high in her perch.

"F-i-n-e," I said, just loud enough for her to hear.

"Lisa, you look very pretty today. I hear you're in the third grade now. Do you like school?"

I was stunned when she said I looked pretty! I smiled, close-mouthed, hoping that my birthmother had heard her say that. And then I felt my grin grow wider and wider.

"I like it fine," I answered, still smiling with my lips tightly closed.

"That's good. What's your favorite subject in school? Do you like math, reading, art…? What do you like to do most?" Her questions kept coming, and she actually seemed interested in the answers.

"I like…ummmmm...math," I answered with some hesitation. I really wanted to say that gym was my favorite, but it wasn't one of the choices she presented and I wanted to be cooperative. Math was the only subject in which I was starting to do well, so of course it became my instant favorite.

"And how do you like living in your foster home?" she continued. "Fine, it's fine," I lied, pushing back all the negative thoughts that burst into my mind and wanted to come out of my mouth. "That's very good, Lisa" she said kindly. Finally we came to the question I couldn't wait to hear.

"Lisa. Is there anything special you'd really like to do this year?" Judge

Bacon was smiling and still looking directly at me. Now she appeared to me to be some sort of fairy godmother in a vision straight from a storybook. She had removed her glasses to talk to me, and I began to notice her blond up-do which was glowing, halo-like, under the recessed spotlight shining directly down on the bench.

Breathing faster and faster as she asked me the magic question, I told myself; *I ain't just going to say no like Jeff and Mark just did. I have to say something. I can't be scared and just say no!*

Then, mustering up all the courage I could conceive while my heart began to pound against my chest, my answer came out louder than anything else I had said that day, "I want to dance."

"You want to dance?" she asked, now smiling triumphantly at receiving a tangible answer.

"Yes, I really do..." I answered hopefully.

Judge Bacon put on her glasses again, picked up her ink pen and began writing on the paper in front of her. When she finished, she addressed my lawyer directly, saying something like, "Make sure Lisa gets to take dance lessons."

"Dance lessons, Your Honor?" My lawyer looked puzzled.

"Yes. Make sure she gets enrolled into a dance school as soon as possible. Is that clear?"

"Yes, Your Honor. I'll pass on this information and make sure it happens," my lawyer answered quickly while writing something in her notebook.

The deed done, I just let it all go. I smiled, showing all my teeth and didn't care who saw. At that moment I saw a brief glimpse of the power my words could have. I felt that someone had listened to me, understood and cared about my desires. The judge had decreed that I would get what I wanted! It didn't matter what anybody said and not even Mama could object. I would be taking dance lessons! As I walked boldly out of the courtroom that day I felt like the only person pushing through those heavy courtroom doors. I was filled with happiness mixed with an unfamiliar sense of pride in myself. Eyes on the prize, I had stepped up and managed to speak for myself.

The very next week I started my dance lessons at a nearby dance school. The school issued me a new dance bag along with tap shoes, ballet slippers and a black leotard and tights that actually fit me right. Mama couldn't give the usual excuse of not being able to provide transportation because of Daddy Graves's work hours. The dance school van was to pick me up and drop me off twice a week at the house. Since Mama wasn't in the courtroom, she never quite understood how it all happened but she hated it mainly because she had no control over the decision. I felt sure that she would never have agreed to it if there had been an opportunity. But without a word, she'd get me ready each dance class day and have me wait in the front hall for the bus.

I now felt that Judge Bacon had become an important player in my life. She was one person in authority who actually listened to me. I began to look forward to court visits. And, true to her word, she always asked what I wanted and made sure I got it. A clarinet and music lessons was another product of her magic wand, and this magical gift opened up a whole new area of involvement in school activities for me. Although my frequent moves to different foster homes made mastery of the instrument a challenge, I was still able to play well enough to be in the school band, and ultimately, a marching band where I mastered the moves more quickly than I had mastered the instrument.

Chapter Eight

ANOTHER NEW START

Word that we were in the final days at the Graves's home took me by surprise. We had been there over four years and I was nine going on ten when Ms. Bell, our new social worker, came to the house to break the news. Mama was on her best behavior as Ms. Bell explained to the three of us that we would be moving that upcoming weekend because the Graveses were moving to their vacation house in Virginia and not taking us with them.

The news sent a wave of anxiety through me and I began to shake violently. I had dreamed for a long time about getting away from Mama but the reality of that happening made me physically ill. I ran to the bathroom, threw up slightly, and then was seized with a spell of dry heaving. Jeffrey and Mark were just fine with this news and didn't say much; we never said much around grownups, just looked at each other and spoke with our eyes. My fear of leaving arose from Mama's many comments over the years. How we would never have it as good as we had it there, how we would eventually find ourselves set out in the streets strung out on dope, and how I was "gonna end up pregnant and crazy" just like my mother. Those scary images ran through my mind until I finally realized that these worries came from a woman who barely ever left the house and was ignorant of the real world outside.

Slowly it dawned on me that I was ready to leave, and I began to feel calmer. And when the day arrived, I took with me the few small brown boxes my foster mother neatly packed with only the clothes she had decided to let me keep. She kept the other things — the dressy clothes she bought using my clothing stipend from the DC government.

It didn't take long for us to start looking forward to our move out of the Graves household. The slight feeling of withdrawal we experienced was quickly replaced by a cautious sense of well-being when we met our new foster mother and understood that becoming acclimated into her way of life would be much different from anything my brothers and I had ever experienced. First of all, I noticed that Mama Primas's pleasantness stuck around even after Ms. Bell left us with her. I was used to being treated one way in front of the social workers and then totally differently when they left. But not so with Mama Primas. This heavyset, Afro-ed, light-skinned woman actually seemed to be genuinely kind and caring! Nevertheless, I remained automatically suspicious of her and barely smiled in those first hours, just in case the bad stuff was going to start up. But by early evening I had loosened up enough to dare to look around the house — a row house in the middle of the block.

I had always wondered what a row house looked like inside and had this idea that because the houses were connected, people could go back and forth to other houses though adjoining inside doors. Mama Primas's house was bigger inside than I expected and to my mind it had everything that the Graveses had except the fancy chandeliers. The big difference was that in this house we were free to walk anywhere; we could even use the refrigerator on our own. Our new foster mother laid out all the household rules for us on that first day, but I certainly wasn't ready to try things out because I feared any misstep might trigger a negative response. Mostly I just stayed put in the TV room and watched cartoons with a serious face and my arms crossed in front of me. But then she told us we could go outside and play until the street lights came on. Not just in the yard, but we could go to the playground a whole block away. When we were certain she was serious about that, Jeff, Mark and I made a beeline for that playground!

In Mama Primas's house, meals were far more informal than we had been used to at the Graveses' house. She actually encouraged our lively conversation during meals, and inevitably, one of us would say something funny enough to make her laugh until she turned red and the tears flowed down her chubby face. She had an exaggerated, operatic laugh which made us laugh right along with her. I couldn't believe that an adult could laugh with kids, let alone, kids like us. I had never in all four and a half years with the Graveses heard either of them straight out belly laugh without a care in the world like Mama. Her laugh convinced me that she was the real deal. I began to feel sure that we could relax and have fun here.

Nights at her house were very different too. What I liked most was that we were all in rooms on the same floor. I had my own room complete with a full size bed, a desk, and best of all, a clock radio. My room was right next to the room Jeff and Mark shared at the front of the house. They had twin beds; two desks and a TV that sat on a wire-frame stand. She had a rule that the boys were not allowed to come into my room to play or hang around. I didn't know it at the time but this rule was a protective measure Mama decided on after she read my official records which included a history of suspected sexual abuse by older boys. However, she did allow me to go into the boys' bedroom because there was a TV in it which we could all watch together.

Mama's room was the largest of the bedrooms. It was across the hall from mine and included a bathroom and walk-in closet. We were allowed to go in there; the first time since living with the Parkers that I was welcome in a foster mother's private space. More than anything else, this trusting gesture on Mama's part caused much of my anxiety to melt away. Within a short time I was transformed from an introverted, depressed little ball of nerves into a happy-go-lucky, energy-filled little girl with a growing sense of confidence. That is, about seventy-five percent of me was that way. I still didn't have the courage or the confidence to let my guard down completely. After all, I still had to deal with the mean people outside of the house who knew my dirty little secret, that I was a foster child.

By the time I was nine while living with Mama, I had improved my handwriting and had revised my revenge list in neat writing on pristine lined paper with no rough edges. I folded it neatly, rolled it up and stuck it in the back of my under- wear drawer. During the Primas years, that list came out only three times and never once to record any injustice by her. Her punishments were reasonable and deserved. My brothers and I had the freedom to do the things that other kids in the neighborhood were allowed to do. We could go to the playground, swim in the public pool, and freely take part in activities in school and church. My nervousness was in remission and I even had friends. Most important, Mama didn't make a point of introducing us to people as foster children.

Mama's name didn't appear on my revenge list, but there was another name that did during that time — *our birth mother*. We hadn't seen her since we last saw her in court when she was informed of our move. The 15-minute visit with her wasn't bad, more like neutral. I remember asking my brothers where Mama Primas was and sticking close by them for protection against our birth mother. But afterward, she phoned Mama, called her names and accused her of being a devil, poisoning us against her, and abusing us. That was when I put her on my revenge list.

Those phone calls were a direct blow to my happiness and brought back a feeling of fear and dread. It was as if I was being beaten all over again; this time not with plaited switches or a leather belt, but with words that left bruises on my soul. I was afraid Mama might decide to get rid of us just to get our crazy mother out of her life. Mama Graves had told us our mother was sick and crazy; now I couldn't disagree. Making those phone calls showed she was deliberately trying to destroy the only normalness I had begun to feel, and now I wanted to hurt *her* in some way. I didn't know why, but writing down her name and crimes against me on my revenge list made me feel much better.

That first year living with Mama Primas was the best I could remember. It proved to me that Mama Graves was evil when she convinced us we would never again have it as good as we had with her. Even Mark slowed down his mischievous behavior at school and never once brought any of his foolishness into the house. When we went to family court that year I was thrilled to see Judge Bacon and for the first time I felt comfortable answering her questions honestly, not trying to hide any secrets about my home life. When she asked how I was doing, I said eagerly, *"I'm fine and I like living with Mrs. Primas."* This was an unusually brief court session because the judge didn't have to deal with Mama Graves's long list of complaints about our behavior as presented through a social worker. Mama Primas had no complaints about us.

During the court session I looked around for one of the many FLOC social workers I had known over the years, but there were none. We were now clients of a new foster care program associated with Catholic Charities, and that made me feel a bit out of place. It had been years since I had seen our oldest brothers Anthony and Winston and I asked our newly appointed attorney if she knew their whereabouts. She gave me the familiar answer of a lawyer new to the case and said, while writing in her notebook, "I can check that out and get back with you."

Of course our birth mother showed up in her usual form, still looking down her nose at our foster mother who she had never even met. In her sly way, she let us know her disapproval about how we looked. This time, it was a ridiculous tactic because Mark and Jeff were dressed proudly in new suits and I wore a new dress. These were clothes Mama Primas had recently purchased for us and I was especially proud of what I was wearing because it was the first time I had ever been allowed to pick out my own clothing.

While I reluctantly joined Mark and Jeff at lunch with our real mother that day, I could see that nothing about her had changed. Scrunching up her face, she carped about my hair and appearance and told us we weren't being cared for properly because we didn't look right. I didn't have much of an appetite and just nursed the hot dog and canned soda we got for lunch while she pestered my brothers for information about Mama Primas. I didn't say a word until it was time to go. Relieved that I was free of her for another year, I sang out happily as I walked away, not looking back, "B-y-e-e-e!"

Seeing her that day had the usual lasting effect on all of us, but this time Mark was affected worse than ever before. Afterwards we noticed a new sadness about him that lasted for weeks. Then one afternoon, while Mama, Jeff and I were together in the TV room, Mark walked in and announced, "Mrs. Primas, I'm running away."

She perked up from her reclined position but stayed completely calm and asked him, "You are? Where are you running away to?"

"To live with our real mother," he said with a flatness in his tone.

As he looked directly at Mama, I thought this was more serious than I had ever seen him. I know she understood this because by now he always called her Mama the way Jeff and I did.

"Okay, but wait a minute." She answered as she got up and walked into the kitchen. Jeff and I stayed put, eyes fixed on the TV. Mark didn't say anything, just pulled his packed duffle bag close to him.

Mama came back into the room with a brown paper bag in her hand. "Here, take this with you and please let me know when you have arrived safely."

"Yes ma'am," he said in a low voice. Then he walked toward the front door. Jeff and I jumped from our seats and followed him saying goodbye sadly as he walked away. "Bye, I'll talk to y'all later," Mark said quietly as he walked out the front door. He was holding the bag lunch in his hand along with round trip cab fare and change for a pay phone call that Mama had given him. Her face was more flushed than I had ever seen. She was clearly worried, but warmly hugged Mark good-bye and wished him luck.

I yelled out angrily after watching Mark do his usual pimp walk briskly up the street and then out of sight. "He's a dummy! A big head stupid dummy! Our mother don't want him 'cause she don't even know where Anthony and Winston is. He's a stupid dummy!"

"I know," Jeff chimed in. "Why would he leave here to go live with her?"

"Cause he's stupid!" I yelled.

"Okay now, Stop that!" Mama Primas cut us off and tried to help us understand what just happened. "Mark's not dumb or stupid for wanting to go live with your mother. She's still your mother."

"She ain't my mother! She ain't nobody's mother!" I protested.

"Stop right now, Lisa! Mark is going to be all right." I couldn't tell if she really believed those words; I sure didn't.

For the rest of the day Jeff and I hung around in the house and watched TV, waiting nervously for Mark to call. Dinnertime came and went and still there was no phone call. In fact the phone didn't ring at all. Mama Primas never once used it and I knew it was because she didn't want to tie up the line. There had never been a time when Mark wasn't in the house with us and I felt extremely anxious that something bad would happen to him. I didn't trust our real mother one bit, so when the streetlights came on, I began to panic. I was also very angry and rammed my thumb into my mouth to prevent saying out loud all the nasty things I was thinking as I stared blankly at the TV and said out loud to no one in particular, *She's the reason we're in foster care in first place. She beat Mark and put all those gashes in his head. She cursed out Mama Graves and I bet that's why I got all those whippins. They never let us visit her because she beat me and Jeff for dripping shoe polish on her precious bedspread. She acts like she cares when she comes to court, but I know she don't because she don't even know when my birthday is. That's why she never gave me a gift or even one single birthday card. She don't care about none of us for real, just her church and herself. She just be fakin' and I can't stand her!"*

Nine o'clock came and still no word from Mark. Mama Primas quietly reminded us to get ready for bed. The quiet in the house made everything feel wrong. I had figured out that all the quiet talking Doretha Ponder had done with Mark that day at court was what made him run away. I hated her for that. And just before going into my room and closing the door, I called out loudly, "We were all fine before she came back around!"

As I lay there crying softly, I thought Mark would disappear the same way Winston and Anthony had and I would never see or hear from him again. Then, just as my eyes were closing, I heard the doorbell. I immediately sat up in my bed and listened closely. I could hear Jeff stirring, and under the crack of my closed door, I saw the hall light pop on as Mama Primas called out, "Just a min-u-te!" It was obvious she had been wide awake. Then I heard Mama quickstep down the plastic runner on the carpeted staircase followed by the sound of the door opening. I could hear Mama Primas's voice but couldn't make out what she was saying. Then I heard Mark. He was crying loudly and trying to croak out some words. "She told me that I couldn't live with her. That I had to leave. I asked her why and she just said to go back where I came from." Mama Primas guided him up the stairs saying sooth-ingly, "It's alright, Mark. You still live here with us."

As I listened to my brother's pain, it confirmed everything I had ever thought about my birth mother. She wasn't crazy, just a mean, selfish, heart-less hypocrite and I would never give her the opportunity to reject *me* again. There weren't enough "Praise the Lords" or "Hallelujahs in the world to con-vince me otherwise.

Chapter Nine

Life Gets Good

Mama Primas took on the three of us as a single parent, but there was one other adult in the house, her younger brother Sonny Jones. He was quick to tell us we were welcome to call him Uncle Sonny. Though he was a year younger than his sister, they so closely resembled each other that they could have passed for twins — the same thing people always said about Jeff and me. Sonny wasn't plump like Mama Primas and his Afro wasn't a blowout like hers, but they had the same curly hair and fair complexion. One more thing; they both spoke proper English that wasn't the least bit forced. Uncle Sonny and Mama had grown up in Kansas. They dressed, spoke and carried themselves differently from the people we were used to being around in DC, and for me that was a big relief.

We didn't see much of Uncle Sonny that first week after our initial introduction. But we knew he was quietly living in the fully furnished and equipped basement apartment right below us and wondered how he got in and out of the house. Turns out he had his own entrance just beneath the left side of the front porch. He also had a hidden backdoor entrance at the back of the house.

Uncle Sonny owned the only car of the house; a clean, well-kept light blue Mercedes Benz with a large silver emblem protruding from its hood. He kept it in a tightly latched one-car garage just beyond the small fenced-in backyard facing the tidy alley. We could see that Uncle Sonny loved his car and we watched as he took it out at least once a week for a short excursion just to run its engine. But other than that, he walked or took public transportation most every time he went out.

Whenever we saw Sonny outside, it was usually in the backyard working in his small garden near the garage, or he'd be weeding his flower bed along the fence. There he tended a line of tall, bright yellow and black sunflowers along with some colorful annuals and a few cherry tomato plants. Some large painted rocks in pastel tones added decor to his plantings, while they also kept us from trampling on his work when we played back there. He always engaged us in conversation and tried to keep us involved for at least fifteen minutes at a time. He showed us how to plant flowers, weed the beds and even how to seed the sunflowers and roast them on the patio grill. I liked it when he showed us these things but was glad it was only for a short time because I was always eager to run out the gate in search of playmates.

My brothers and I had been talking for weeks about venturing down to the basement. We wondered what Uncle Sonny's apartment looked like and why he was always so quiet down there. I certainly wasn't about to go by myself into another basement where there was an older male unless my brothers were there too. I couldn't stand the thought of finding myself in another Gavin type of predicament so I waited for my brothers to make the first move. Sometimes we'd be fooling around and one of us would open the basement door leading from the kitchen to the carpeted staircase. It looked dim and shadowy down there, and we dared not flip the light switch. But we did dare each other to run down and right back up without being seen. No one picked up the dare; we would just close the door and laugh, playing off the situation while still desperately wanting to know what it looked like in Sonny's place. Since he was always nice to us, we didn't want our nosiness to mess up the relationship.

Finally one day, Mark just boldly marched down the stairs like it was nothing, while Jeff and I stood at the top with the door wide open just looking and listening in astonishment. We heard Mark quietly calling out, "Uncle Sonny! Uncle Sonny!" Then we heard faint voices but couldn't make out what was being said. We stood there puzzled for a couple of minutes waiting to hear or see more. Finally, Jeff bounced down the steps in twos and began calling out, "Uncle Sonny, it's me, Jeff." Then Jeff disappeared from sight and again all I could hear was muffled talk. A minute behind Jeff, I bounced down the steps calling out Uncle Sonny's name. Once down the steps, I turned the corner and could see daylight shining in from the open back door. There were no lights on, just whatever sunlight was coming through the windows. There stood Uncle Sonny, stirring something in a pot on the stove while Mark and Jeff were seated casually at a counter that enclosed the kitchen. They looked comfortable as if they had been there many times before.

"You might as well have a seat too," Uncle Sonny said to me in his nonchalant way. I looked behind the counter carefully at each new-looking appliance in the neatly organized kitchen. On the counter was a bowl of fresh cherry tomatoes and assorted shelled nuts. A light garlic smell filled the air as he lifted the lid off a pan of sautéing vegetables. The only thing I didn't see was any meat. Sonny seemed to anticipate my question and told us, "You know, I don't eat animals".

We looked at each other wide-eyed and then laughed. One of us asked, "You mean you don't eat hamburgers?"

Uncle Sonny answered, "I don't like eating meat. I'm a vegetarian." Our facial expressions said, WOW! But our mouths just said, "Oh!" And that was all that was said about that subject. It was the first time I had ever heard the word vegetarian and now it felt like Uncle Sonny was even more different then we had even imagined. While he and my brothers talked, I spun around on the stool and looked around the place.

Beyond some black and white Asian partitions I could see a full wall of shelved books, magazines in a rack and newspapers. From my stool, I stretched my neck to see all I could — mainly large floor pillows and a full-size futon. All of this looked very odd to me. Uncle Sonny's apartment reminded me of a place on the then-popular TV show, Kung Fu, which we three watched every Saturday. I wanted a closer look, so I asked to use the bathroom, then walked slowly across the long room trying to appear as un-nosey as possible while I took in every detail of the place.

There were no lights on and I thought, *Dag! Why don't he like lights?* I could see well enough with the help of daylight coming in the windows and the open door but it still seemed quite dim down there because the front porch blocked most of the light from coming in. As I passed the Asian partition I saw that there were even more books than I had first thought. But what made my eyes pop out of my head was the bronze smiling Buddha statue surrounded by incense burners and a single pillow.

What the hell is that? I muttered to myself as if I had just seen something I wasn't supposed to. Then I ducked into the bathroom and turned on the light. Looking at myself in the mirror, I thought; *this place is weird*. I didn't have to use the toilet, so I just stood in the room for a minute and flushed it before walking out. I quickly walked back over to the counter to sit down, but before I got there, Uncle Sonny looked at me and said, "Avez-vous lavé votre mains?"

"Huuhhh?" was my only reply.

My brothers giggled, making me think I was the only one who didn't get the joke. Then Uncle Sonny repeated the words and quickly translated them into English. He said, "Did you wash your hands?"

"Hah ha ha ha ha!" Jeff and Mark laughed loudly.

"Y'all need to stop laughing because you ain't know what he said neither!" I rolled my eyes dramatically, then turned to Uncle Sonny and said, "Oh, I forgot."

I retreated to the bathroom and not wanting him to think I was nasty, took at least thirty seconds to wash my hands.

The subject changed when I was seated back on a stool and Uncle Sonny announced, "I stand on my head for thirty-minutes every day."

"Stand on your head? Why?" I chimed in.

"I practice Yoga."

Then one of my brothers asked, "What's that?" By now we were hanging onto Uncle Sonny's every word.

"Uncle Sonny, are you Chinese like Kung Fu? Was that Chinese you said to me?" I asked.

"No," he answered in his matter-of-fact way. "I'm black just like you all and the language I was speaking to you was French."

"O-o-oh!" I cooed. And then I said in an asking kind of way, "It sounded pretty, I want to talk like that."

Then Mark sang out, "I want to learn how to stand on my head for thirty-minutes!"

"Me too!" Jeff and I joined in.

From that day on, we always went down to the basement expecting to learn something from our mysterious Uncle Sonny and he was always ready with something new for us. He was defiantly different from any person we had ever known and we enjoyed being around him. First, he began teaching me random words in French by using them in our conversations. He soon had all of us standing on our heads with no effort at all.

Uncle Sonny was soft spoken and let us hang out with him even when he didn't expect it, but we knew that when he did his version of light parenting, he was serious about trying to teach us something useful. Uncle Sonny's ideas and lifestyle were way different from anything we had ever seen. He was a black man unafraid to laugh or be different. I trusted that and soon I was able to hang around the basement with him and not worry about a thing.

For the entire time that we lived there on Thirteenth Street I never saw Uncle Sonny get outwardly angry. But the time when he drove all four of us to my dance recital in nearby Silver Spring, Maryland, I learned an important lesson after complaining all the way about the rumbling of his prized light blue diesel car, "Why is this car so loud? It's hurting my ears. Uncle Sonny, you need to get your car checked because it makes too much noise!"

Mama Primas never said a word. But when it was time to leave the recital that evening, we headed home in a taxicab. Though she never said anything to me about my behavior, I knew that it was because of me that Uncle Sonny didn't pick us up. I knew that I must have hurt his feelings and I felt bad about that. Despite this awareness, I waited a few weeks to apologize for criticizing his car. He accepted the apology and we never mentioned the incident again.

Uncle Sonny was not always in sight, but he was always aware of what was going on. One day I flew out the back door running as fast as I could, tripped over one of those large pastel rocks, and was launched face forward into the corner of the garage. I was out cold but when I came to, I was in Uncle Sonny's arms. He was carrying me into the house and calling, "Sis! Sis! We need to take Lisa to the hospital right now!" As I lay there limp in his arms, my face hurt and was swelling quickly, but somehow I felt like smiling. Uncle Sonny drove all of us in his car to Children's Hospital where I spent the rest of that evening being fussed over.

Mama knew that we had been making our way uninvited down to Uncle Sonny's apartment and had become regular visitors. Always competitive, we kids one-upped each other by bragging to her about each new thing we had learned from him and then showing her our newly-acquired skills like the headstands and the full splits he did so effortlessly. She knew too, that we were equally enthusiastic about our *Speak and Spell* and *Scrabble* games with her and showed wide-eyed wonder at the magic of the *Ouija Board* she introduced us to.

One day I seated myself at the dinner table and smartly announced to Mama, "I'm not eating animals anymore. It's gross and I want to be like Uncle Sonny. I'll only eat fresh vegetables, bread and nuts. Oh yeah, and cereal. I'll eat cereal too." Mama Primas smiled and said calmly, "OOH! You are?" I answered. "Yes, I'm a vegetarian now." And without protest she allowed me to pass on having the baked chicken that night. "Well I'll eat your piece of chicken," Jeff called out agreeably. I was underweight and anemic according to my last doctor's visit, but Mama stayed cool and never brought that up.

The next few nights when she cooked pot roast, lamb chops, liver and even hamburgers, she watched without comment as I left what was supposed to be my portion of meat in the serving dish. But the night that broke me down was the night she blazed up the cast-iron skillet and laid a row of center split hot dogs in it. That night, Mama and the boys were chattering away, the TV was on in the kitchen, the round condiment carousel was full, and the table was set; it was just the way I loved dinner to be at Mama's. And, before us on the table was my favorite dinner; hot dogs, pork-n-beans, potato chips and lemonade. I was the first to reach out and grab two hot dog buns and two slightly charred hot dogs — cooked just the way I liked them, slathered with ketchup, mustard, and a topping of relish and the center split filled with sauerkraut. Naturally, I opened my mouth as wide as I could and chomped into the end of the hot dog, filling my mouth to the max. As my jaws worked away on this huge load, Mark said, "I thought you didn't eat meat no more, Lisa!"

I looked at him and rolled my eyes and neck with attitude and before I could fully swallow, I launched out at him in my well-known sassy tone, "Hot dogs ain't meat, so mind yo' business, little boy." After a big swallow, I looked at Mama Primas and said in the most refined, literate way I could, "Mama, this dinner is *deee-spicable!*" Mama Primas had already blushed a bit at my comment about hot dogs not being meat, but now she couldn't control her reaction. It was as if her big Afro got heavy on her head which fell straight back with the sheer weight of the thing. Then she began to howl with laughter at the top of her operatic voice, "W-h-h-oooooooooooooo! "W-h-h-oooooooooooooo! "W-h-h-oooooooooooooo! Mama just laughed and laughed as if she would never stop and both my brothers followed suit by holding their stomachs and rearing back in their chairs shaking with laughter to match hers. I wasn't sure what it was all about, but this was so much fun that I also began laughing uncontrollably. I had never seen an adult laugh so hard and so happily over something I said. We were all laughing with her and at how her laughter changed octaves when she caught her breath, turned red in the face and used her napkin to wipe the steady stream of happy tears from her eyes.

My favorite dinner had now turned into a spontaneous party for our little family. I had never before seen an adult seem so happy and willing to let down her guard. The only kind of *getting happy* I had ever seen adults do was in church when they raised their hands above their heads and shouted, "Praise the Lord" then jumped up and down until their large hats and sometimes their wigs flew off.

Finally, Mama caught her breath and said with a grin, "Lisa, you are something else, girl. A little riot!" Then she explained to us that using the words we learned in our weekly *Scrabble* games was a very good thing and to never stop trying new words. "But, you should make sure you know the meaning of a word before you use it, ok?" I was still basking in the fact that I had sparked so much laughter and said proudly, "Okay, Mama!" She then made it a point to let me know that she wasn't so much making fun of me for my misuse of the word *despicable* but it was more that she loved my beautifully-timed delivery which seemed planned for its ironic humor. Then she looked at me with a sincere face and added, "Just brilliant, Lisa."

Before we moved to Mama Primas's house I had never had a real friend. My new foster mother noticed right away that I had some serious social issues and she tried to reassure me every chance she got that I was completely safe in her home. But I was still turning to my brothers for a sense of safety and resorting to thumb-sucking for comfort. In those days, I was perfectly content with being in the house or going to the playground alone and swinging on the swings. For the last four and a half years I had learned to be my own best friend and still wasn't sure how to be someone else's. Of course, I thought of Grandma Arrington as a best friend and fondly remembered those times when I played alone in her little kitchen, talking to myself as I played. At those times, she often peeked in while I played and said jokingly, "Now Lisa, it's all right if you want to talk to yo-sef and carry on. It's when you start answerin' yo-sef that they call ya crazy. Alright? Ha ha!" I got the joke but, after she told me that, I was very careful not to let anybody else see me playing like that because

I didn't want to seem crazy especially since I was seeing Dr. Livingood and was sensitive about letting anyone know that.

I may have been content with being a loner but Mama Primas sure wasn't willing to accept that it was my preference and made it her mission to somehow snap me out of what she referred to as my "funk." My brothers and I had quickly formed a bond with our new mama and enjoyed our family meals and the learning games she played with us. We happily started out going to church with Mama every Sunday until she noticed that we were bored out of our minds. We were used to going to church, sitting quietly, and staying awake until the service was over with no complaints. And compared to going to some of the Baptist churches we went to before, Mama Primas's Simpson Hamline United Methodist up on 16th Street was a cakewalk. The services were chill, the people were friendly, and services were only an hour and best of all, nobody got on your case if you nodded off for a few minutes.

But Mama understood that children needed to be around other children and had heard that some of the kids in the neighborhood were going to the church a block up Thirteenth Street so she walked us up to Peoples Congregational United Church of Christ to attend one of its many events. The next Saturday Mama Primas met with the youth activity coordinator, Mrs. Allen, who welcomed my brothers and me. Then she assigned us each to a youth member in our own age group to show us around. That was when I met Minyon.

Sticking close by Mama Primas, I was the last one to be assigned. Both adults could sense my ambivalence about leaving my new guardian's side so Mrs. Allen told my guide right in front of me, "Minyon, please show this young lady around the church and introduce her to the other youngsters. She will be attending Sunday school starting next week so show her the classroom and who her teacher will be."

"Okay!" Minyon replied and without hesitation said to me, "Come on, let me show you the fellowship hall first. I was going there anyway because they have refreshments set up and I need something to drink."

Minyon was walking fast and I could see right away that she knew a lot of people because whenever we passed people while walking in those long halls they would call out, "Hi Minyon!" in a way that seemed as though they really missed her even though they had just seen her the week prior. She'd greet them back by name and then add something like, "Oh, this is Lisa. She's new so you will be seeing her around too." They'd politely speak to me and then Minyon would begin walking fast again so I would quickly wave goodbye and try to keep up with her. Everybody knew and liked her and it didn't matter how old they were. The older members would stop her briefly and wrap their arms around her and tell her how pretty she looked followed by, "How's your father?" And Minyon always answered, "Fine. He'll be in church tomorrow."

Minyon's father was one of the oldest and most well-known members of the church. In fact, people would even say that he was the father of Peoples Congregational and Minyon was its Princess. There was even an area in the church courtyard dedicated to him where he had planted a large overgrown rose bush which he called The Minyon. Though Minyon was eight going on nine, her father was well into his sixties and used a walker after suffering a stroke. Later he had to use a wheelchair. But, despite his physical limitations, he attended church almost every Sunday.

After meeting Minyon that day, I looked at going to church in a whole different way — as a fun way to spend every Sunday. By letting us Ponders go alone to that church Mama Primas trusted us in a way that I had never experienced so I was determined not to ruin her trust by behaving badly and did my best to control my natural sassiness. Being friends with Minyon was easy. Although she was a year or two younger, we both had the same height, complexion and slender body type. But those were our only similarities. She was not in the least bit shy or afraid of anybody or anything and that's what I admired the most about her. I wanted to be able to look people in the eye just like she did and speak without worrying about how people perceived me.

When Minyon and I found out we lived just around the corner on the same block, we were thrilled. She began picking me up on Sunday mornings so we could walk to church together and I went to her house to play jump rope or ride her bike almost every day. Out of the many middle class kids at the church who Minyon had more in common with, she chose to be the tightest with me. I often thought to myself; *How could this popular girl be my friend? Her hair is long, pretty and always perfect, she has all those pretty clothes, she is so feminine and cute and everybody loves her. Why does she even want to be friends with me? My hair is too short. I only have a few plain clothes. I don't have any other friends and I act like a tomboy. And, most of all, I'm a stupid foster child.*

It had been clear to me that these were some of the reasons I didn't have friends and why some kids and adults never hesitated to let me know it. Minyon ignored all of these details about me and encouraged me to join all the things she was involved in at church, so eventually I took a chance and joined the Junior Dance Troop. I had been reluctant, but finally joined after she spent months teaching me two of the featured dances that included all the girls in the troop. Minyon had been taking Jazz, Ballet and Modern dance since she was very little which was evident in her stature and walk.

I often said to her, "You're going to be a real dancer when you grow up, aren't you?" But Minyon downplayed her skills as if it were no big deal. I admired all that she could do and her extraordinary confidence, but what I liked most was that she made me feel her equal.

Minyon's mother allowed us to play within the short distance between the stoop in the front of her house and the fifty-yard sidewalk straight cornered by alleyways on each end of the block. Mama Primas gave me much more freedom to move around the neighborhood than Minyon's mom gave her but the fun Minyon and I had far outweighed any restrictions and limitations. It was only when Minyon wasn't home or was sick and couldn't come out to play that I went to the playground or swimming pool just to have something to do. I often got bored while out on my own but when we were together, things were never dull. Even when we had nothing planned we always managed to figure out something even if it was just talking our heads off.

At times we would stroll up and down the block talking about our day and once we got started talking, we ran our mouths like grownup gossips. The stories we shared were so full of hyperbole and animation that if people walking on the other side of the street happened to look over at us doing our wild gesturing, they would probably think we were having a fit. We didn't care because we were in our own little world. Most of the funny stories came directly from that everyday reality show, the DC Public School experience. We quickly realized and confirmed with each other that the things some of those kids would say and do was beneath us. Our favorite things to talk about were what we saw when parents of misbehaving kids had to come to the school to retrieve their suspended children.

"Oooh, Girl!" Minyon would begin. "You should have seen what happened at my school today." I'd lean closer and say, "Oooh, what?" Then I hung on her words while she talked nonstop and I listened and laughed, filling in some spaces with "Ooohh!" as she continued with stories like this one:

"These two boys got into a fight on the playground and one of them was fighting just like a girl. The other one started dragging him around the playground by the seat of his pants. Then, gurl, guess what? … The first boy started crying 'cause the other boy got him down on the ground. Everybody saw that fight 'cause they gathered 'round in a circle. And guess what else? … They were sixth graders!" We were both in the fourth grade so it was a big deal to see 'big' kids fighting like that."

I would say something like, "Da-a-a-a-g, you were lucky to see that fight."

"I know!" Minyon would answer like it was nothing and continue without hesitation.

As the story continued, Minyon's theatrical movements often had me so wrapped up in what she was saying that I could imagine the whole scene as if I had been there myself.

"Two teachers finally grabbed both boys off the ground and took them to the office. But what was really funny was when the mother of the boy who won the fight came up to the school to get him. Gurl-l-l, she was so ghetto, with some house slippers, hair rollers, and a scarf on her head. Pink and some black rollers were all sticking out the sides of that scarf."

As Minyon spun the story, I would sit there and drop my mouth open.

"She couldn't even keep those slippers on her feet without sliding each foot forward like she was skating on the floor. Plus… She was dirty! Then she started cursing out the teacher because her son said the teacher grabbed him. But that's because the teacher didn't want him to fight her."

I would fall out laughing at Minyon's description and we would shake our heads in disgust while agreeing, "I'm glad my mother don't look and act like that." It felt good to know that Mama Primas was a mother I could feel proud about.

Chapter Ten

Having a TV in the boys' room was a special treat for us and we shared it gladly. But there were a few times when my brother Mark would make a big fuss about an upcoming boxing match and say, "Ali is coming on at 8 o'clock, so betta not nobody be messing with the TV."

Jeff didn't really care. He'd be too engrossed in putting together one of his model cars or something, but I always made it a point to say something smart like, "No you not, because Dance Fever comes on and I called the TV. Plus, you not the boss anyway, MARK"! Then Mark would say, "See man, that's why can't nobody stand you, because of that smart mouth." And I'd give him the glare and say, "That's why nobody can't stand you, 'cause you a ugly fool."

Then Mark would get up in my face and fake buck at me like he was going to hit me if I even moved. And then I'd buck right back at him with my fist balled up just like his, and I'd say, "I dare you to hit me, boy!"

"Watch!" Mark would say and then he'd threaten me as he walked past, purposely bumping my shoulder. I always knew that was coming, so as soon as he passed me, the palm of my windmill slap would land right between the center of his shoulder blades.

But when 8 o'clock came, all three of us would be happily sitting close together in front of the thirteen-inch black and white TV eagerly waiting for Howard Cosell to announce the boxers entering the ring. As soon as Ali was announced, Mark would jump up and start throwing punches and doing his rendition of the Ali shuffle. He swore to us that his moves looked just like Ali's. Then Jeff would get up and move around doing his own thing, but was careful not to challenge Mark's technique.

Mark would brag, "I'm too fast, I'm too quick, and ya'll can't even see my punching coming!" Then, without even throwing out a punch, he'd laugh and say, "See, you didn't even see it that time, I'm too quick and I'm too fast just like Ali." Then he'd chant like Ali;

> *"Float like a butterfly sting like a bee!*
> *I'm the Greatest of all time!*
> *You can't hit what you can't see and I'm so Pretty!"*

When Mark started that chanting, I'd roll my eyes and neck while calling out, "Oh no, you ain't!" After that, I'd just watch Ali and Mark for a bit, and then Jeff and I would get up and do everything Mark did. "See, I got it, don't I, Mark?" I'd say hopefully. At first he'd say, "No! You ain't got nothing! Plus, you just a girl anyway." None of this mouthing off bothered me; I just kept practicing. I figured if I learned the moves, I could really learn to fight.

After I mimicked Ali and Mark for a while, my brothers became kind of impressed with my footwork and hand speed. It was the first time they both acknowledged something I could do as well as a boy, and I was really proud of that. It made me a die-hard Ali fan with a secret urge to try some real boxing when I grew up a bit more.

I got my chance to experience boxing sooner than I thought. The school year had come and gone — one of the best I'd ever had. Being able to stay in one school, in one class with one teacher and no interruptions for moves to new foster homes was unusual for me. Besides participating in any and all of the church events I was eligible for at Peoples Congregational Church, I figured that summer would consist of my brothers running back and forth to the Upshur pool and playground while I hung out with my new best friend Minyon at her house just around the corner. Mama Primas didn't much like that plan. She knew it wasn't going to work and thought if we weren't doing a planned activity, learning something or being productive, it just wasn't right.

Catholic Charities had given Mama Primas the idea of sending us to summer day camp. I had never been to a summer day camp before and even though I was open to it, I was nervous that I might not fit in. But I had heard kids at school talk about what they did and how much fun they had at summer camp and I was eager to go because it sounded normal. I loved any normal I could get.

The Y van picked us up in front of the house every weekday morning that summer at 8:00 AM and we stayed at camp until 2:00 o'clock. This was perfect for Mama Primas because it gave her time to go up to the church and take care of all her secretary duties. But it didn't take much time before I decided camp might not be for me. Most of the kids enrolled there were from that neighborhood and knew each other. They weren't interested in meeting or welcoming outsiders, so I never let my brothers out of my sight. As long as I could keep them in my sight, I felt I was okay.

There were only a few activities included in our daily routine at the Y. One was the three-block hike to the elementary school cafeteria for the nasty government-issued hot lunch program. The second was the two-and-a-half block walk to Benjamin Banneker public swimming pool — we kids called it 'the DC bathtub' — which was located directly across the street from Howard University. After the daily swim, we spent the rest of our camp hours inside, gathered around the Y pool table, mostly as spectators watching the activities of the older kids or junior counselors.

As I watched some older kids playing pool, it felt like I was watching a television program with a lot of profanity, suggestive sexual content and commercial interruptions. Two of the older kids were joneing on each other by ripping on each other's mothers until they almost came to blows. There was the occasional reprimand by one of the few adults who were supposed to be in charge. They would occasionally peek in on the teenage counselors and yell something like, "You s'posed to be watching 'em, not messin' around!" Messing around usually meant the counselors were either playing pool or outside in the alley by the emergency exit door puffing on a joint followed by a chaser, a Kool cigarette. I instinctively knew they were smoking reefer because Mama Graves had always grumbled about young people smoking dope. "No-good-street-hoodlums on the back of the buses and on the street corner smoking strong, stinky smelling reefer and it ain't make a bit of sense," she would grumble. She was right, it did stink, and it hung around on their clothes long after they slunk back into the Y flashing their sly smiles.

We were all considered "at-risk kids"— even the summer workers who were supposed to be watching over our activities — but I always felt that those kids were way more at-risk than my brothers and I, if only for the fact that when they left the Y they had to walk through one bad neighborhood to get to an even worse one where they lived. When I lived with Mama Graves in her fancy house, I often consoled my unhappy self by thinking I was better off than other kids because of the house I lived in. But in the short time we had been living with Mama Primas, she had taught me something of much greater importance than the appearance of the house I lived in. She convinced me with her caring and her respect that I was smart, funny and beautiful even if I didn't have two pennies to rub together.

The number of campers in the program ranged between ten and twenty on any given day. We Ponders were 8 to 14 years old. When it rained, the lunches were brought over to the Y and we ate in the auditorium where we had just been playing. Rain meant we wouldn't get to go to the pool either, and so we milled around aimlessly in the loud, echoing spaces between the auditorium and the rec room. On one rainy day, Mark and a group of boys found two pairs of boxing gloves stuck away in an old locker. They were tattered, filthy, and bursting along the sides, revealing dirty sponge-like pieces of crumbling padding leaking out through the burst seams. To those guys, finding these was like finding pure gold, and soon we were all expecting to see a fight and crowding around a group of boys who were already forming a ring around two older boys.

In no time, there was a crudely organized system of bouts lined up for our entertainment. I noticed that the bigger, more aggressive boys were choosing less aggressive boys to fight with. Those boys usually ended up on the grimy stage floor balled up in the fetal position and praying that their opponents wouldn't forget that this wasn't a real fight and start kicking and stomping them. Each fight stopped when one self-appointed timer shouted out, "Ding! Ding!" Then the winner raised his hands above his head and claimed his victory while also offering the same trouncing to another boy who was at the same skill level as the bout's loser.

Everybody was into it, even the girls. It was one of the few times all the campers took part in an activity together other than going to the pool and eating lunch. Mark and his buddies had spontaneously organized an activity we all could be a part of. I watched as some boys became corner men, carefully pouring out a bit of warm soda into their fighter's mouth between rounds. An older boy — the clown of the bunch — appointed himself ring announcer and introduced each fighter by pointing out every messed-up thing about him.

His commentary had the crowd rolling on the floor with laughter while also pissing off the fighter just enough to make him more eager to mix it up in the ring: "In this corner we got big Moe wearing some dirty-ass shorts his mutha cut out of some ol' jeans he shudda thrown away a long time ago, his brother's funky blue t-shirt that he had on yestidday — because I saw him in it — and some mismatched socks, like nobody can tell they different just 'cause they all rolled down and shit!"

One kid appointed himself the Don King-like bout instigator and ran around fast-talking between fights getting kids to agree to match-ups: "Kevin, you gonna fight Larry? 'Cuz he say he gonna kick your ass!" Kevin immediately got all pissed-off and shouted, "He say what? Well, fuck that Larry! Yeah, sure I'll fight him!"

Then, just to seal the deal and whip up the crowd, the junior Don King yelled, "Yeah! You know he been wantin' to fight you since fifth grade so y'all might as well go ahead and get it over with!" The deal finally set, he then announced: "Everybody! Shut up for a minute, Larry and Kevin gonna fight next!"

And then there was my brother Mark. As finder of the gloves, he was in charge of them. When the fighters pulled them off, they handed them to him and he reverently put them on the next two fighters. On two occasions Mark even donned them himself to fight. Both times, his opponents gave up within seconds, shaking their heads and mumbling, "That boy is crazy as shit in the ring. Hell no! Take these gloves off!"

Soon there were only a few boys left who hadn't fought; younger ones like my brother Jeff who were more interested in bouncing an old dirty tennis ball off the wall or terrorizing girls by chasing them until they'd have to turn around and pretend to fight the boys off. As much as these younger boys enjoyed watching their big cousins and brothers in there duking it out, they had no interest in getting in the ring themselves. So the bigger boys gave them a pass and waved them off, at the same time making sure to call them a bunch of punks and pussies so everyone could hear.

At first all the girls were just standing in the observers' circle. Girls from the neighborhood laughed and cheered and talked all kind of smack while shouting out which boys would beat which. But when they started talking about what they would do if they were in there fighting, Mark called out, "Hey... Y'all wanna fight?"

"Yeah!" The group of girls sang out like a gospel choir. A boy in the crowd shouted, "Go ahead and put the gloves on then!" This was right up Mark's alley. He wanted to keep the boxing going on for the rest of that day if possible. Before we knew it, girls were in the center of the circle flailing away at each other both verbally and physically.

I had been watching from the sidelines and thinking the whole time about what I would try and how tight I would look if I had a chance to get in there and box. But those girls weren't like me. Most of their fighting was done with loud, hostile insults and the actual physical fights only lasted a minute or so. They didn't care who they fought either. It could have been a sister, cousin or best friend. It was all the same to them. The trash talking and constant zingers back and forth made it seem like they hated each other but they didn't. This was pure theater for them. As soon as the fight was over they were back up being friendly in each other's faces like nothing ever happened.

Mark laced a pair of the gloves on one girl's hands and she stood there without an opponent, waiting for someone to step forward to fight. Suddenly, Mark ran over to me and grabbed me by the arm. "Cm'on Lisa, it's your turn!"

"What? No, get off me, Mark!" I shouted, yanking away from him.

"Cm'on Lisa! Man, you know you can beat this girl. Just do what you been doin' in the room when we were watching Ali!"

Mark shoved the soggy, gritty gloves on my hands and wrapped the laces around my skinny wrists triple the number of times needed for a normal-sized arm. Suddenly I was standing, terrified, in the center of the circle about to fight a complete stranger. I stood quiet and stunned while she ran her mouth, telling all her friends she'd kick my "skinny little ass." I saw that she was only a few inches taller than me but she was way thicker around. A neighborhood girl, she knew everybody while I knew only my two brothers. There was no smooth way to get out of the situation and I knew that if I left the ring, the bossy girls would bully me until the end of camp that summer. It was all Mark's fault! I stared at him with the most hateful stink eye I could muster. Then I looked for Jeff in the circle but couldn't find him. Nobody was going to save me from this one. I felt my cheeks filling with air the way they did when I was mad at that bitch Mama Graves. Then the human gong gave the signal to start. "Ding! Ding!"

My hands were so small I had to hold on tightly to the folded creases of the slimy loose material inside the gloves just to keep them from moving around on my hands or possibly flying off while I was in the mix. "Come on, fight me!" My opponent taunted as she squared up face-to-face, almost touching her nose to mine. "Come on, girl, hit me first so I can tear you up in here!" she boasted.

She scored a quick punch, and as I stumbled backward, the crowd gasped, "O-O-hhhh," boosting up what she had just done. I wasn't hurt, but they had oohhh'ed her at my expense and I hated being embarrassed. Ignoring the nauseating stench of mildew and sweat from the gloves that was filling my nostrils, I raised my hands beside my cheeks and found the bouncy platform of the balls of my feet.

"Uh-oh! Look at her. You done got her mad now!" one of the older boys laughed out. I wasn't mad, but I was embarrassed and needed to undo that Oohh that had been done to me.

Now Mark was jumping around and yelling over everybody, "Do like you do in the room, Lisa, do like you do in the room! Fast hands, and get out of the way like I showed you!"

Suddenly it all came to me and I started to feel like I was doing what Mark said. By the 30-second mark, I had avoided all of my opponent's attempts to hit me in the face when all at once, like a human windmill, face-down and eyes closed, that girl came rushing forward and I had no place to go. All Mark's techniques and all my thoughts of boxing like Ali instantly left my mind.

"You ain't kicking my ass!" I blurted out. Bracing myself and determined not to move backwards like I had before, I landed double the number of wild windmill swings she flung at me. The palm of my glove landed on her over and over again. I could feel the light thud of her gloves landing on the side of my arms as I stood tall and banged away until she fell down. But like a spring on a sprocket, she was back on her feet without missing a beat. She was keeping her head down and I was sticking with my winning game plan.

Don't stop. Don't stop, no matter what, I kept telling myself. The crowd was going crazy, cracking up laughing at our technique and at the same time cheering us both on. I was dead tired but I knew that if I stopped she'd get the best of me. Then with a sudden loud bump, her butt hit the stage floor. I stopped and stood ready, waiting for her to recover instantly again, but she didn't. She just stayed there exhausted, trying to catch her breath.

"I told y'all, I told all-a-y'all my sister was gonna beat her ass!" This was Mark doing his rhythmic Ali imitation. He ran over to me while the girl was stretched out on the floor, then pointed and laughed in her face. "Ha-a-a-a… that's what you get!" Then he grabbed my arm, held it up in the air and bragged loudly, "My sister, the champ. I told all y'all not to mess with us Ponders. My sister *won!*"

I was happy but barely smiling and mostly relieved I didn't get hurt. Mainly, I was telling Mark to take those disgusting wet gloves off me right away. He did, and proudly. Then Jeff came towards me out of the crowd and said, smiling, "You ok, Lisa? You did good!" I shook my head signaling that I was OK and he went back to whatever he had been doing. When I looked over again at Mark, he was all puffed up like a rooster.

Chapter Eleven

One day Mama Primas told us she was going to retire from her job and move back home to Kansas with Uncle Sonny. We had been living happily with her for almost four years and although she tried to sound upbeat about her news, it was a horrible feeling to know that she was leaving us behind. Seeing that Jeff and I were very upset, she tried to paint a prettier picture and said, "You will be living at this really great house up on 16th Street."

Mama Primas wanted to make sure we understood that she wasn't giving us back because she didn't love or want us anymore. She explained there were rules in the foster care system and it just wasn't possible to reassign a DC foster kid to someone in Kansas. It was plain to see that she was as hurt by the situation as we were, and that made us work harder at being positive.

This time, we would pack our own clothes in the lightweight three-piece luggage Mama had picked up for us from Kmart. It was our first real luggage — her thoughtful replacement for the humiliating plastic garbage bags of clothing that we had arrived with. The overflow would go into several small boxes she had brought from the church. She would allow us to take everything she had given to us over the years and more, including the five-book boxed set of *Hardy Boy Mysteries* downstairs in the TV room.

When Mama Primas told us we'd be leaving, I had assumed it meant the three of us, Jeff, Mark and me. She explained only where we'd be living, that our social worker would deliver us there, and that everything would work out fine. After overcoming the shock of having to leave, I told myself that at least I still had both my brothers. But the thing she hadn't told us was that Mark would not going with us. All our previous transitions had been deliberately designed to be quick and final and without much discussion, so the way this news was delivered shouldn't have been surprising. After all, it was the slick foster textbook way of doing things. But this time it was our beloved Mama Primas shocking us with such terrible news.

To my eyes Mark had always seemed to stay in the kind of trouble that called for punishments much worse than something written in a file or having to stay in his room for a few days with no television. There had been those times when he was placed in a reform school for a few months to "prevent him from getting into any real unlawful activity." At least that's what we were always told. We knew that his main issue was getting into fights at school. And we knew what an effective fighter he was. At home, things with him were as normal as with any fifteen-year old boy. Predictably, Mark hung out with his older buddies and had little to do with Jeff and me outside of family activities. But we all loved one another, and the last thing we wanted was to be separated. So when we learned Mark wasn't going with us, we broke down crying. Tears streaming down our faces, we cried, "Why? Ya'll didn't say that!" We hadn't seen this coming. Mark's belongings had been packed up and stacked neatly downstairs just like ours, as if we were all leaving together.

The social worker told us to calm down and explained that the new place already had three kids and adding the two of us would fill the place to capacity. She then added that because Mark was fifteen, the foster mother didn't want to take on another teenage boy anyway. My emotions were all jumbled up. I was shocked, sad, and outraged, feeling duped out of yet another brother. Once again I was on my way to another strange house with one less brother and might never know why or where he would end up.

In those final days with her, Mama Primas had reminded me to continue going to the library two or three times a week and emphasized again that I was a smart little girl. Coming from her, those words had made me feel good because I knew she knew what smart really was. She not only had high school and college diplomas but also a master's degree from a very well-known college. From the day we arrived at that neatly kept row house in the center of 13th street, till the day when Mama Primas broke that heart-breaking news to us, I had considered her the perfect mom for me.

After we left Mama Primas's house, the sense of stability that I had slowly regained since leaving the Parkers completely dissolved. Living in those two homes had given me a true sense of what being home felt like, but then, in both cases, in the snap of two fingers we were packed up and shipped out without any real explanation at all. I guess I misunderstood those conversations with Mama Primas about me graduating from high school and going to a good college. I had failed to understand that she didn't necessarily mean that I would be doing these things while under her care. At the time, "going home to Kansas" sounded like a good enough excuse and I accepted it, but when Jeff and I were settled into our next home and learned that it was another hateful version of the Graves household, I became angry that Mama Primas had allowed this to happen.

This time the change would send my life into a tailspin. Once again I would have to transfer schools, join a different church and discard all my friends as if they never existed. It was as if a big eraser had rubbed out whole portions of my life leaving me with a blank page on which to start writing a new story. Sometimes I'd even find myself confusing people, places and events. Was my mind playing tricks on me? I had trouble knowing what or who was real and what was fake. But worst of all, Mark was gone and we had no idea if we would see or hear of him again.

That Saturday when Jeff and I stepped on the front porch of the big house on the corner of 16th and Webster Street, I experienced an eerie feeling of déjà vu. It had been seven years since we landed at the Graves's house and waited for the front door to open. This house was exactly one block down the street from Simpson-Hamline United Methodist Church where Mama Primas had been the secretary and attended regularly. We were to live on DC's "Gold Coast," a section along 16th Street with a reputation as the neighborhood with big extravagant homes, churches and embassies. Mama Primas had joked with us a few times before we left, saying teasingly; "Aren't you lucky? You will soon be living like rich kids!" She followed this comment with a little laugh and a slick grin. This was yet another one of the tactics she used to keep us optimistic about having to leave. I knew she was being sarcastic, but the idea of living with rich people just as Little Orphan Annie did was, for me, a hopeful thought tucked far in the back of my mind.

As we stood anxiously outside the house, a short salt-and-pepper-haired black woman in her sixties opened the door slowly and said to come in. Lurking behind her was a short, heavy-set, dark brown-skinned woman with black hair who took over the introductions. She seemed like a bodyguard or some-thing and I disliked her immediately. She forced a big smile on a face that was-n't used to smiling and said, "I'm Lovey Lomax and this is Mimi Long." After a couple of minutes passed, she beckoned to us with her index finger and gave us our first order, "You two, come with me." As we followed that ugly pear-shaped troll out of the room, a sense of dread rose up in my heart. It was ob-vious that she was the one in charge, despite the fact that Ms. Long was considered the primary caretaker in our new foster arrangement.

Ms. Long stayed in the living room to give our social worker the usual half-hour drop-off interview. In the meantime, Lomax yelled up the stairs for Sean and Dena to come down. They were also foster children, an eight and ten-year-old sister and brother. Lomax told them to give us a tour of the house, several times describing it grandly to us as a "seven-bedroom, three-bath and two-powder-room house." I figured we were supposed to be impressed so, in a slow-monotone, I obliged with a "Wow." I was glad to see that there were two kids close to our ages, but was becoming very uneasy because I had sensed right away that Ms. Lomax was one scary bitch. Right from the start, her bossy tone and unattractive posture had waved a big red danger flag right in my face. Ms. Long had a much more even demeanor and seemed to be sin-cere. She was quiet and relaxed but the fact that she let Lomax run the show when it came to us foster children seemed like very bad news. After the walk-through, all four of us kids strolled toward the corridor where the grownups were finishing up. We could hear Ms. Lomax talking in what I later came to know as her teacher voice. Suddenly she loudly announced to Ms. Harris, "We're sisters!"

"Ohhh...?" Ms. Harris answered. It seemed like one of those long, I-don't-believe-you ohhhs.

Hearing this, the four of us kids looked at each other as if some sort of telepathic force had taken control of our minds and we broke out laughing in one sudden burst. Jeff whispered, "Psych! I don't think they sisters!" We laughed again.

Then discretely pointing towards Ms. Lomax, Dena said, "Shh... before she hears us!" In that very moment of shared amusement a trusting bond had formed that would bind us together until the day we would inevitably be sep-arated, taken from one foster household and deposited at another.

We were all foster children but our differences were very pronounced. Dena and Sean were considered beautiful children because they had fair skin and "good hair." They also had family close by and had only been in the system for a few years with definite plans of returning home on a set date, which neither one of them knew.

The brother and sister never came off as snobbish or thinking themselves better than we were. But Ms. Lomax favored them, and didn't hesitate to do all the comparing throughout the time we lived in that house. She made it her business to point out each of our differences from head to toe as if Jeff and I were foster children because of the way we looked. She also bragged about how smart they were, especially since they were attending John Tyler Elementary, the school where she herself taught fifth grade. But to those two children, their lot in life was just as bad as ours and they couldn't wait to get out of the Long/Lomax household.

After Ms. Harris left us, we met Pierre, our other new foster brother, who had just recently turned eighteen. He came back from walking Toby, Ms. Long's large black mixed breed, pride-and-joy dog. Pierre rushed Toby over to the basement stairs and quickly closed the door before the clumsy canine realized that Pierre wasn't coming down with him. Introductions were briefly made and then Pierre quickly shot back outside.

Ms. Lomax made it clear that Pierre fell into the beautiful people category for the same reasons Sean and Dena did. We later learned that she routinely told anyone who would listen that he was her son even though it was obvious their family trees grew in completely different pastures. Anyone could see that it was another one of her bald-faced lies used to justify her insistence that he go everywhere she went.

Lovey Lomax never cared what anybody thought because she considered herself the all-knowing, smartest person in the house. She and Louise Graves were just alike when it came to that caste system crap. They were both dark-skinned evil women who possessed none of the features they placed the most stock in and unknowingly wallowed in their own self-hate when they criticized people with features like their own. It was these two women who were responsible for making me all-too-familiar with the concept of black self-hatred.

My first week with the "sisters" threw me for an emotional loop and I fell into a familiar depression, crying whenever I was alone at bedtime or in the bathroom. I felt that I had died and come back in somebody else's life. It seemed to me that someone was playing a cruel joke by alternating heaven and hell every few years just to see how much I could take. Things were so confusing to me that I gave in to the silence which had been my best friend at such times.

The freedom I had enjoyed while living with Mama Primas had been stripped away with no warning. The school, church and the playground we played at while living with her were all within walking distance, but now Lovey Lomax declared them off limits. We had to give up everything we knew and loved and were expected to adapt immediately — the way foster children were expected to. We were told that because Sean and Dena had a "real" mother they were allowed to call the sisters Aunt Mimi and Aunt Lovey. Somehow, our "real" mother didn't count. I wanted to call them that too because I didn't want anyone in the street thinking Lovey Lomax was my mother. She was what kids called "ass crack ugly." At times, she would act so ghetto that you'd think she was the stereotypical loudmouthed black woman with no education and something to prove. So I just opted out of calling her anything and said "excuse me" if I needed to get her attention. She made us go to John Tyler, and made us wait for her in her classroom every day after school. All the kids at school knew that we came with her and often asked, "How you stand having that ugly bitch as your mother?" We would say, "We can't!" When they talked about her, I always made a point of saying, "She not my real mother!" I began asking her, "Why can't we just keep going to school where we were?" She answered in full voice, "You not gonna live at our house and tell us what you gonna do!"

Mimi was a more acceptable parent figure. A retired nurse, she was a petite, dainty woman who took pride in her stylish yet conservative appearance. She never raised her voice and used variations of tone and pitch to get her message across. Her signature line when new foster children moved into her house was, "Now don't tear up my house!" followed by a short sermon about how it was bought and paid for by her, and how FLOC didn't own anything in it. She was mild compared to Ms. Lomax and in return we liked and respected her. But as for living like Orphan Annie, the excitement of Gold Coast living was over before it started. I knew that no matter how big or fancy the house we lived in was, we were still the same old malnourished, Medicaid card-toting, free lunch-eating, hand-me-down-wearing foster children we always had been.

In the first week we were at that house, I saw Lomax smack Dena across the face for carrying the wrong pocketbook to church! She said, "I told you to get the white pocketbook!" Then she hauled off and smacked her across the face. I could immediately see the red mark she left on the child's light skin. I already felt that Dena and I were sisters and ran to her and rubbed her face saying, "Are you okay? She betta not hit me, she betta not!"

I remember feeling strong and defiant in that instance, but only a month after my arrival, Lomax slapped me in the face, too. I hadn't had enough time to put up my guard to stop it and instantly felt the warmth of blood gushing from my nose. To spite her I made a point of swinging my face around quickly so the blood would hit the curtains. Dena had heard the blow from the other room and said later, "She hit you, didn't she?" I said, "Yeah, just go in and look at the curtains. You'll figure it out." I thought angrily, *Bitch, that's a mess what you did*. Now I knew just how it was going to be with her.

But Lovey wasn't the only bad guy in our soap opera. Pierre was regularly molesting Dena at the time and I witnessed it. I had gone up to the bathroom and was planning to scare Dena playfully as she got out of the shower. I just stood outside the door and without knocking first, burst into the room and saw that Pierre was penetrating the little girl anally. He ran out of the room immediately and I was left with Dena who was pleading with me, "Don't tell, don't tell…" with fear burning in her eyes. Although I wanted to tell on him, it is hard to explain just how hard it is to do so in situations of abuse like this. Mainly, when you are a foster child, you are scared about where you will have to go next because of the situation you have reported on. It could be an even worse situation than the one you are currently in. By now I was a pro at keeping secrets.

Mimi stayed in DC with us that hot, hot summer while Lovey went to Florida, taking Dena and Pierre with her. When Lovey came back, Mimi made a generalized complaint about our slowness in pulling weeds in the brutal summer heat. Hearing that, the ugly-ass devil Lovey came out that screen door so violently that it hit the back wall of the house and seemed like it would fly off its hinges. She was yelling at the top of her hateful lungs: "Get down to the basement right now so you can get what you deserve for giving Mimi trouble!" Something snapped in me then. I knew we had done nothing wrong and I knew I wasn't going to take a beating from her without a big struggle. In the basement, I screamed at her to stop hitting my brother and let her know that she would not be laying a hand on me. She told me to shut up and get in the basement where she was administering the beatings. "Take off your pants and sit on the edge of that chair!" she screamed. I kept up the noise until she finished beating Jeff and Sean. I didn't move; just stood and waited for her to come close. Jeff was whimpering and begging me, "Please, just take it, Lisa. It will be over soon so just take it!"

I shouted at him, "Why? I ain't do nothing!" Just then she drew back the belt to hit me too. I grabbed the belt and quickly wound it around my hand. I braced myself as hard as I could and wouldn't let go. I had never felt this kind of strength. She struggled to get the belt back, but couldn't. After a few seconds, she realized I wasn't letting up and started ranting; "You got to get outta this house! Your stuff will be on the porch in the morning waiting for the social workers! You'll soon be living in the streets where you belong!" Then she dropped the belt and stormed up those basement steps like a big hulking bear retreating into the forest.

I was terrified about what would happen next, but at the same time, I was admiring this strong, determined self. I thought back to those early whippings in Mama Graves's damp basement after which all I could do was cry and scribble things in my revenge list. Remembering that last stand with Mama Graves when I refused to cry and cringe while she beat me, I became calmer and even more determined than I was then. I could help myself now; I no longer needed the revenge list to help me work out the rage and humiliation.

I often wondered what would have happened if anyone had discovered my angry revenge list. Would that person have had me put away for life? Or would they have read it, sympathized with me, and rescued my brothers and me from our endless hell? It doesn't matter anymore, but I know now that keeping such a list is what saved me until I was strong enough to stand up for myself.

The next morning when my stuff was not out on the porch, I realized that Lomax had been bluffing the whole time and I had called her out on her bluff! This was the last assault Lomax would dare attempt on me and I was proud of that.

Chapter Twelve

FOSTER PEDICURE

The night before leaving the "sisters" felt like Christmas Eve to me. I couldn't wait to see my social worker, Ms. Harris, pull up in her little blue Datsun to get us the hell out of that house. I had taken enough of Lovey Lomax, and after her failed attempt to whip me down in that basement dungeon, I knew for sure that she was eager to see my black ass gone. Right after I grabbed the belt to keep her from lashing out one lick at me, she swore before God that I was going be out of that house "SO FAST YOUR HEAD WILL SWIM!" That meant *that night* and I believed her. But in reality it had taken two whole months to find another home for Jeff and me.

The morning we were picked up with our few belongings, we didn't have a clue where we were going to end up. Both of us were glad to be leaving and prayed that things wouldn't get any worse before the door closed behind us. Most of all, though, we were sorry we would be separated from Dena and Sean. We four had vowed to be each other's eyes and ears in what we considered *the never-ending punishment* and we regretted that those two would now have to fend for themselves against Lomax.

By then, Jeff and I had learned a lot about how to look after ourselves and had each grown a few inches taller and outgrown the only clothes we had. The thought of buying us new clothes had seldom occurred to our caretakers — unless you count the few nasty old used things that Lovey had picked up for us from the thrift store on 14th Street. I despised used clothes because they never fit me right and they always seemed to have a smell that stayed in them even after they had been worn and washed many times. I remember mumbling to myself frequently, *When I get grown and have my own money, I'm gonna have the best clothes, shoes and even underwear! Shoot!*

That stuff will fit me perfect so everybody will know these are my clothes, not somebody else's.

Mama Primas's gift of luggage to us before we left her house was meant to allow us to move to the next foster home with a measure of dignity. But on that tense last day at the Long/Lomax household Lovey took great pleasure in throwing everything we owned into a couple of heavy duty garbage bags and one or two old banged-up cardboard boxes. She just took everything out of the drawers and off the hangers, balled them up and threw them into the garbage bags. We never knew what she did with the luggage Mama Primas gave us. Her final act of aggression was saying to Ms. Harris with a sarcastic tone in her voice, "Their "luggage" is all labeled and ready to go!" Hearing that, I laughed out loud, finding it funny, but when our young social worker looked at our "luggage" she simply frowned and shook her head a bit and then quickly caught herself and returned to neutral. Lomax left the room quickly without saying goodbye and then I heard Mama Long lightly making her way down the carpeted staircase. She was as relaxed and gracious in that moment as she was when we arrived on the first day. I got a strange feeling and wondered how much she really knew about what Lovey had been up to with us. Was she clueless or did she know and simply not care?

Soon we were out the front door and heading north up 16th street. The "sisters" episode had finally come to an end, but we were surprised to learn we would be living only eleven blocks away from them. I was worried. *What if we have to run into them again?* Soon we were pulling our sorry-looking garbage bags and boxes from the car and placing them on the porch of an average-looking house. As we did this, the door opened, revealing two teenage girls in the doorway, their blank looks tinged with surprise. Behind them, standing in the darkness was a tall, thin, sickly-looking woman peering out at us. Seeing Ms. Harris, she produced a fake smile, baring two rows of perfectly sculpted dentures. Clarise Wooten motioned for us to come in and started boasting to Ms. Harris about her many years of service as a FLOC foster parent, and pointing out that she had been raising the same four fosters since they were little.

Jeff and I fidgeted as we waited by our things for the long self-serving résumé to come to a close. The speech she was giving to our social worker was of the sort we had heard many times before. Like Mama Graves and Ms.

Lomax, she was notorious for giving herself accolades for her foster parenting skills. I felt my stomach turn at the similarity among the three of them. Ms. Harris listened politely for a minute and then made no bones about the fact that she was there to take care of business for Jeff and me. She got right to the point.

"Ok, now let me introduce you to Lisa and Jeffery Ponder," she said, smiling. "Both children will be entering the sixth grade this school year. We managed to get all of their belongings into my little car so it shouldn't be a problem getting them settled in right away."

Wooten recognized that her opportunity to show off was over and quickly answered, "Okay, Kisha and Darlene, you can show Lisa where her stuff will go and Daniel, you can show Jeffrey.

Unlike most of the social workers we had over the years, it seemed that Ms. Harris actually took a real interest in us and in her job. She often asked us how we felt and wanted to know how we were getting along in the Wooten house. She listened closely to what we said but, of course, we were guarded about telling the truth about our situation for fear that it could lead to something worse. Ms. Harris was a young, good-looking, confident black women straight out of college and ready to make a difference in the world. But to foster mothers like Lomax, Long, Graves and Wooten, she was a potential troublemaker. From the start, when she thought we couldn't hear her, Ms. Wooten often complained about Ms. Harris's "nosiness" and her habit of taking us out for lunch to talk privately. Mama Wooten's preferred alternative would have been for us to stay in the house where she could overhear our conversations and interrupt or edit them to cover her tracks.

It didn't take long for Jeff and me to see that we were considered intruders in our new FLOC home. No sooner than Ms. Harris had driven away, Kisha, the youngest of the girls — remembering the light-skinned Dena and Sean — commented to Ms. Wooten: "Aww Ma, I thought we were going to get the cute light-skinned kids from that house!"

Darlene started belting out a made-up song,

Boxes and bags, boxes and bags,
I got to get me some big boxes and trash bags.

Her solo was followed by the girls' whoops and belly laughs and their slapping five on both the front and black-hand sides.

Mrs. Wooten ignored the girls' antics and started reciting a list of house rules as she pointed to our rooms and what beds we were to make up for ourselves. She never bothered to introduce us to the others, but continued to explain about how things in that house worked. Apparently we were to learn to do chores, cooking, laundry and whatever else we needed to know as we went along day-by-day. Then, after about 15 minutes of instructions, she disappeared, leaving us to figure most things out for ourselves. Jeff and I knew then that we would have to protect one another like never before.

Mama Wooten's foster children were the twins, David and Daniel, their younger sister Kisha, and Darlene who was not related to them. When they entered the foster system, the twins were seven and Kisha was five. Darlene was a little older than Kisha. The four of them had been in residence for ten years and were firmly bonded as a family. Now teenagers ranging from fifteen to seventeen, they were not only older but also a lot bigger than Jeff and I were. There was no doubt about who ran stuff in that house — them! Ms. Wooten was in residence but certainly not in charge.

Soon we would begin calling her Mama as we were expected to address all our foster mothers. In each place we went it was considered a sign of disrespect if we didn't. This home, on the other hand, was completely different than any we had been to before. Though the house was on Montague Street, a middle class neighborhood straddling Fourteenth and Sixteenth Streets, it possessed little charm and was furnished with only basic, low end necessities. The living environment meant nothing to Mama Wooten as she rarely entertained company in the house except for the regular all-night card games she hosted. Outside of those card games she spent most of her time in her bedroom. On weekdays she could be found lying in bed watching her "stories" on TV, and crocheting toilet paper covers and triangular shoulder throws to sell to church members. She seldom interacted with any of us kids. If the telephone rang she always answered in a sickly voice as if she had a good reason for being in bed as much as she was. When she left the house, it was usually to attend Sunday church service where she shouted to the glory of the lord and danced around the aisles in a state of pious rapture, often speaking in tongues. Her church day started at eleven o'clock and ended around four, followed by a fellowship dinner. Other than that, she was largely inactive.

Our social worker had to make a special home visit just to enroll Jeff and me into our new elementary school located only a block away from the house because Mama Wooten simply did not exert herself for things like that. But she had to do the grocery shopping once a month. For those trips she painstakingly loaded me, Jeff and the two girls into her canary yellow Impala and headed to Shoppers Food Warehouse to buy groceries followed by a stop at the local Murry's Steaks where she always picked up a dozen half-smokes and a box of frozen beef patties. The fallacy was that the ten bags of groceries she bought for the month lasted only into the second week. By then, lunchmeat sandwiches on stale leftover bread were the only option open to us.

Food preparation was left to the two teenage girls who had no culinary skills and no concept of kitchen hygiene. One of Darlene's techniques was to make hot sandwiches by singeing the lunchmeat directly on a dirty gas burner. The smell that this produced was enough to turn my uneasy stomach, and I often went without any food at all. On some occasions when there was absolutely no food in the house, Mama Wooten gave the older kids money to buy us all meals from McDonalds. Mama Wooten certainly wasn't keeping track of our overall nutritional level because she never ate with us children, preferring to eat in her room from a tray of carryout food brought in by one of the teenage girls.

During those first few weeks on Montague Street, my mantra was, *as long as no one touches me, I'm good.* I told myself that if anybody in that house laid a hand on me or my brother, they would be in for a wild fight. It was clear to me that the subtle and not-so-subtle bullying by our foster siblings would always be an issue. I developed insomnia while keeping a watchful eye out because I simply didn't trust anybody in that house but Jeff. Mama Wooten's notion of parenting was to let our foster siblings take charge of getting things done, so the lack of adult supervision meant that the unspoken threat of violence by her teenage guard dogs lingered in the air all the time. As the days passed, Jeff and I became even closer than ever and kept a constant eye on one another. We put our heads together every day just to stay one step ahead of our biggest fears — abuse and separation. And we agreed that Mama Wooten was a foster mother in name only and if we didn't take charge of our own lives the other kids in the household would dominate us. Because of the abuse that had been done to me in the other homes, I was always on an acute alert for approaching signs of physical and sexual abuse. To me everybody started out as a suspect. Jeff was less worried about that and was more concerned that we weren't getting all we needed, mainly food. At school he would make it a point to get the free breakfast and lunch as he had at Clark Elementary.

Jeff and I were both placed in the sixth grade at our sixth school in seven years, Brightwood Elementary. The next year, we attended Takoma School on the far northwest end of DC and as a result were farther away from home for a longer period of time during the day, a fact which delighted us both. Takoma reminded me of West Elementary, the school we had attended during our happy days with Mama Primas. Both schools went from pre-K through 8 and both had open space classrooms, which meant there were no walls dividing the classes. I loved that arrangement because I could look across and see my brother any time I wanted. The only minus was that I despised walking the three-mile roundtrip to school. There was no provision for giving us bus tokens to use on cold or rainy days, and as we walked those three miles each day, I'd complain to Jeffrey about how unfair it was that we had to walk while our foster siblings were issued bus tokens for getting to schools closer to the house than ours.

"They just do us wrong like we don't even matter," I'd say dramatically, then adding, "I can't wait till I get grown so I can take care of my own damn self." Then Jeffery would say something like, "Don't worry about it Lisa, we can take care of ourselves now."

Soon we worked out a way to make the most of our daily commute. We'd have speed-walking contests to see who could reach the school's front gate first. Jeffery figured out a technique of walking only on the lines of the sidewalk, which allowed us to hold a conversation and walk without missing a beat. But he always won by a few steps, and I always thought of an excuse why I lost.

"Your legs are just longer than mine, that's the only reason you keep winning," I'd complain. But one day I came within a step of beating him and he proclaimed, "Okay, I don't want to race walk no more."

A few weeks later we began running. Jeffery would beat me at this by a half a block or more until the day came when I came within inches of beating him. And, just like the speed-walking contest, the running came to an abrupt end. Those were probably the only two instances in which I ever got mad at my brother and I had no problem with letting him know how I felt. But I could not stay mad at Jeffery for long. By the time we'd make it home, all my irritation would have faded away. Now I look back and see my brother Jeff as my first sparring partner who kept me on my toes and made me earn the possibility of winning!

Unlike the kids I'd fantasized about being like on TV — the ones with good families who were given a weekly allowance — we never had money and never thought we could get any. People just weren't handing money out to kids like my brother and me, so we constantly talked about what we were going to buy when we got old enough to work. I imagined myself dressing like the models I admired in the magazines I saw on the newsstands like *Seventeen, Glamour* and *Vogue*. Jeff talked about wanting to have enough quarters to play video games at the neighborhood arcade and winning the chance to get his initials up on the high scoreboards of his favorite games.

I'm not sure exactly how this all started but one day we got a chance to do just that. We played video games at one of the local arcades on Georgia Avenue by cashing in every quarter and every dollar we had in our book bags. But it wasn't *our* money. It was the thirty-five dollars in cash that we had collected from customers we sold candy to for our annual school fundraiser. I think at first Jeff and I had agreed to spend only a dollar apiece and somehow replace the money in time to deliver the candy to our customers. But we had the time of our lives dropping quarter after quarter into those machines that afternoon. We even got to put our initials on the high scoreboards of *Pac Man, Centipede* and *The Phoenix*. For those few hours, I was no longer Lisa Ponder the foster child, I was one of those rich kids on TV having fun the same way they did. The only thing missing was a mall where I could buy something pretty for myself to take home in a shopping bag.

That day, our 4 o'clock curfew came and went and before we knew it, six o'clock had arrived. What excuse were we going to give for being so late? After spending all the money and gobbling up every bit of fun we could, we now had to worry about being in trouble. Sure enough, trouble arrived. When informed of our absence, Mama Wooten actually arose from her bed and put on street clothes to drive around the neighborhood looking for us. Jeff was the first to spot Mama Wooten's yellow car and watched her pull up to the

Georgia Avenue corner where the arcade was. We heard her shout, "Jeffrey and Lisa, Jeffery and Lisa!" Then she drove alongside us, yelling out the window until we could no longer ignore her and slowed to a halt. She demanded that we get into the car and when we climbed in she grilled us about what we had been doing.

"We were hanging out in the arcade," we said truthfully. Kisha glared at us from the passenger seat. She seemed more disgusted with the fact that we hadn't come home on time than Mama Wooten was. We knew that if it were up to Kisha we would have been whipped and punished. I never regretted missing curfew or having so much fun with my brother as I did on that day. Jeff and I have both been haunted for all these years by our crime of stealing the money we had collected for the candy we never delivered to our customers. I have always worried that anything bad that befell us after such a heinous act was richly deserved. To this day, I believe in Karma.

Then Jeff came up with an idea of how to make some honest money for us both. This time he didn't want video game money. He wanted to have money so that he could buy something for us to eat whenever we were hungry. Jeff was afraid of being hungry, was tired of us having to scrounge for food and didn't like it when I refused to eat because of the unclean conditions at the house. He called his plan *hustling*. When the hustling began, our food nightmares were over. The first day he hustled at the Safeway he said, "Lisa, I'm going to make some money real fast so go over there and wait for me."

I was worried and asked, "Make some money, how?" But I obediently walked over to the curb and sat on the black steel rail that kept the shopping carts from rolling out into the parking lot. Then I stood and watched as my brother approached several women and spoke to them. I couldn't hear what he was saying and was starting to get anxious. *Oh God! He's going to get us in trouble for messing with people!* After being ignored or refused three or four times, Jeff got the nod from one woman. After nodding her head at him she walked into the parking lot while Jeff stood back by her shopping cart which was crammed full of groceries. When she pulled her car up to the curb where he was standing, Jeff rushed to the back of the car and pulled up the trunk.

What in the world is he doing? I worried. Jeff then began carefully taking each bag out of the cart and neatly placing them in the truck of the car. As soon as he was done he rushed to the woman's open window where she had a crisp new dollar bill waiting for him. He quickly reached over and took the dollar with a polite thank you. Before the woman could drive away he had spotted his next customer.

Woo, he actually did it, I thought. I had only been standing on that curb for a few minutes and Jeff had already made some real money. His hustling went on for about a half hour during which he raked in more than three dollars. Then he said, "Come on Lisa, let's go in and get something to eat before we go home." I was smiling broadly because it was a rare event when I got to go into a store and choose something for myself. I saw my brother in a completely different way after that day and wanted to learn from him. Almost every day after school Jeff went to the Safeway and hustled money. I liked that he had money in his pocket and he made sure I had a full stomach before we got home. After a while I got in on the act and began hustling people he missed while helping someone else.

"Excuse me, Miss, may I help you with your bags?" I'd ask in the sweetest voice I could. After that the person would give me the once over, probably thinking, "As little as you are?" I quickly learned that people who weren't in a hurry were the best targets. They probably knew it would take longer for us to carefully put their groceries in their cars than if they did it themselves. But they were willing to let us do the work and were generous with their tips.

Jeff and I became an efficient team. We learned to play off each other. And when it came to the money, Jeff told me, "Lisa, don't let nobody else know you have some money."

"Why? You think they'll try to take it from me?" I asked. And before he could answer, I huffed, "Puh-lease! I wish somebody would try to take my money. I'll beat their black ass. I don't care which one of them it is. Humpf… I *would*, too!" Then I wound my neck around with all the attitude I could.

"No, just don't let them know because all they're gonna do is try to be real nice to you so you'll buy them something and then they gonna be mean right after they get what they want. So don't even show them! Jeff knew all this because it had already happened to him when his school friends learned he had some money.

Because there were slow days when it looked like nobody was grocery shopping, Jeff came up with the idea of hustling at the gas station and asking customers if he could pump their gas for them. By then, I didn't at all mind.

I liked the smell of gas and it made me feel grown up doing such an important job, or at least at age thirteen I thought it was important. Business at the gas station wasn't usually as good as it was at the Safeway so sometimes we would split up and work both places. Then we'd stop off at McDonald's after and get hamburgers and fries instead of our regular diet of Little Debbie's Oatmeal Cream Pies and a cold twenty-five cent soda from the Safeway. Jeff never worried about being broke or hungry in those days. Having our little hustle made living at Mama Wooten's house a little more bearable for both of us.

As much as Jeff and I looked out for each other, our biggest wish would have been to get along in the house without a threat of any kind lingering in the back of our minds. But we knew our foster siblings. They were stuck together like glue and in their minds we had invaded their space. The feeling of being pushed out, rejected or abandoned is a feeling that sticks with most foster children until they are finally emancipated. I know I have felt that way. So instead of focusing on the other foster kids in the house, I concentrated on my relationship with Mama Wooten and began to clean her room and run little errands for her. I realized that the more helpful I was to Mama, the nicer she was to me. I wanted to be liked so I tried to please her by being a good helper. I regularly cleaned her room which was always cluttered with takeout food bags, dirty dishes and anything else she didn't feel like taking down to the kitchen or throwing away. *Euw! How can she stay in this clutter all day?* I repeatedly asked myself. It bothered me more than it did her so I tried every-thing in my power to control the growing mess before things got too bad.

After a while she began to ask me to assist her with organizing her cro-chet work so that it would be ready to be sold by the next week. She was really good at crocheting and I was impressed by her skills so much that one day I picked up a ball of yarn and watched and tried to copy everything she did. I had learned a little crocheting and knitting from Mama Primas but didn't get too deeply into it because I liked playing outside better. Mama Wooten saw that I was struggling to catch on to her stitch pattern but hadn't gotten very far. After I sat there fumbling for more than thirty minutes, she broke down and taught me a triangle pattern she was using to make her multi-colored shawls. Now I was on a mission to make my very own dark blue/light blue shawl with hanging tassels and all. It took a couple of weeks of me coming into her room on weekends to complete my very first wearable crocheted project.

I thought often about Mama Primas and wished she could see what I had done. I knew she would have made a big deal about it, bragging to all her family, friends and church members of how her bright daughter had done this wonderful thing. That wasn't going to happen with Mama Wooten. But she showed her approval the best way she could without creating any tension for herself or me from the other kids. A slight smile and the promise to let me make another if I wanted to. I would just have to be happy with that, and I was.

Before long Mama Wooten had me doing something for her on a more personal level. She had caught onto how badly I wanted to get along and made me her own personal pedicurist. The square plastic dishwashing pan was kept in a corner next to the nightstand on the opposite side of her bed. Whenever she asked, "Lisa! Take the basin into the bathroom and let the water run until it gets hot. Then, put some dishwashing detergent in it so I can soak my feet," I happily did what she wanted. At these times she spoke more nicely to me than she normally did and I welcomed that. For me, any niceness was worth a lot. At her request I'd dart straight to the bathroom to do what she asked. After a while, she said something like, "I need to soak these calluses, then I want you to take one of those razors and get all the dead skin off for me." So now I was officially her pedicurist.

None of the set-up bothered me. But it was reaching down into the murky water to pull out one of her waterlogged feet that made me want to throw up and I had to train myself not to frown up my face when the bottom of her foot was pointing at me. But when the water had cooled below room temperature and the once-hard chapped and rough skin was now white, loose and wrinkled, I dutifully took a deep breath and went to work. Before what she began to call "doing my feet" began, I had never even handled a razor. Inside I screamed, no! because I couldn't stand the thought of accidentally cutting into her foot and seeing blood spew everywhere. The razors had a protective edge to prevent me from cutting myself yet I still was terrified of slicing into one of my fingers so I was extra careful. I'd gently angle the blade and scrape down to the towel under her foot. A thin layer of soaked skin the width of the razor would gather onto its edge and I'd wipe it on the towel. Every few seconds I would look anxiously up at her face to make sure I wasn't hurting her and see that she was crocheting along happily. The first five or six times she told me, "Do my feet," I would be careful and pray that nothing went wrong. Though I wanted to get along, I still didn't trust her and could picture the lie she would make up to tell FLOC explaining why she couldn't walk and that it was all my fault. So the more she required these revolting pedicure sessions, the more resentful I became. I was beginning to see that doing Mama Wooten's feet didn't make things any easier for me there in the house. It was just another chore that I was expected to perform.

Jeffrey hated the sight of me in the room working to get every piece of dead skin off her feet, clipping and filing her toenails, oiling and finally paint-ing her disgusting thick yellow toenails with two coats of clear polish. One day he felt so sorry for me that he volunteered to help. He had watched me enough times to know what to do and Mama Wooten was just as happy now that she had two of us doing her feet on command. On our walk to school Jeff and I often talked angrily about how gross it was to dig the toe jam from between her toes and nails. Then to somehow make ourselves feel better for putting up with it, we managed to talk of it as a funny in-joke between us.

After spending so much time with Mama Wooten, I realized that she was easily influenced. She was frail, weak and didn't really have any real friends. Her sole identity — other than her screamin', shoutin' behavior in church — consisted of having the house with the most foster children in the agency and winning the award from FLOC for that, along with saintly bragging rights.

In addition to hustling bags at the Safeway, pumping gas at the gasoline station and our new friendship with a girl on our street named Metisse, Jeff and I began to relax a bit more in our own living situation. We had been in Mama Wooten's home for almost two years and had made it clear that we were not going to fall for any funny business from anybody. The money we earned after school gave us newfound confidence. It meant not having to beg, borrow or steal from anybody. The empowerment of having a mere two dollars in my pocket opened me up to a kind of freedom I had never felt before. But we both knew that the only way we could hold on to our freedom was to keep up our hustle. We had each other's back and I felt al-most as confident about things as I had living with Mama Primas. Our foster siblings could recognize the change in our behavior. We were no longer bending to their will because they were the ones we had to rely on for food or anything else we'd need in that house.

But the longer we stayed at the Wooten house the more I realized things were not measuring up to the FLOC standard of living. I guess that was one of the things Ms. Harris sensed when she first delivered us to the home. I know that is why Mama Wooten was extremely uncomfortable with us having her as our social worker and finally complained about her to the agency until she was taken off our case.

In the early days of FLOC, the main mission was to place children with loving, caring couples or individuals who showed a sincere interest in taking care of needy kids. Often the people who expressed a willingness to help couldn't meet the qualifications because their living arrangements weren't up to snuff. That's when FLOC sometimes stepped in and offered one of their homes to the prospective foster parent. Mama Wooten sold them on the idea that she was a good candidate for this arrangement and was granted the use of the house she had now been living in for more than ten years. This meant that unlike any of the other foster parents I had already lived with, she had no financial responsibilities as far as the house was concerned.

Just like Mama Graves, Mama Wooten told us not to tell about anything that went on in that house. You knew that everyone would hate you if you told and I was a master secret-keeper. But I wanted to be everybody's friend, so I had this vibe that there was a line other kids shouldn't cross; asking too many questions or making fun of me. Kids knew that if they messed with me verbally, I was always going to jone on them back, but more cleverly. I had already scoped everyone out, anticipating that someone might start to jone on me. So when a kid started making fun of my ratty clothes or shoes, I would tear that person's ass up verbally. I would read them from top to bottom and tear into them, starting with: "Well, at least I don't..." I got a reputation for being good at this, so people would leave me alone.

There was a new girl at my school. People were messing with her at first. I wasn't messing with her because I always wanted to be friends with other kids. But she came up to me one day and said, "Bitch, you had those pants on yesterday!" I immediately answered, "I *know* you ain't talking, Felicia, with your eyes popping out of your head. And look at your Jerry-curl hair.

You look like a pit bull poodle!" She just stood there listening. And then she said, "Hummm..." and I knew she knew she was busted. I mean, you can't say anything back to that. So instead, she and I became friends.

I had to just work with what I had by keeping my clothes clean and switching around the few things I owned. Because I was sensitive about my crappy wardrobe, I became better at joneing than anyone. Kids would listen to me when I got on a roll and they'd crack up laughing. They didn't mess with me because they knew how I could jone.

My new friend, Metisse was attractive and had the best clothes, pretty hair and was light-skinned. But her nose was considered a really 'black' nose, and she was slue-footed, so kids joned on her a lot. I think the girls were jealous and the boys liked her and wanted her attention. After Metisse joined Jeff and me on the walks to and from school, the distance seemed like nothing. Sometimes she used the tokens she had saved up for weeks so that we could ride the metro with her on cold or rainy days. I wasn't used to selfless gestures like that and, for me, it sealed the deal on our close friendship. Everything about who Metisse and I were as individuals was different, but our wanting to be friends was genuine. She was the first best friend I had since Minyon. The same way Minyon and I did way back when, Metisse and I loved to laugh and talk every second we were together. She made living on Montague Street much easier by giving me something to look forward to every day and together we made going to our new school actually fun. Our words were like medicine for each other as we talked candidly. I even trusted her enough to tell her about what was going on with me at home. When I told her we were foster children she hadn't a clue what that even meant. But by the time I told her about how Mama Wooten and our foster siblings were she felt as protective of me for living there as I was about her when we were at school and kids were joneing on her.

Metisse was having a more difficult time than I was with being teased and bullied. She also had difficulty adjusting to the differing teaching methods of the four teachers we had. She always avoided confrontation, but I was willing to indulge in it and our classmates learned quickly that she had some mouthy backup when I was around. She had not needed to defend herself in her previous school but the kids at the Takoma Campus in DC had a much harder edge than the middle class kids from Shepherd Park where she had previously been. Fortunately, Takoma was mild compared to many of the area school choices where the kids were basically running the place. Metisse and I began talking our way through the problems we were having at school which made going much easier and more fun for us both. After a while we even began calling each other cousins as a symbol of our closeness.

She only lived three blocks away from Mama Wooten's house so we walked her all the way home before we continued on the next few blocks. Initially, the rules were that we had thirty minutes to make the trek from the school to home — or else. But when Jeff and I started making our little extra money hustling grocery bags at the Safeway and I made a new best friend, we ignored the rule and Mama Wooten didn't seem to notice or care.

One Christmas, Metisse got a brand-new Atari 5200 console and some games and invited both of us up to her apartment. This was the first time I'd been invited into anyone's home since leaving Mama Primas's and I was excited. That invitation took our friendship to another level. I had thought about inviting Metisse to our house around the corner many times. But the way our foster siblings acted, I knew they would have immediately recognized how nice Metisse was and instantly taken it for weakness, and that would have sent me into protective mode. Going to her house was obviously a much better idea.

Metisse was a good hostess. She invited us in and offered something to drink and often even a snack, which were usually cookies or Doritos, which we always happily accepted. You could tell right away from the look of the furniture and the way the place was arranged that Metisse's mom had class. Their apartment was clean and neat with just the right lived-in feeling. There was nothing phony about Metisse's lifestyle, which showed in the way she lived, dressed, and as I would quickly find out, how her mother was. Girls sometimes bullied her because she came to school dressed so nicely. I never understood that because I was accustomed to being teased for the exact opposite reason. She would wear fresh new polo shirts and the latest designer jeans and I would be in the same old two or three pairs of over-washed corduroys or some off-brand pair of jeans which had been handed down to me and which never quite fit. Nevertheless, both of these wardrobes were the butt of jokes.

Metisse's mother was a school teacher and she and Metisse had a good life. After we started hanging out together and I went to her apartment after school, her mom provided me that mother thing that I craved. I had never wanted to be a person with a revenge list. I knew I was a good person. But I knew without a doubt that I was an unwanted person. Metisse and her mom took me out of that other self. Her mom used to ask if we got our homework done. I loved it when she did that; it felt so good to have someone actually care about what I was doing.

Metisse's invitation to come over and play video games turned into an everyday occurrence. Jeff started out coming over with me but he soon got tired of hanging out with us girls and ventured off on his own. Often he would stick back behind at the Safeway and make money during the hour or two I was hanging out at Metisse's. There, she and I played video games, talked on the Mickey Mouse phone she had in her room, or searched through and clipped out all the latest fashions from her magazines: *Seventeen, Glamour, Harper's Bazaar* and *Vogue*.

Metisse's room was always messy, her clothes thrown everywhere. To her it was no big deal, but I couldn't imagine having such gorgeous clothes and shoes and treating them that way. I could see that Metisse's mom put much thought and care into picking out everything her daughter wore. That kind of attention was what Metisse had become used to and I paid close attention to all the wonderful things her mother did for her. I often suggested that we spend some time cleaning up her room just to please her mother and Metisse would look at me as if I was half crazy and go back to playing Pac Man.

While in the Wooten foster home I completed the 6th, 7th, and 8th grades, enjoyed having Metisse as my best friend and went to church every Sunday with our next door neighbors Reverend and Mrs. Henderson. To me, those were big accomplishments and I was proud of myself and my brother for making it this far. Living in that house wasn't easy but I did what I needed to do to survive without getting too messed up physically or mentally. When Jeff and I first got to the house in October of 1980, we had upped the current count of foster children in the home to five. A sixth foster child, David, was one of the twins. When we came to live there, he was away, living at a Job Corps program near Baltimore. When he returned to the home, that four-bedroom house was a really tight fit for six teenagers. Mama Wooten was in the master bedroom, David, Daniel and Jeffrey shared a room, Kisha and I shared a room and Darlene, the most demanding girl, had her own room. The set-up was working, and we managed to share one bathroom down the hallway with very few problems.

But in late 1981, things got way overcrowded and more dysfunctional in the house. Mama Wooten decided to capitalize on her FLOC home and rent out rooms to boarders. Ahead of time she warned us, "I don't want y'all talking about what goes on in this house. It's nobody's bidness, especially those nosey white people down at FLOC. Okay?" It could have been Mama Graves talking at that point, because the words and the attitudes were so alike. We knew she was mainly talking to Jeffery and me because the other kids remained silent and looked to us to answer. "Yes ma'am," we said in a chorus.

Then Les arrived. He was an 18-year old boy fresh out of a minimum security Wilderness school for boys. Housing a boy this age with young teenage girls was a clear violation of FLOC rules, but Mama Wooten instructed the three of us girls to clear out our rooms on the second floor and move everything we owned up to the attic. It was the first time I had ever been up there and was amazed by all the untouched dust that had settled there over the years. We jammed each of our twin beds flush to the wall in a corner of the room in hopes that the space would appear big enough to accommodate the three of us. The dusty, mildewed stench made me queasy during the first few nights I went to sleep there. My eyes watered and my throat itched every night when I tried to cope with the dust that still remained even after we had tried to thoroughly clean the space. The boys remained on the second floor. This time David and Daniel shared a room and Les and Jeff were in the other. That left the front room just next door to Mama Wooten's for her new tenants, a twenty-two-year-old woman named Barbara and her two-year-old son, Li'l Tony. Barbara was a meek, reserved woman and it was clear to me she had been through a lot. The other thing I noticed was that she dressed well which sparked immediate jealous feelings from Kisha and Darlene.

Barbara was very protective about her young son. You could see that she was an attractive woman despite her obviously bruised cheek and faint black eye showing through her pancake makeup. Mama Wooten was happy to have her as a tenant for the set price of $200 a month including the babysitting fees she charged her to take care of L'il Tony while she went to work. One day Li'l Tony's father showed up at the front door and Mama Wooten invited him in.

Tony did what he needed to do to get past Wooten and find out which room was Barbara's. Next thing we knew, he had pushed his way into her room. Minutes later, Barbara began to scream, "No Tony, Stop! Leave right now, p-l-e-a-s-e!" We heard his low muffled baritone voice between slaps and bumps coming from the room. This disturbing activity brought joy to Kisha and Darlene. They laughed and made jokes about what they thought was happening blow-by-blow. Mama Wooten didn't react to what was going on until she heard little Tony cry out in fear," Mommy! Mommy! H-h-a-a-a-a-a-a-a-w"! At that point she finally slinked out of her bedroom and knocked on Barbara's bedroom door. The commotion quieted and she said, "Barbara! Y'all can't be in there acting like that around that boy," as if Barbara had somehow provoked the whole thing. She called through the door, "Mrs. Clarise. Tony ain't even supposed to be near me. I have a restraining order against him." Then we heard her say to Tony, "How did you find out where I live?" And he replied in his thug voice, "Don't worr-bout it Bitch, Ima always know where you an' my son be stayin'!"

Things quieted down and Tony picked up the child who laid his little head on his father's chest while leftover whimpers from his throat faded away. While the girls snickered and took pleasure in the whole scene, I tried to show Barbara some support by offering her a glass of ice water. "No, that's all right, Lisa," she said sadly.

For me, this abusive scene was another dark lesson for me to heed: *Never marry a man who might beat my ass, no matter how good he looks.*

Only weeks after that incident there was another knock at the front door. Mama Wooten shouted, "I'll get it!" I should have known something was up because she had got up and was dressed that day. The middle-aged woman standing at the front door was yet another new tenant with bags in hand. This time a tour of the basement was being given and we knew she would be moving in. This new tenant was Ms. Latrelle. She stayed down in her basement apartment most of the time but when she came up, she acted standoffish. Her basement quarters weren't even as nice as our attic situation and I always got the feeling that she didn't like Mama Wooten. But when I saw her in the kitchen or knocked on the basement door to see if I could come down to wash clothes, she was always friendly to me.

My stay at Mama Wooten's came to an abrupt end not long after Les's arrival at the home after he left Wilderness reform school. He was very outgoing and impressed all of us by smoking a handmade corncob pipe. This 6-foot-1, light-skinned, flirtatious and outwardly charming young man seemed to awaken Ms. Wooten from the deep sleep she had been in during the years we had been there and we saw her take an immediate interest in him. Kisha and Darlene were also smitten by this young player, but they hid their secret crushes from one another and provided their attentions to him privately. I was not interested in being any more to him than I was to Daniel and David, but, like my other past abusers, Les was cunning and slick and he expected all the women in the household to fawn over him. He took my resistance to his attentions as a personal insult and his lack of success with me pissed him off to the point of violence.

When we were alone in the house one day, Les chased me down and as I struggled to escape upstairs, he snatched my foot, pulled me down and dragged me towards him — my ribs painfully bumping down the steps — as he tried, pants open, to do what he had long been wanting to do. Sheer terror somehow gave me the strength to break free and run to the bay window with the intention of breaking through to the front porch. In that instant, I saw my beloved brother approaching the front door and I screamed at the top of my voice, *"J-E-E-F-F...!"*

With Jeff's arrival, Les instantly backed off, allowing me space to immediately sprint out the front door and run to a neighbor's house leaving Jeff on the porch, completely confused. The neighbor, Mrs. Green, was the FLOC foster mother of a little girl whose hair I regularly cornrowed for five dollars every two weeks. She welcomed me into her home with open arms and listened to the story I blurted out between sobs. She did not doubt me for a second and immediately picked up the phone and called FLOC to report my story. I never set foot in Ms. Wooten's house again.

Chapter Thirteen

After our abrupt departure from the Wooten household, Jeff and I were sent back temporarily to the Long household to live. This time Lovey Lomax was no longer living there and that was a relief. But very soon Jeff was sent to a foster family somewhere in Maryland. It was then I knew the Masterminds — those faceless bureaucrats who were behind the ripping away of what was left of my family — had finally won. Ms. Long told me with a half-smile on her face, "They took Jeff away 'cause he's a bad influence on you." Anyone who had anything to do with such a diabolical plan was now officially on my shit list. Jeff and I had been a devoted pair for a long time, and his absence hurt me more than I could say. We still saw each other at FLOC once in a while, but that was it. The good part is that although he was angry and troubled, he had landed in a good place. His new foster mother — Mrs. Jordan — was a true Christian woman who was good to Jeff and patiently worked to get him out of his funk. Her husband was a drinker, but not an abusive one, and Jeff was to stay in that home until he aged out of the foster system.

Now, at age 15, there was another surprise for me. I was going to another foster home. Hearing this, I imagined thick black ooze seeping its way out of my body and encasing me with the defensive shell of a Brazil nut. *It's on! If they think I didn't care before, just watch how I really don't give a fuck now!*

I had become an expert in sniffing out the phoniness of potential new foster parents. The McLeaches, who were next, were no exception, especially Kelly, that phony-ass Christian I was expected to call Mama. I felt sick to my stomach as I watched her four-foot-eleven porky body waddling toward me with her compliant husband, Johnny, limping along at her side on his shortened leg. Right away, that nasty little voice inside me started growling as I waited for them to approach me. While I leaned against the wall with as much attitude as I could show, that dark inner voice started telling me; *Same shit, different day.*

Watching the pair coming closer, I told myself, *There's nothin' boutchou I haven't already seen. Donchu be gettin' in my face! OK, now I gotta say somethin' to 'um...*

"Hi, how you doin'?" I drooled those phony words out along with a smile just as fake as I could muster to match theirs.

Ms. Brinker — my social worker for the last two moves — made a big deal of announcing dramatically, "These are the McLeaches!" I said nothing in return, just kept staring at Brinker, my glazed eyes sending her a message; *Don't even try it!*

Brinker knew me well enough to know I was apt to speak my mind or show-off at a potential foster mother's expense. In the past, she had even let slip a surprised laugh or two at my bold displays of attitude. But this time, it seemed she was trying to overlook my games and get me to impress these strangers. In the past, she always took me to the foster parents' home to meet them and have them look me over, but this time she had arranged for them to meet me at the FLOC office. It was an unfamiliar routine, but there was no doubt in my mind what was up and I wasn't having any of it. After all the formalities and yada yada yadas, I grew even more impatient and breathed loud sighs that sometimes came out as one long hum. Then suddenly, the "interview" was over and the McLeaches were officially on their way to a new source of foster parent income.

"Okay, let's go," Mrs. McLeach announced, in a hurry to move the process along more quickly and get out of there.

"Where to?" I said as the feeling of dread began to well up in my throat.

Brinker broke the news that I would be moving to Fort Washington, Maryland with these two strangers. Hearing these words, I could feel my face go blank as I leaned forward to get into her face a bit. "*R-e-a-l-l-y,* where *is* that?"

Silence. Finally, Ms. McLeach pushed closer to me, spacing out her reply with a dramatic emphasis on each letter as if talking to an idiot: "In... P ... G ... County...where...we...live."

All I knew about Prince Georges County was that Jeff was placed out there when he left Mama Long's house. *Oh, so they shipping all us foster kids outta DC now?* I was lost in feelings of confusion and disbelief. What a perfect trick they had played on me. *They planned this. They planned this. They planned this...* the words repeated out over and over in my head while a familiar tingling sensation began to wrap my body with its heat. A tight knot inflated and filled the back of my throat while unwanted tears slowly welled up and began to run down my face. Mr. McLeach saw this and briefly retreated out of sight, bringing back one of the cheap, coarse orphan-brand napkins from the snack table just outside the meeting room.

No longer able to act tough and cool, I lost control and completely covered my face with the rough napkin. I stayed that way for a while, realizing that a whole new fear was upon me. I was long past the point of being scared of foster parents, social workers, psychologists, shrinks — and even my terrifying mother. This was a new kind of fear. This time it was *distance!* So *that* was to be my new tormentor; distance from everything I had known all my life! Suddenly time sped up and, before I knew it, all my stuff— the little bit of shit I owned —was piled in the trunk of the McLeaches' ancient sun-bleached brown hooptie.

As we drove away, the McLeaches' questions began to hurtle toward the backseat where I half-reclined like a rag doll. I could tell that my one-word answers frustrated Mrs. McLeach. But she was not willing to reveal her true colors too soon by showing anger or nastiness, so she tuned the radio to a gospel station. *Oh god, she's tone deaf,* I thought as I listened to her shout the words she knew and substitute tuneless humming for the ones she didn't. Mr. McLeach began chatting to her about church and last Sunday's service. Her frequent outbursts of "Praise the Lord" caught me off guard and I thought; *Another one of these Holy Spirit fake-me-outs!* My inner voice was getting louder and more desperate and I aimed my hate-filled glare into the back of their fake-pious heads. Then, before they could turn and notice, I looked out the car window instead.

Searching for something familiar in the passing scenery, I noticed that the city was fast disappearing behind us as the hooptie sped toward alien land. As we moved forward just one or two notches over the speed limit, it seemed that my life was racing backward and would soon drop out of sight. *I wondered; Is this how it feels to die?*

The McLaine house was a three-bedroom rambler perched at the top of a ridiculously long flight of concrete steps. The house faced the woods and was hidden at the deadest dead end of a small community of cookie-cutter houses. As I took in the unfamiliar scene, I wondered idly how Mrs. McLeach could still be so fat after climbing those steps every day. There were two other girls at the McLeach house, Sharquitta and Shawna. I could see immediately that Sharquitta was the star of the show because she was Mrs. McLeach's real daughter by another man. She was a light-skinned kid of almost exactly my age.

After several trips up and down the thirty or so steps with Mr. McLeach, all my worldly goods were squeezed into the tiny bedroom next to Sharquitta's and across from the couple's own bedroom. My new foster mother stood in the narrow hallway with her hands resting on the second fat layer just under her triple E's and without any expression she directed me to enter a tiny undecorated room. There I was to share a bed and a closet with Shawna, the less-than-average-looking thick, dark brown-skinned twelve-year-old FLOC foster child who played a poor second fiddle to Sharquitta's stardom. The bed filled most of the space, adding to my impression that the room was originally intended to be a walk-in closet. My clothes were to be comingled with Shawna's by doubling them up on a few bent wire hangers to be hung on a tiny closet pole and stuffing the folded things into a few inadequate drawers in a space that seemed more like an indentation in the wall than a usable closet.

Only the basics were provided for us fosters at the McLeach house and I didn't blame Shawna for resenting the requirement to share with a complete stranger what little space she had been issued by her foster parents. I knew my arrival was an intrusion into the world she had become accustomed to during her year with the McLeaches. Despite her learning disabilities and many serious behavioral problems, she had managed to mesh perfectly with this family. In fact, it even seemed that she saw nothing wrong with the fact that Sharquitta had an ample room decked out with a matched bedroom set and a reasonably-sized closet full of nice clothes. Shawna was a survivor and had formed a valuable alliance with Sharquitta long before my arrival. She wasn't about to let my arrival interfere with the strong bond she had carefully forged.

Sharquitta's soft tan complexion gave her a push just over the line of average-looking. The same applied to the way she dressed; she had enough clothes in her closet to never have to wear the same thing twice for at least two weeks and that was important in high school. The mushroom hairstyle she wore framed her face and gave her a kind of innocent yet slightly adult look which went right along with the way the rest of the ninth-graders at Friendly High School looked. There was nothing charismatic about her so it was good she had kept many of her friends from elementary school. Her C-average grades fit perfectly with the intelligence level her public thumb-sucking underscored. I came to think of her as mentally sub-par.

The isolation of the first few months of living out in Fort Washington, Maryland sank me into a depression as deep as the one I experienced after I was moved to the Graveses' from the Parkers's. History was repeating itself as I changed schools and churches and traded in those friends I had managed to claim. And there was no certainty they would be replaced by new ones. With these changes, my protective shell hardened and my bad attitude went into third gear.

When I finally talked to Jeff, I was happy to learn that he had settled more happily into his new home in Suitland, Maryland with the Jordans. After a long hard six months of adjusting, he realized how lucky he was to have landed there. His many initial acts of disobedience had never discouraged Mrs. Jordan. Angry and rebellious at first, he refused to accept any love that was offered to him, but in time she patiently broke down his defenses. Her sincere kindness was the ideal for a foster mother and was reminiscent of the way the Parkers had treated us. She was a rarity in many ways because she lived out her religious values and actually cared about those she considered "her children." Jeff became a fixture in her home as the couple accepted more children in need of help. The list included special needs children in wheelchairs and a range of physically and mentally disabled children who cycled through the home on a regular basis. The way she was the first day Jeff introduced her to me was the way she remains until this day. She is no phony Samaritan; she is the real deal.

I still had the clarinet that Judge Bacon, my fairy godmother in judicial robes had miraculously arranged for FLOC to purchase for me. I was proud of having that instrument and lovingly vacuumed the inside of the case. Mostly, I wanted desperately to learn to play it well, so I signed up for marching band although I knew no one. I wasn't a good clarinet player because I had not had any consistent lessons and had to play by ear, often faking the notes. But I could march! I just watched what the others did and learned the routines quickly. And the best part was that being in band meant I didn't have to go home right away after school.

Right from the start, Ms. McLeach had her eye on that clarinet and wanted to know how much it cost FLOC to buy it for me. She must have thought it could bring in some bucks, because after I was removed from that unhappy household, she called me and begged me to take it to her place of work. I feel sure that she planned to sell it. I still don't know why I complied with her request. It was mine, and her taking it was theft, pure and simple. I guess the only explanation for my passivity was that by then I was accustomed to the theft of my meager belongings by falsely entitled foster parents. This was just another instance in a series of thefts of my meager belongings when I left a foster home. Apparently, I was expected to "pay" my foster mothers. My party clothes, an unused child's toy tea set, new luggage, a used bicycle, a vintage denim jacket, the clarinet; it seemed these were viewed as taxes owed to my oppressors.

When band season was over I tried out for the track team and found that I was a good runner. I hated the practices, but quitting wasn't an option; the choice was either run for two hours in the cold or go home right after school. I had learned that the busier I stayed, the less I had to focus on the fact that I was lost in that place without a way into the city. The two Metro buses that went back and forth to DC ran from seven to nine in the morning and five to eight or nine at night and were not a possibility for me.

Even after a long and tiring practice, I hated walking into the McLeach house in the evenings. It always felt like there was something funny going on; perhaps because in my absence I had been the main topic of conversation for the McLeach women. Their studied indifference towards me made me miss Jeff terribly and long to see or at least talk to him.

My participation in the McLeach family activities was limited to going to church. While there, my foster parents pretended that we were an ideal family and Ms. McLeach spent her time yelling in tongues, her head bent back to let out those strange words bubbling up from her throat: "Oohlalarama mala lamsamu schleramarema!" Watching the spectacle, I used to look around the church and think; *Everybody up in here goin' straight to hell if this is what they all doin!*

Kelly McLeach set herself up like the holiest saint at church and then, the next thing, we'd be at home and she'd be starting fights and having tantrums about some little thing around the house that didn't please her. "You think because you stay after school every day you don't have to do no chores around here? You wrong about that," she'd shout at me, usually with a mouth full of spraying food.

Seeing that mouthful of half-chewed food, I would raise up one side of my lip in disgust and say, "No, I don't think that. I do chores here like everybody else." I tried hard not to speak with an attitude, but I couldn't control the look on my face — and I know it was filled with sneering attitude. Soon these petty exchanges escalated into arguments that I was never willing to back down from.

Sharquitta's constant attempts to make things personal never failed to raise the level of hostility, and she'd jump in saying, "Why you getting smart with my muva?" I would get indignant and answer, "Whachou mean? I ain't getting smart. She asked me a question and I answered it."

Then Sharquitta's eyes would roll — with Shawna following in an exact imitation — and then she would move closer to out-and-out war by challenging me, "You keep getting smart with my muva and…"

"And what?" I'd say, staring hard into her face. At that point, Mr. McLeach always jumped up to stop what he figured would soon turn into a fist fight.

After things quieted down, Sharquitta would mutter under her breath to me, "You keep talking to my muva like that and I'm gonna punch you in your face." Most evenings, this was the kind of under-the-breath snickering and talking-just-loud-enough to be heard that generally shut down the family dinner.

"Phuuha… You ain't gonna do shit to me," I'd mutter in the same way while getting up to put my plate into the sink. As I walked past with the toughest athletic walk I could muster and showing her my hardened muscles, I would add a few more fighting words like, "Ya'll don't want none-a this." As far as I was concerned this ended the conversation, at least until the next night.

I admit there were many nights when I was the shit disturber, not Kelly or Sharquitta. For instance, one particular evening I confronted Ms. McLeach with, "When can Shawna and me get some new clothes?" Instantly, that fat woman stiffened up, bugged out her eyes, and squawked, "*WHAT?*" I responded with complete confidence in the rightness of my cause; "*NEW CLOTHES*. You just got Sharquitta some!"

With this my foster mother turned red-faced and looked more ready to rumble than I had ever seen. So much so that she stopped chewing her cud long enough to concentrate on the exchange. I had known I would be starting something before I even asked the question but went ahead anyway just like I had planned while making my last turn on the track that afternoon.

She spat out a defensive reply, "Sharquitta's father sends money every month for her. That's why she gets new clothes. I can't believe you got the nerve to ask me something like that!"

Now Shawna was thinking I got her in trouble and became indignant, saying to me, "Why you puttin' me in it? I ain't say nothin." Without missing a beat I said, "Why you steppin' and fetchin', Shawna? I'm just saying. Ms. Brinker said foster kids get a clothing allowance every month and I ain't seen no new clothes since I been here."

Now Ms. McLeach was furious and shouted, "That's a lie and I'm gonna ask that white woman why she tell you something like that when they don't give us enough money to do nothing with in the first place." She sat back with her jaw clenched and waited for Mr. McLeach to vouch for her. But he wouldn't do it that time or the many other times when she expected him to back up her lies.

I heard them arguing behind the closed door of their bedroom that night. Johnny McLeach was trying to be diplomatic with his wife without sounding like he was actually taking my side. He wisely suggested that she buy Shawna and me a few clothes just to shut me up.

The truth is that Johnny was the only one in that house who took an interest in what I was doing. He would pick me up from some of my late band practices and often showed up at track meets, especially those at other schools. I never expected anybody to come and support anything I did, so it always felt especially good to know that there was somebody out there just for me. He'd let me see he was there with a quick shout and a brief wave,

"Hey Lisa!" I'd turn and wave with just enough smile to show some appreciation and go back to whatever I was doing. The fact that I loved having him there was a personal secret that I never shared with anyone. I feared that it could become just another carrot for Kelly to dangle in my face with the threat of taking it away at a whim.

Because I ran the second or third leg of the two-twenty and four-forty, my races fell somewhere in the middle of the meet and that meant I would be there for at least another hour, but Johnny McLeach always stayed on to watch me. There were a few times when I was recruited to run in some of the sprints due to an A-Team member's absence. I never won any of them, but the few times I came in second, I could always hear him yelling at the top of his lungs, "Go Lisa, You got her! Catch her, girl! Go!"

In the beginning, he often seemed to me to be a milquetoast type of guy who didn't rock the boat when it came to his wife. But I learned that there were times when he put his foot down for what he believed was right, and times when he spoke out against the blatant favoritism she regularly showed toward Sharquitta. I began to think of him as a good guy who gave me the only moral support I was to receive in that household. The ride back home after my races was when I got to see a totally different Johnny McLeach. His more relaxed body language and personable conversation gave me the idea that he thought I was okay. There was no sexual bullshit in his behavior either; his attitude felt very fatherly to me and I began to view him a lot differently than I had in the beginning. I remember one spring day when he apologized for things that had happened in that house. It was about a week after my sixteenth birthday and I was sitting out on the front stoop. He sat down beside me and started to talk. After some beating around the bush he got to the point and said he was sorry that there was no mention made about my recent birthday.

"We could have at least got you a card or something. I feel real bad about it because it isn't right." he explained sadly.

I looked up and gave him a smile meant to show it didn't matter as he continued, "It was wrong that Sharquitta was treated right and you didn't get nothin'. 'Specially with her birthday only one day after yours. It was wrong the way you were done and I'm sorry."

I didn't say anything because I didn't want to break out crying in front of him. I shook my head to let him know I understood and continued breaking and throwing pieces of a twig I was holding in my hand. After he walked away, I quietly said to his back, "Thanks."

Now I was really confused. Was he trapped like I was? Did he have to play a role to get along the same way I did and if so, why would a grown man put up with that? I was beginning to understand why he spent so much time down in his meticulously organized workspace where he kept all his fishing stuff. Why, he was an outsider in that house too! He'd spend hours down there making fishing lures and preparing for his next fishing trip. When he wasn't in the basement you could find his head underneath the hood of that crappy old Buick. At least once a week he'd be outside tinkering with it. Despite his constant attempts to keep it running, I never felt comfortable riding long distances in that piece of junk, especially after he and Kelly would occasionally arrive home late due to car trouble.

Years after I had been removed from the McLeach household, things finally made more sense to me. I ran into Johnny McLeach on the street and he told me he and Kelly had split up after she and Sharquitta had physically attacked him just as they had gone after me when things began to heat up.

I had only one friend when I lived with the McLeaches. Wendy was a white girl I met in Ms. Arboch's guitar class. We were brought together by our love for Prince and the Revolution, Billy Idol, and rock music in general along with the fact that we were the only females taking the class and we loved that there were two band members in the Revolution named Wendy and Lisa and therefore declared ourselves honorary members of the group. Because I didn't have many clothes it was impossible for me to fit in with my style and peer-obsessed classmates so I sought an alternative style which I usually invented as I went along and which Wendy greatly admired.

She introduced me to the punk rock scene in DC and we hung out at her house on the weekends and colored and spiked our hair with red and purple unsweetened Kool-Aid and extra-hold Aqua Net. We tore holes in our jeans and accented the look with black combat boots and flannel shirts layered over rock and punk band t-shirts we bought from Smash! — a punk rock novelty shop in Georgetown — with money given to us by Wendy's mother.

Even though I was still into the growing hip-hop culture of Roxanne Roxanne and Lisa Lisa and the Cult Jam, the punk culture was also one I could identify with. It was made up of a ragged bunch of rebellious kids in need of attention and a decent family life. It was a culture of parties, shows and walking around looking as alienated as we felt. I was lucky to have a friend like Wendy who was off-beat enough to understand that my foster child history made me a natural in this scene. Wendy and I called each other sister and vowed that we would die for each other, borrowing the name of a Prince song, *I Would Die for You*. We knew that if one of us got into any trouble while we were together, the other would kick ass at all costs. My friendship with Wendy made my living at the McLeaches' much easier. When I was with her — which was most of the time — I was able to escape my real life circumstances and add a punk layer to my protective shell.

Wendy had friends with cars who accepted me as easily as she had. As a part of my indoctrination into the Punk Rock scene of Georgetown, we went to shows at the 9:30 Club and the Hung Jury Pub where some of the most well-known bands played. We'd thrash around in the mosh pits of the dance floor and aimlessly walk the lengths of M street and Wisconsin Avenue. Our final stop would be the Burger King where everybody ended up after shows. Then we sat down by the Canal with our feet dangling over the edge of the stone wall.

Wendy exposed me to the music of bands like Bad Brains, Circle Jerks and the Exploited. The aggressive and violent nature of the music invigorated me. They stood for the things I was feeling although half the time I didn't even know all the words. The leather, combat boots, spiked jewelry and extreme, colorful hairstyles looked crazy to outsiders, but the peace within our offbeat group gave me comfort. We even did regular things together like shopping for and experimenting with makeup and potential hairdos.

Wendy lived with her single mother in an old dilapidated house plunked down in the center of a plot of land that had been handed down through her family. Her mother was an attractive young cashier at the supermarket just across the busy highway from the house. The rare occasion Wendy ever spoke of her father would be to mention only the short distance between his nice apartment and the hovel in which she and her mother were forced to live. Wendy and her mother seemed to me more like sisters than mother and daughter. I admired their relationship and consistent level of respect for one another. Their household was the direct opposite of the McLeaches' where there was zero tolerance of my mistakes, mishaps or lapses. It seemed to me that Wendy's mother gave her daughter the freedom to be a teenager and to commit mistakes and never held these over her head.

The buildup of dirt and dust footprints across the wooden floors of the place exaggerated the extreme age of Wendy's plantation-style farmhouse. No matter how much we'd vacuum and wipe the surfaces, the build-up would be right back in two or three days. Even if the wind blew just a little, the leakiness of the wooden slats and floorboards allowed the outside weather and debris from the overgrown plot outside to seep into the living space. When the dirt got in, it mixed with the hair and dander of their big friendly mutt. So the house was never clean, but it was a different kind of unclean; more like camping-style dirty. Spending weekends over there reminded me of the camp days with the teachers at FLOC learning center and summers at Camp Goodwill. I never minded helping to carry wood for the potbelly stove that kept the house remarkably warm in winter.

Even though Wendy wore braces, she smiled often and gave the outward impression she hadn't a problem in the world. She was how I wanted to be. When I first met her I knew she wasn't one of those snobbish, judgmental girls that I wanted nothing to do with. Friendly High in Fort Washington was full of those girls back then. There were no *real* rich kids there like there were at Deal Middle School in DC, yet many of the kids did their best to make everyone think they were rich. Where you lived indicated your social and economic levels just like in DC, so the ones who lived in Tantallon, the newest of the middle class developments with big houses was always the best name to drop. On the other hand, when a tough kid said, "I'm from South View," a low-end apartment development, you were supposed to understand that they weren't to be messed with.

Wendy was a shapely, one hundred-thirty-pound blond who wore her hair cut just below her neckline. We were the same height but I was "straight up and down" with a boyish, athletic figure. She never focused on things like my skin color, religion or net worth. Instead she would say things like, "Why is your skin always so smooth and clear"? To this I would answer, "I don't know. I just wash it with a bar of soap, nothing special. "Then Wendy would say, "I hate my skin! This acne is gross and gets on my nerves." I would tell her, "You look fine, don't worry about it."

Wendy envied my skin because I didn't have to suffer the major breakouts she often had to deal with. I thought it was pretty cool that her mom allowed her to wear makeup. But Wendy didn't like the idea of having to get up early in the morning just to cover the raised red blemishes with makeup before she went anywhere. To make the acne less obvious she added accents of eyeliner, artistically-placed shadow, and a flat pink lip color. At sixteen she had become an expert in the makeup arts.

Back at the McLeaches' I was still halfheartedly trying to manage the most difficult task ever — simply getting along with my foster family. The adults left for work together in their hooptie at 6:30 a.m. each morning and Shawna's bus would come to pick her up at about seven to make the long trip to Accokeek, Maryland. The bus which picked up Sharquitta and me at the very top of the hill arrived at seven thirty. But she generally didn't get on the bus. On my way out the door, I often saw her twenty-something boyfriend driving up to the house for a day of sex with her and I knew she wouldn't be going anywhere; certainly not school.

Sharquitta seldom showed up at school, but at home she played the role of diligent student by getting homework assignments from one of her friends in the neighborhood. When she realized I knew what was going on, her aggressive, hostile behavior toward me underwent a big change. She became nicer, more accommodating. I knew this was her way of keeping me from telling on her. But I appreciated not being messed with and didn't care what her reasons were. In fact, the events leading up to my removal from that home actually started with a rare sisterly moment when Sharquitta asked me, "Will you go with me to Ma and ask her if we can have birth control pills?" Even though I knew the answer, I asked fake-innocently, "Why?"

She had rehearsed her answer, "Because I have a boyfriend now so I just need them in case." Then she quickly added, "Of course, we're not doing nothing but... Can you just go with me to talk to her?"

That night when we sat down to talk to Ms. McLeach, I waited for Sharquitta to take the lead and ask her question, but she didn't. After a long pause in which we both sat there looking stupid, I just came out with it: "Me and Sharquitta want to know if we can get some birth control pills."

In an instant, that woman pushed past Sharquitta faster than I had ever seen her move and got right in my face: "Lisa, I don't know what you and that white trash girl are out there doing but Sharquitta don't need to be poppin' no pills! If you want them, I don't care, but she don't need'em!"

I stepped back and looked for support from Sharquitta, but she had disappeared as soon as her mother came after me. I had been played! I turned and laughed in my foster mother's yellow screaming beach ball face and decided not to be angry. After all, I had nothing to lose over the birth control issue. I didn't need any pills.

A few months later, Ms. McLeach started the conversation at dinner with, "As y'all can see, Sharquitta is gaining weight and...well, she is pregnant." You'd think I was the only one at the table who hadn't already noticed Sharquitta's predicament because I was the only one to raise my voice in surprise: "Whaaa...?"

But then Shawna started to laugh and Mr. McLeach took on the *I KNEW IT* expression. There was nothing else to say at the table that night as Sharquitta acted like nothing at all was wrong. But I felt Ms. McLeach's hatred towards me heating to white hot. I basked in the glory of Sharquitta's misfortune for weeks. But then the Kelly McLeach volcano erupted and my time in her house came to a dramatic end.

Wendy's mother had been teaching her to drive ever since she was fifteen. One day, living up to her promise to teach me to drive too, Wendy took her mother's car and we went to the Friendly High School parking lot for a lesson. When we returned to the house, we had to face her hysterical mother who had been calling around looking for us. She had even called the McLeaches.

Wendy told her mother the truth: "I took Lisa up to the lot to teach her to drive." When her mother cooled down a bit, she asked evenly, "Why would you do that when you don't even have your license?"

"Because I promised her," was Wendy's tense reply.

"Don't do that again Wendy, there is supposed to be a licensed driver in the car."

"I knooowa!" Wendy said back with a good deal of attitude.

It was the first time I had ever seen the two of them exchange heated words and I felt sorry for being the reason. But then the strangest thing I had ever seen happened: it was over. Things went back to normal. I had never seen anything like it. There was no leftover feeling of anger, disappointment or disgust hanging over us. I understood instead that her mother's emotions came from the uncertainty about our whereabouts and safety. Now that we were back and her mother had chided her, we went right back talking like nothing ever happened.

That same evening when I got home Ms. McLeach couldn't wait to confront me about the incident. "I heard you and that white trashy girl went out and stole a car. I already called your social worker. Hahahah! And she always thought you were Miss Goody-two-shoes."

I was indignant. "What are you talking about? We didn't steal no car!"

Then she began yelling at me: "You did because the white girl's mother called me and said that y'all were out half the day!"

"That's not true. You're making that up. We didn't steal a car. We borrowed Wendy's mom's car."

"Oh, shut up and go in the room. And don't ask to go back over there no more either!"

"What do you mean?"

Now she was feeling her power: "You heard me. Don't ask to go back since those are the kinds of things y'all do together."

I met her threats with a rush of emotion, "You ain't got to worry about me asking you nothing. I'll do what I want to do!"

My psychiatrist had been working with me at my school, but when Ms. McLeach learned of this she insisted on always telling her side of the story. So he had begun having family meetings as well as my individual meetings. Kelly was like Mama Graves in that she was threatened by anything I might say in private to a psychiatrist, so my meetings with him became less productive and more guarded as I felt she was listening in on us. One day after a family therapy session, I was upset and my allergies started bothering me. I went into my bathroom, locked the door, and started casually running a razor blade along the length of my forearm. Seeing the blood pooling in the shallow razor cuts somehow gave me relief from the tension and anger I had been feeling.

I honestly didn't want to cause anyone pain. My question when privately cutting myself was always; *Why do I want to hurt myself?* Sometimes I thought it was because I really didn't like myself. But really, I think it was more about releasing the emotion. If you are a boxer and work out with the punching bag, you hit it repeatedly for several rounds, trust me, at the end there will be no more fear, doubt or anger in you. When you are a little girl with nowhere else to go, you might sit down and say, "Would anyone care if I killed myself right now?" At times when I did this, I would stop myself and say quickly; *But I don't want to hurt myself.* But then you might cut or hit yourself and find that it was something you could take. You'd say to yourself; *Well, I'm still here. Whatever they want to do to me, I can take it because I can take this cutting.* It is weird. You would give a sigh of relief and tell yourself; *Whoo, I'm glad I can take it.*

In a lot of ways cutting is like boxing. Because after you get out of that first fight, you do the same. You say to yourself, *Whew... I made it through!* You are so glad you got through the fight, and even better, you were able to hit back! That's why discovering boxing was so good for me later in my life. I didn't have to just take the abuse; I could hit back without getting in trouble! Seeing someone lying down after I hit them always made me step back and look inside myself, asking; *what am I doing?* Sometimes that made me question whether I was a good person. But boxing gives you a format for realizing that you and your opponent are in the situation together —both have agreed to hit one another — and knowing that makes you appreciate what you did. The thing that made me feel a bit guilty is that I would be looking at an opponent and thinking; *You just got an ass-whipping that I would have loved to give to someone back when I was a kid.*

Later that night, my serious allergy issues were getting worse and I started to rifle though the medicine cabinet in the hall bathroom to find medicine to help me breathe. Finding there was nothing there for me, I knocked on the couple's bedroom door to get help. Mr. McLeach opened it.

"I can't sleep because I can't breathe when I lie down. Can I please have something for it?"

He went to their bathroom to find a pack of over-the-counter sinus medicine. But suddenly Ms. McLeach bulldozed past her husband yelling, "What do she want now?" Turning to me, she screamed, "Get away from my door and go to bed!"

I answered back, "Get the hell out of my face, lady!"

Mr. McLeach then held his wife by the shoulders as she pressed forward threatening me, "Ima gon' bust you in your face!"

Suddenly Sharquitta showed up, got into the mix, and threatened to hit me too. I was on a roll now and baited Sharquitta with exaggerated laughter, "HAHAHAHA! You just mad 'cause you got pregnant!"

By that time Ms. McLeach was within an arm's length and hit me as hard as she could in the face with her little fat fist. Sharquitta was next in line and punched me too. I restrained myself from returning the blows and instead started screaming at the top of my lungs — louder screams than I thought possible! I felt defenseless and alone and only those ear-shattering screeches could upstage the tears that were now flowing freely.

Those threatening words and the blows that followed took me right back to Mama Graves's house. I could almost hear the words she used to shout at me as I sat on those kitchen steps when I was six — words that were supposed to make me shake with fear and beg for mercy. Words like, "Ima tear you up when we get home, Ima skin you alive, Ima slap that smirk off you face, Ima slap you so hard you head will spin, Ima knock the devil out of you, Ima kick your ass, Ima mess your little ass up, Ima bust you in you face."

What happened at the McLeach house was really nothing new to me. But it was new to those two as they finally got to live out the fantasy of what they had long wished they could do to me. But Ms. McLeach had nothing on Mama Graves. Mama Graves's threats hanging in the air long before the physical act of beating me happened were worse because they created so much anxiety. They were the threats that would come early in the morning leaving me to walk around all day with them until just before bedtime when the whupping often took place. I had been training psychologically for years to deflect powder-puff blows while bobbing and weaving with my own little arsenal of verbal zingers just waiting for me to let them go as soon as I saw an opening. So, in my sixteen-year-old mind, there was nothing they could do to me that had not already been done except kill me, and to some degree I welcomed the finality of that notion. As far as I was concerned I was supposed to be dead by then anyway.

I had been going to church all my life and was taught that "you cannot enter the kingdom of heaven if you take your own life" but no matter how many times I was baptized I didn't feel saved from the hell I was already in. I assumed it was inevitable that one of these people I had to live with would kill me on purpose or by accident. All the holy-rolling foster mothers who swore Jesus was their Lord and Savior and preached words from the Bible whenever they had an audience had convinced me that I was going to burn in eternal damnation.

It was really beyond my youthful understanding that so much pretending went on at church. Every Sunday or significant church holiday, these people would play dress-up and talk to one another as if they were practicing a monologue in a mirror. It was amazing to witness these so-called "Christians" or self-proclaimed "New Samaritans" really trying to pull one over on God. It was as if the clothes they wore completed their transformation but as soon as those clothes came off, the devil was back in full effect. I could spot the hypocrites as soon as they opened their mouths and started praising the lord. I knew in my heart that there had to be a God if only because I was still in one piece. But my inner church followed one golden rule: *Whatever they give, give it back ten times more, good or bad.*

There was a lot going on inside of me in those days. I teetered back and forth between being the kind, loving person I knew was buried somewhere deep inside me, or wreaking havoc on the people around me before I ended up becoming a sad victim who didn't have sense enough to strike first. I worried that the anguish balled up inside me for so many years could actually cause me to kill a person if I were to lay a hand on them. I guess that was what made me think a second longer before I took a threat as a real assault and struck the first blow. But, I would be telling a boldface lie if I said I never thought of giving the beat-down to any of them if given the chance; all one hundred and five pounds of me tearing through their flesh with my fist and making them *shake with fear* and *beg for mercy*. I was far beyond being green in the department of being threatened and hit by people who should know better.

After Kelly McLain's volcanic eruption and the hitting, I took more of the allergy medicine than I should. As I lay on my bed, my mind had been racing and my heart felt like it was about to burst out of my chest. I was trying desperately to figure out a way to get out of that place. At the same time, I was becoming really drowsy. I began to worry that I had overdosed on the sinus medicine. I started crying, trying to think of a way out. My heart was racing out of control and I was terrified. Had I tried to commit suicide? Or was I just too upset to care how much medicine I had taken? I was in panic mode now and started wildly splashing water in my face. Afraid of what might be happening to me, I began to demand that someone take me to the hospital. This feeling of bursting, terrified panic was all new to me, and I truly thought I was going to die.

The McLeaches took me to Southeast Community Hospital and by the time we arrived, Ms. McLeach was covering her butt like a real pro. She told the people at the hospital that I had taken an overdose of Triaminic in an effort to kill myself. Not satisfied with that lie, she added, "After she stole a car!" When the nurses emptied my stomach with an emetic and saw that I was all right, they immediately transferred me to the psych ward as a suicide risk.

Dr. Cornell came the next morning to see me in the psych ward. I told him I didn't like being locked up there and tried to convince him that I had not tried to kill myself. Nevertheless, he said that it had been reported that I was suicidal, and the rule was that you had to stay a week after a suicide attempt. There were some messed up kids in that ward and I briefly found them amusing, but I hated being locked up in there with them. Nighttime was the worst; I worried about what horrible things could happen to me in there.

After a week in the ward, I went to the attendant and asked her if Dr. Cornell had called and added that he was going to take me out of there the next day. She got all full of attitude and bugged out her eyes, staring at me in disbelief. Raising her voice, she said "No, you're *NOT* leaving tomorrow! Didn't you steal a car? You got problems, gurrl..." I went to my room and started bawling my eyes out. I wondered what lies Ms. McLeach had told about me that could ruin my life. I cried and cried. The next morning, Dr. Cornell came just as he had promised and I was so glad to see him that I gave him a big hug. When we walked out of the place together, I couldn't resist some sweet teenage revenge. I told that attendant, "Here's my doctor. I told you I would be leaving today!" Then I gave her the full physical show of attitude with rolling eyes and full body language and it felt really good.

I think about my own children and I imagine someone treating my child the way Ms. McLeach treated me. I remember all the times I was scared to say something to her for fear that something bad would happen. She was a hateful woman who cloaked herself in all that phony religion. A part of me still wants to get my lick back at her! How could an adult hit a young defenseless girl?

It feels so bad when I remember how that foster placement ended up for me — in a psych ward! If I saw Kelly McLeach again, I know I would give her a fair chance to apologize. But I doubt she would do it. It is scary to think how she could have changed my life in a very bad way.

I was never to return to the McLeashes after that. My knight on a white horse, Dr. Cornell, who looked to my eyes as fine as Smokey Robinson, took care of that. He knew there was something inside me that just had to come out. And years later, when I reconnected with him as an adult, he told me, "Lisa, you made people uncomfortable because you always called them out on their shit."

Chapter Fourteen

Case #: T 513.276.6

Lisa was placed with the McLeaches on 01/17/84.
She has had numerous foster care placements
which have resulted in her having difficulty with
maternal figures.
    Lisa's progress with the McLeaches fluctuated.
Sometimes she felt and acted as a family member and
at other times she felt like an outsider. She had a
particularly difficult time adjusting to Mrs.
McLeach and vice versa. Mrs. McLeach had difficulty
presenting herself as an authority figure which
Lisa needed.

                                — Social Worker

    Lisa was found to be alert, coherent, well-
oriented, open and cooperative. She seemed remorseful
about the ingestion of 6 allergy pills, but was
not suicidal. I recommended that she continue with
individual and family therapy concomitantly.

                                     — Doctor

I was in the teen psych ward as the direct result of the scene at the McLeaches'
house. My one-week stay ended on a Monday when Dr. Cornell and Mrs.
Brinker both arrived at the same time for my release. I had been there only a
week, but still, I was in every sense of the word *dry*. Dehydrated and chapped,
my skin was flaked with ashy dead skin that obscured the true brown tone of
my complexion. Without any regular application of oil, my hair had become
brittle and broken from brushing. My mouth felt cottony and my brain empty.

My eyes felt stuck open until I made a conscious effort to blink and then I imagined they were making a flapping sound. I hadn't been required to take any sort of medication while in the ward, but I hadn't been able shake the floating feeling I got while breathing the helium-like air that the psych ward seemed to spew.

I could tell that my doctor and social worker had talked about me before coming to meet me, but I was relieved and happy to see them even if they had been discussing my flaws. At that time, they were the two adults in my life that I felt I could trust. Despite my positive feelings about them, my automatic protective let-down shield had stayed up just in case they didn't show up to get me out of there.

Before we could leave that nightmare place, the two had to take care of paperwork. While they did that, I remained quiet and subdued, aloof from the technicalities they were discussing with hospital administrators. But once outside, I sucked in deeply to let in all the fresh air that would fit into my lungs and tried to exhale the stale hospital smog that had been smothering me. Because of the pathetic way I looked, I was content to blend into the background and hoped no one would notice me in such a torn-up state. Mainly I was self-conscious that Dr. Cornell had to see me looking this way. I couldn't wait to see him at our next session so I could show him I was back to looking respectable again.

"Okay Lisa I'll see you on Wednesday at the office on Sixteenth Street," he said to me, smiling as if everything was completely normal. And I waved to him as he walked across the parking lot after we found Mrs. Brinker's car. Once we were inside the car, Mrs. Brinker began to fill me in on my future. "As you probably know, you won't be going back to the McLeaches'…" Before she could complete her sentence, I began to mockingly rejoice in the news. "Yes, Yes! Good! Thank God, and Praise the Lord!" My possible return to the McLeaches had been a great worry on my mind during the whole week I was in lockdown. I knew that going back to that house would have been impossible for me to bear.

Mrs. Brinker just smiled at my reaction and continued. "What do you think about moving to Wheaton, Maryland?" *As if I really have a choice!* I thought before answering, "I don't know! Is it in the middle of nowhere?"

"No, it's nothing like Fort Washington," my social worker replied. "There's a Metro nearby. You can get it right at the station in Wheaton Plaza

Shopping Mall." I thought for a minute and answered in a more positive tone. "Well, that's cool, as long as I'm not stuck in the middle of nowhere. I never want to be stuck like that again!"

At sixteen, I was done listening to all the adult bullshit being spoon-fed to me as if I lacked the ability to respond. It was foster kids, not their foster parents, who endured the yearly court visits, met regularly with appointed shrinks for extensive psychological evaluations, and were defined by official files that took everything we ever said or did and everything we were unfairly accused of and put it under a high-powered microscope. It seemed to me that everyone who dealt with us was *appointed*; certainly no one was holding up a hand to volunteer out of the goodness of their hearts!

Yup! I had the *Foster Parent Racket* figured out. To me it was like being a part of a crime syndicate. If you ratted on a foster mother you had to be re-located into the foster protection program so you wouldn't get whacked. Those foster mothers were the knee-busters who came after anybody who in-terfered with them getting their check.

When we pulled up in front of a tiny rustic storybook-looking house in a lower middle class, mostly white neighborhood in Maryland, Mrs. Brinker turned off the engine and we sat in the car and talked. She told me this would be what was considered a 'temporary placement' and warned me that I should make the most of it. She added that I was being placed with a middle-aged couple fairly new to the foster care system who had adopted two young sisters three years prior.

At first I was really worried about how bad I looked after living on the ward for that week. I knew from vast experience that first impressions never go away. But when I laid eyes on Frank and Sette Wiggins I was no longer concerned. Sette was a black woman with a hard face and unfriendly eyes who was first to the door. Her dark brown complexion was dingy and unkempt as if having good skin didn't matter to her. She tried to produce a smile, but for me, looking at her was like looking back in time at Mama Graves on an unre-hearsed day at a FLOC function; everything about her physical appearance and carriage screamed *insecure*. Noticing her unpleasant voice, I still tried my best not to judge anything about her until I got a sense of who she was inside. Then, trying to seem open and friendly, I extended my ashy hand to shake hers. It was then that I sensed she was hesitant about even touching me.

Frank Wiggins was an average Kenny Rogers-looking white man complete with a salt and pepper beard. He had on a pair of faded jeans and a polo shirt and could have looked halfway decent if his clothes didn't look rough-dried as if left for days to dry in a ball in the washing machine. His Docksiders were wet and stained around their worn edges indicating that he probably had been cutting wet grass earlier in the day. To me, he seemed more relaxed and natural than his wife. I didn't sense any of the negative vibes from him like those his wife was sending into the air. While Sette went to call in the two girls to meet me, he talked easily to my social worker. I felt neutral about him at the time; it wasn't until later in my stay at that house that he befriended me in much the same way Mr. McLeach had — in a fatherly way, with no funny business attached to it.

At eight Olivia was a bit taller than her sister Kim who was a year older. Her hair was loosely braided into two pigtails held together by large ball twists. She was smiling and shiny with sweat from whatever game she was playing before I arrived. But Kim was different. She was not smiling and seemed uncomfortable and nervous. The two were blood sisters, but one could easily assume that one biological parent was different for each. Kim carried an aura — dim and withdrawn — that felt very familiar to me. Her dark brown skin was dull and lifeless just like her hair which was in randomly arranged self-service plaits separated by a web of crooked parts.

I didn't like what I was seeing and feeling. Clearly, the two girls were cared for differently. As I noticed this, I was aware that my expression might have changed from trying-hard-to-be-nice to complete disgust. I cut my eyes over to Sette and let out a deep long sigh to demonstrate that I had noticed. *Man, I can already tell this bitch ain't right. She's another Louise Graves and this ain't gonna work for me.* Our eyes briefly met, then she quickly looked away and barked out an order to Kim, "Show her where to take her things and give her some sheets so she can make up that bed."

The little girl replied, "Yes ma'am," and scrambled to grab one of my small bags off the floor. I blocked her and said firmly, "That's all right, Kim, I got it. I can take my own things. Thank you anyway." My response had enough implied message for everyone in the room to see that I wouldn't hold back when something bothered me.

I followed Kim to the top of a narrow flight of creaking stairs muffled by an old worn-out shag carpet. Those stairs and that carpet defined the appearance of the whole house. Claustrophobic and lacking in charm can't even describe the tightness and dinginess of that place. It was an unfinished do-it-yourself project that felt like a bunch of band aids were holding things in place temporarily until repairs could be started. Where there had once been a living room on the first floor, there was now a master bedroom partitioned off by an unfinished and unpainted sheetrock wall. Just behind this room was another one I assumed had once been a dining room. At the back of the house there was a door leading to a small eat-in kitchen with a table for six. As we entered the bedroom I was to share with my two new foster sisters, Kim explained, "This is my bed, that's Olivia's and the one next to the wall is for you. I'll go down and get you some sheets, OK?" I noticed that her voice and posture had lifted a little as soon as we got out of her mother's sight. "Okay. Thank you, Kim," I said gently, thinking; *She could be me at this age.*

There was one closet and a chest of drawers that the two girls shared. And there was a night stand with a lamp and a small four-drawer dresser that had been set aside for me in that crowded room. After unpacking my things I located the bathroom and started to wash off all evidence of the hospital. Attempting to remove any signs of dryness from every inch of my body, I conditioned my skin with petroleum jelly. Then I hot-curled my hair, bumping every strand of my hair and then raking through it with my fingers.

One thing was clear to me. My nightmare departure from the McLeaches' house and my stay in that hospital ward had changed me. I was no longer interested in waiting and hoping that things would work out. No longer afraid of the unknown, I knew for certain that I had outgrown my tolerance for being abused and lied to; I was no longer willing to put my fate in somebody else's hands.

This was my eighth foster home — my eleventh move through the system — and I was a not-so-sweet sixteen. But I was determined to try to accept my circumstances more open-mindedly, realizing that things could be worse than they were. I tried my best to remind myself of my social worker's advice and make the best of a not-so-ideal situation. But that was a tall order; it was hard right from the beginning. My attitude toward Mrs. Wiggins was already warped and it would only get more toxic each day. The more I witnessed the blatant favoritism she showed toward Olivia over her sister Kim, the rage inside of me grew from the reels of flashbacks of the bad-old-days with Louise Graves passing behind my rolling eyes. I was seeing and experiencing the same old shit over and over in home after home and I was sick of it. I refused to acknowledge Sette Wiggins as my foster mother, or anything else.

The altercation with the McLeaches had left a terrible taste in my mouth and I wasn't about to give another so-called foster mother a chance to punch me in the face again. As the days went on, I would hear the girls referring to their parents as Mom and Dad, but BULLSHIT was how it all translated through my ears and I would think, *There must have been a two-for-one deal at the adoption agency when they got those girls, because even the neighbors say how bad Sette treats Kim.*

Kim was a little skinny girl just like I was, but the way she lowered her head and tucked her body into itself like a scared dog cowering, tail between legs, whenever her mother entered the room made her look even smaller. I promised myself; *As long as I'm here, Sette ain't getting away with nothin'.*

I often looked at Kim and remembered praying to God for someone to rescue me from Mama Graves's grip. Sette's overt way of criticizing and degrading her while in front of me and anybody else was only worsened by the sneaky way I knew she physically abused her in private. I felt so sorry for my foster sister because she was the only one getting the so-called discipline Sette was handing out. As for me, my attitude and body language downright dared her to put her hands on me.

Much like Daddy Graves, Mr. Wiggins was clueless to what was happening when he wasn't around. So I began confronting the woman on the unfair treatment between the two girls. One day I asked her, "How come Olivia gets to play all day and Kim does nothing but fulfill your assignments? Dag! Kim, do this! Kim, go get that! Clean up here and move that there. Always slapping that girl for something, but I've never seen you even yell at Olivia. That's messed up. I'm serious too. That's real messed up." Sette denied it all, shouting, "No, No, I don't do that!"

Sette hated my outspokenness. I knew that everything I had wanted to serve up to Kelly McLeach before I left Fort Washington I was dishing out to Sette instead. One day, feeling cheated as a sixteen-year-old having to share a bedroom with a nine and a ten-year-old, I blurted out in front of everyone in the kitchen, "Does FLOC know about your two boarders living here?" I was referring to the fact that the room right behind the Wiggins' bedroom was occupied by a forty-something year-old woman and her fourteen-year-old daughter, Kiki.

I had touched a raw nerve. My comment was enough to make even Mr. Wiggins mad and Sette get up from the dinner table and storm into her bedroom. It was a question I already knew the answer to but I asked it anyway. When Sette left, I muttered, "Yeah right, us foster children aren't the only ones who lie. It always comes down to making a quick buck, doesn't it?"

I knew I had to stop that kind of outspoken rebellion. I needed to get busy and make the best of my situation as my social worker had suggested. All I really needed was a source of basic shelter and a place from which to go to and from school. At school I joined the concert band which performed and practiced after school hours, and Wheaton Mall was but a short bus ride away. Recreation centers and activities for teens were everywhere. When I was alone and there was nothing I had to do, I could catch the bus to the mall or take long walks around the neighborhood. It was Mr. Wiggins who noticed I could use some wheels. He mentioned to me that he had a ten-speed bicycle that he used to ride all the time but it had just been sitting idle for at least a year.

"You can have it if you want it, Lisa," He offered after wiping it down and inflating the tires.

I couldn't believe he was sincere and said, "I can?" The look on his face gave me my answer; I threw my right leg over the seat and mounted the bike, thanking him enthusiastically and smiling for what must have been the first time I had cracked even the slightest grin since coming to that house. This bike would be my escape from the close confines of that house. I knew that with my "Hi/Bye" attitude toward the Wigginses, I was lucky to be getting anything, let alone a sleek pair of wheels. Once again, in the tradition of Daddy Graves and Daddy McLeach, I was the recipient of a kindness from a father figure with no strings attached and it felt good.

Having that bicycle made me feel different. Now I owned something of worth, not just some old, ill-fitting used clothes. Having received such a coveted gift, I lightened up my attitude a bit and tried to get along while in the house. Though I saw how much Sette resented her husband's perfect gift to me, I could see that she was happy that the bike took me away from the house for many hours that I might instead have spent inside, just coiled up and waiting for her to cross the line with Kim.

Now I was free to go where I wanted, and that made living with the Wiggins bearable for the rest of my short placement with them. I also enjoyed Wheaton High School. It was unlike any of the schools I had been to before. For the first time, I didn't feel like I was lost in the sauce and had to find my own way out. It didn't matter if I was a black foster child. Those teachers were strict in a true caring way. They figured out where I was behind in their subjects and told me how to catch up.

My favorite class was English. The class was reading *Animal Farm* when I joined it and I had to work hard to catch up. This was one of many books on a reading list we'd be required to complete before the end of the year. When I first saw that list, I was scared. Back then nobody talked about dyslexia, so all I knew was that I was slow and struggled through the assignments each night, never quite completing the required number of pages. But I was enjoying what I was reading even if I frequently needed to go back over a page to fully understand it. To my relief, we usually reread the assignment in class, and this allowed me to catch up and be ready for a surprise quiz or a discussion. Reading, though difficult for me and a cause of some anxiety, nevertheless became a source of enjoyment while I was at Wheaton High, however briefly, and this was a great gift to me, just as the bike had been.

One morning, Sette opened the refrigerator, caught a glance at something inside and almost jumped to the ceiling while screaming at the top of her lungs, "Wooooooooo-Woooooooooo-Wooooooooo! OH MY GOD, who put a damn snake in the refrigerator?" Everyone ran into the kitchen to see what all the noise was about. There was Sette floundering around, huffing and puffing. Mr. Wiggins opened the refrigerator door, looked, and then pulled out a long, shiny, heavy-looking black snake from the lower shelf. It definitely looked real, but a second look confirmed it was just a rubber toy. I stood by the stairs watching as she flopped around and then I laughed boisterously. "Ha ha ha haaaaa. That's messed up!" No fan of snakes myself, I stayed far away from this one, just in case it sprang to life. And as I stood there, I noticed someone else taking a lot of pleasure in the sight of Sette's discomfort. It was Kiki, the boarder's daughter. She was standing in the doorway, hands over her mouth to hide the snickering. By now, Sette was shouting, "I KNOW WHO DID THIS TO ME! YOU KNOW I'M TERRIFIED OF SNAKES AND YOU *WOULD* GO AND DO THIS. NOW YOU ARE *OUT* OF HERE!" I figured she was accusing Kiki, and that made sense to me, given the girl's guilty demeanor. But then Sette got into my face and repeated her accusation, and it dawned on me that I was the suspect.

I quickly shouted back, "Naw, not me! You got the wrong person!" Sette wasn't hearing it. She yelled back like a five-year-old blaming her sibling. "*YOU DID SO!*" And of course, I couldn't resist answering her back. "Not hardly! I can't stand snakes and wouldn't touch even that nasty-looking fake snake!"Her answer raised the conflict to a new level. "You did, and now you've got to get outta this house."I grabbed my backpack and stormed past her out the door to catch the school bus. As I sat on the bus, I knew with great certainty that the Wiggins phase of my life was all over and Mrs. Brinker would probably be waiting for me when I got home that evening.

It took a week for Mrs. Brinker to arrange my next placement. It didn't matter to me. I had been packed for a week, waiting to move on. But when she told me I would be returning to a place I had already been, I felt the panic setting in. There were no places I had been that I wanted to have anything to do with again with the exception of Mama Primas's. I knew that wasn't possible because she had moved to Kansas more than six years ago. Then Mrs. Brinker asked, "Lisa, do you remember the Parkers, Ida and Raymond?"

I was completely surprised. "The Parkers who we lived with back when I was real little?" My social worker smiled as if she was watching me open a Christmas gift. Then she said, "Well, they are living in DC and got in touch with FLOC to inquire about taking in some children. I told them about your situation and they are eager to see you again. Isn't that great?"

"Wait, what'd you say? The Parkers from the country?"

"Yes, the same couple that had you and all your brothers. I talked to them last week and they wanted to know how you and your brothers were doing. I told Mrs. Parker that I only knew about you and you could tell her how to find out about Jeffery. What do you think about that, Lisa?"

"I don't know except that's a hell of a coincidence." I sat there trying to put together the pictures in my mind of how things were when we lived with the Parkers way back then. Finally I said, "I'm not little anymore. I hope they don't expect that little girl they once had because she no longer exists." All the nasty things Mama Graves used to say about me and my brothers after living with the Parkers banged around in my head as I sat staring at the floor.

Man, I don't want to get all country again, I thought. But most of the memories flooding back were happy. Being picked up and carried around, pretending to plait Daddy Parker's hair and having the comfort of family. *So why am I feeling so ambivalent about this whole situation when I need a place to live? I'll have nowhere to go if I don't stay with them.* Still, it was as though I was looking for a reason to reject the whole idea. I knew the Parkers really did love us Ponder children. I remembered consoling Mama and Daddy Parker as tears rolled down their faces before we rode away from them in Mr. Keeney's car and I told them, "Don't cry, we'll be right back!" Moving back to the Parkers seemed both good and bad. But I was not ready to hear any more bullshit from some untried new foster parents who didn't give a damn about me. So what was bothering me?

Chapter Fifteen

The Parkers hadn't changed much from the way I remembered them. The sincere hugs they gave me when I arrived at their apartment melted the coolness in my body language and I let loose a little and hugged them back. It was the first time I had been hugged by a foster parent since leaving Mama Primas and I definitely wasn't used to the touching. But unexpectedly, I was still experiencing an uncomfortable feeling about moving back with them and couldn't quite put my finger on it. All the good memories of living with them before were still in my mind but I couldn't help that little feeling of anger directed at Mrs. Parker. I knew it wasn't Mama Graves's remarks about the Parkers not taking good care of my brothers and me; those cruel words no longer carried any importance.

The Parkers' apartment was a nice size and far nicer than where I had been living with the Wigginses. Mrs. Parker was a meticulous housekeeper and just as I remembered from when I was little, she took care of everything around the house. She was the first one up in the morning and there was always something cooking on the stove. I made sure the Parkers understood I was almost sixteen and that they treated me accordingly, giving me the same freedom that I had at the Wigginses' house. The only difference was that I no longer had the bike Frank Wiggins gave me. Sette had made it clear that I would not be taking my beloved bicycle nor the cool well-worn vintage jean jacket her husband had handed down to me while I was there. I was accustomed to foster parents not letting me take everything that was mine when I left, but this time having to give back the bike was especially hurtful. I loved that bike and planned on having it forever. Nevertheless, given the experienced and hardened foster child that I was, I got over the disappointment in a big hurry.

It was good to be back in DC because I knew how to catch the bus and quickly learned the subway system. This time I would be going to Eastern High School, which was within walking distance of the house. I felt lucky to be going there because Eastern had the best marching band in the city. I was thrilled to be a part of the high-stepping "Marching Machines." That band was going places and I looked forward to going with them. In fact, that year, I would march with them at Disney World in Orlando, Florida. In DC, our street parades attracted crowds which filled the sidewalks, grooving to the sound and waiting for us to march by playing our renditions of everything from R&B to the Go-Go sounds of DC's finest local bands. I also joined the softball team and the Army JROTC armed drill team.

Dr. Cornell began making home visits in the Parkers' apartment. Mama Parker was different from the other foster mothers because she gave us complete privacy and never interfered or tried to horn in our one-hour sessions. As far as she was concerned I really needed the therapy. After all, I certainly wasn't the sweet little girl she once knew.

At first, all I did was go to school, participate in school activities and come home. I understood that I was no longer in the gentler suburbs of Wheaton, Maryland. I was in northeast DC where the crews had control of the streets and bad shit was going down all the time, making me steer clear of anything that seemed shady.

Mr. Parker worked as a maintenance man for a management company and soon after I moved in with them, he found a three-bedroom row house only blocks away on 15th and D St. There was a liquor store on the corner and a lowly storefront church on the block, but the house and neighborhood seemed fine to me.

I didn't like the idea of not having my own money although Mr. Parker slipped me five or ten dollars from time to time. So when softball season was over and I was finished with band for the year, I went looking for a job. It didn't take long to find one at a frozen yogurt and fruit stand at the newly remodeled Old Post Office Pavilion downtown. I cherished that job as a server/cashier and always had plans for my paychecks even before I got them. Those plans always included going shopping in Georgetown to buy the clothes I had never been able to buy. I thought about all the times Wendy and I went to Georgetown to window shop and how I longed to buy those fashionable items in the windows. I wanted the beautiful shoes and boots and vowed to myself that someday I would have the money to shop there. Now I had a job and I was doing everything right. At least, I thought I was. During school nights I'd get home around 10 pm and Mama Parker didn't really seem to mind letting me in the front door at that hour. But when I began working at the Little Tavern in Georgetown and coming home on weekends at midnight or later, she had a real problem with my late arrivals. She'd say, "I'm not used to opening my door up at 12 o'clock at night for anybody and I'm not going to start now."

I quickly defended my position, saying, "I have to work. I'm keeping my job so don't even try messing with me about that. If you don't want me to disrupt your sleep, just give me a key so I can let myself in." But Mrs. Parker said, "I don't give my key out to anyone." It was as if she were talking to a stranger. To me this was a suspicious, "Where-were-you" type of question and I was offended. After all, I was standing there with my smudged, grease-smelling uniform stuck to my skin after a six-hour shift flipping burgers and she was wondering what I had been up to? The place stayed open and busy for 24 hours, which meant I often had to work past eleven o'clock at night. Because I rode clear across town on those long empty bus rides, I'd arrive back on the southeast side sometimes as late as one in the morning.

I continued to work and the problem about the key was never resolved. But at the end of my eleventh grade school year, I got the news that we would be moving again. This time the house was on the other side of East Capitol Street on 16th and C street Southeast. All that summer I worked my job in Georgetown and felt free to come and go. During that time, I couldn't get past the negative feelings I had been having since moving back with the Parkers. Sometime near my eighteenth birthday I began to recall the details of something that had happened to me while I had lived with the Parkers in the country.

For many years, I never talked about the sexual abuse I saw and personally endured during my years in foster care. But I finally found the strength to speak openly to my former social workers and my childhood psychiatrist and told them that I was sexually abused in various settings while in the care of foster parents. I guess revealing this painful secret was my way of saying *I wish you could have somehow noticed my pain and rescued me.* But I know that there was no evaluation they could have done that was strong enough to penetrate the psychological wall I had built to protect myself from what I had seen and endured. As a child I was embarrassed and ashamed about these things that had happened to me; I felt that my entire body was covered with the nastiness of it all.

I had no idea of the concept of sexual abuse back in those days, but what I did know was that there were things done to me that did not feel right. Still, I guarded the secrets as if they were my own and not someone else's twisted reality. I had told Mama Graves about Gavin's explorations of my body and saw that she did nothing to stop it. And so I guarded these secrets along with the secrets of foster physical and mental abuse I dared not expose for fear of terrifying consequences. The irony was that, by staying silent, I ended up carrying the heavy load of my predators' guilt.

You might ask; *Why didn't you tell somebody?* People only ask such a question when they themselves have never been abused. I can only say that I don't know, even all these years later, how an innocent child could even begin to understand where the guilt lies when an adult or an older child does something bad to them. Also, there was always my overwhelming fear that some kind of punishment would follow if I told the truth.

While I was living with the Parkers for the second time I remembered the details of being sexually abused as a very little girl. I was four then and living in Virginia on the Parkers' small farm when Suzette and Wanda, the two teenagers who babysat my two brothers and me, took playing house to a whole new level. Our renovated home was in a row of houses and trailers with well-kept backyards and pruned fruit trees. But beyond those houses lay a wooded area where residents dumped their old kitchen and bathroom appliances and other discarded refuse from home repairs. The woods gave us a hiding place away from adult rules and prying eyes and for a short while I loved going there. The girls showed my brothers and me how to lean old plywood boards and doors up against trees so that no one could see us there and disturb our play or tell us to behave ourselves. For us, there was freedom and fresh air even among the piles of rubbish.

Suzette and Wanda started our play sessions with many suggestions of fun things to do, and somehow *play house* was always the final decision. They helped us choose who would be the mother, the father, the aunt or the uncle. They said we could do whatever we wanted and this included cooking on the old beat-up stove, driving a car, sleeping together, and seeing some 'nekked grownups.' I always chose cooking so I could be just like Mama Parker. The girls helped me fill soda bottles with water and gather small piles of dirt for making mud pies in jar tops. They showed me how to wait for the mud patties to dry and then dump them out just the way Mama Parker made layers for her cakes. I felt privileged to hang out with them and kept busy sweeping my 'kitchen' with a nearly straw-less broom while pretending the dust I kicked up was smoke from the oven so I had to quickly take out the pies before they could burn. Playing and getting filthy was something that just went along with living on that little farm. I knew Mama Parker wouldn't get mad at me for being dirty.

Our 'house' provided a kitchen for me, but it also created a maze of rooms beyond where the girls could carry on other, more grownup activities. While I was content staying involved in cleaning and baking in my 'kitchen', I could hear the older kids talking and playing. Suzette and Wanda kept me feeling safe in the kitchen by calling out once in a while to reassure me that they were nearby. But one day things got too quiet, and I called out to my brothers. Suzette appeared from behind the partition and said, "You got enough dirt, Lisa? Come, let me get you some more of the good dirt." But I wasn't so easily put off and wanted to know where everyone had gone and began wandering through the maze. Suzette said, "Everybody else went to bed but you wanted to cook so we let you."

"I want to go to bed too. I don't want to cook no more," I whined. "Okay, but you got to be real quiet and lay down," she answered.

The pretend bedroom was behind the partition farthest back. The girls had spread old soggy blankets and crusty drop-cloths there and called it the bed.

"Now Lisa, these are your brothers so they can't be your husband, Okay?"

"Okay." I agreed.

"It's alright because you're the aunt anyway so you just need an uncle."

Then one of the girls volunteered to be the uncle to secure my spot in the game.

"You want to play, don't you?"

"Yeah," I answered eagerly and flopped down obediently on the pretend bed. By now, the happy voices of play that once filled the pretend kitchen had been replaced by low whispers.

One girl said, "Before you get in the bed, you got to take off those dirty clothes, okay?" Without hesitation I got up and pretended to take off my clothes. The girls were fully dressed, so I was following their lead. "No, you are too dirty so you have to take off your clothes for real," was the response.

I knew I was dirty, but I still refused. Mama Parker was the only one who ever took my clothes off, so the suggestion that I take them off in front of them made me feel like I would be doing something wrong. As I lay on the pretend bed fully clothed, I could feel the fun draining out of me. I wished I was back playing in my pretend kitchen with the old rusted-out stove and dried-out mud patties. What I had first imagined as a bed was now what it was, a pile of dirtiness crawling with bugs. Everything had turned serious and confusing, and my smile had disappeared.

"I want to get up now. I am tired of being sleep." I announced.

"No! Lay down and close your eyes!" The nice voice had turned mean and I began to cry.

"Okay, okay, okay! You can get up if you stop crying, okay?" I stopped crying immediately. Then came the second part.

"I'm the uncle and you are the aunt so lay down and close your eyes," one of the girls demanded in a nicer voice. I refused.

"Okay, then we'll take you back to the house."

"I don't want to go in the house yet."

"Then stop being a big baby!"

"I'm ain't no baby!" I protested.

"Then lay back down and just close your eyes."

I did what I was told. Not long after I closed my eyes, I could feel the large gritty hand of one of the girls reaching into my panties. Touching and rubbing the outside of my small bottom her hand felt around as if it were searching for something at the bottom of a bag. Nothing hurt so I just kept my eyes tightly latched. As she started to remove my panties I braced my legs together, hoping they wouldn't tear away, but they did. Now itching and squirming, I could feel a large finger tampering with the outer layer of my opening. It felt odd and confusing.

What is happening? I wondered. I wasn't scared because I knew my brothers were close by and staying quiet just like I was. My eyes were closed but I could imagine everything her hands were doing. Then with more aggression, she forced my knees apart and exposed me to the open air and her busy, moist tongue.

Terrified, I sat up, opened my eyes, and blurted out, "I want to go home!"

This must have scared her because all the bargaining was over and she whispered frantically, "Okay, just shut up and Ima goin' take you home."

As she adjusted my clothes and brushed debris and dirt out of my hair and off my bare skin, both girls began to talk at once, "You can't tell nobody about our house. Okay? If you do you gonna get in trouble and yo Mama is gonna get real mad at you so don't tell her and nobody else, okay?"

Within minutes, the girls were back to being the girls I liked being with. As we walked through the row of yards towards the Parker house, I wasn't as eager to go back home, and was feeling more generous toward my babysitters.

"Okay. I ain't gonna tell," I reassured them.

I continued to work and come home late to the Parkers, and the problem of Mama Parker refusing to give me a key was a problem that was never resolved. Instead she continued to get up and open the door for me. Sometimes she said "H e l l o" with a sarcastic note to it and I replied in the same vein with a drawn out "Th a n k s", to match her attitude. Other times, we were cordial to one another.

All that summer I worked my job in Georgetown exercising all my freedom. But, still I couldn't get past the negative feeling I had been experiencing since moving back with the Parkers. Eventually I started to remember the scenes with Suzette and Wanda back in the woods in Virginia. Once my memory started to unfold, I began to see the details as plain as day and realized that I somehow had believed that Mama Parker had known what was going on with the girls. In my mind, she was the perfect mama, and it was her job to protect me. But she had failed. Blaming her had led to my feeling of anger, and her refusal to give me a key to the house added insult to injury. This wasn't going to be another one of those times I'd beat myself up for keeping quiet about something. It was time for me to step up and lay it all out for her.

One day I came straight home from school without even a stop at the corner store for my usual Coke and a bag of salt and vinegar potato chips. I felt nervous and quivery, and thought I might back out. I contemplated the many different ways to confront her. My initial thought was to approach her in a peaceful non-blaming manner but my emotions didn't allow that. As soon as I got past the, "Can I talk to you for a minute" part, the true feelings I had been blocking for all those years burst forward. My words came out like a fiery ball of sadness, anger, hostility, and nauseous flutters.

I stepped in the room and challenged her, saying, "Why did you let Suzette and Wanda do that to me?"

She smiled agreeably and said, "Suzette and Wanda? You remember them, Lisa?"

"Yeah I remember them nasty bi-i-i…" I caught myself, not wanting to blurt out the rest of the word. But with the same hostile tone and raised voice, I got a little louder.

"Yeah! And I know they remember me, too, after what they did to me."

"What in the world are you talking about Lisa? What did they do?"

I was shouting mad now. "You know what they did and you ain't do nothing about it. That's messed up because mothers don't let that shit happen to their girls!"

Mama Parker sat up straight in her chair giving attention to every word that came out of my mouth. "Lisa, what did…?"

Tears started to stream down my face as my angry words lashed her like a whip. "YOU KNOW WHAT THEY DID! YOU HAD TO!" I accused her.

Mama Parker persisted. "Calm down and tell me what they did then I can tell you if I knew or not!"

"They molested me!" I shouted.

"THEY WHAT?"

"You heard me! They did it more than once. I remember everything!"

"Awww… Lisa, I didn't know about any of that. I wouldn't have let nothing like that happen to any of y'all if I knew." Her eyes welled up and her body slumped in the chair as she wiped her face with the paper towel she held.

Seeing her genuine reaction, I began to soften and lowered my voice. I believed her. She was different from the others; truthful and sincere. Even though I didn't like that bullshit with the key, I knew she wasn't lying or faking. She felt my hurt and was genuinely upset. I wanted to tell her everything because I needed to get the years of blocked pain out.

Sitting there at the table with Mama that afternoon as I told the story and sharing our raw emotions made me feel like a daughter again. Though she had done nothing wrong, I forgave her and myself at the same time.

Chapter Sixteen

INDEPENDENT LIVING

May 14, 1986

... during the initial stages of therapy Lisa was
emotionally labile, had poor interpersonal relations,
and was self-destructive. Over the first year she
made several suicide gestures and was hospitalized
for observation on one occasion.

The past two years have seen considerable im-
provement in Lisa. Her self-destructive impulses
have diminished to the point that they are no
longer a central concern in therapy. In February,
it was decided that Lisa had progressed suffi-
ciently to begin the work of termination. At that
time it was felt that she had gone as far as possible with this therapist. Given her history of poor
interpersonal relationships with women I suggested
that Lisa would benefit from continuing her therapeutic efforts with a female therapist.

The concerted effect of the separation from the
Parkers, her 18th birthday, and the impending termination of therapy has left Lisa very shaken, and
has resulted in a regression in her behavior. While
such regression is to be expected in terminating
any successful therapeutic relationship, Lisa is
responding to more than simply the ending of our
work together. She is again in the position of having significant persons "abandon" her. I should add
that FLOC is one of these "significant persons" in
her life in that the agency has provided the most
consistent support she has known.

While this may be an intensely anxious period

for her it may also be a time of considerable emotional growth. While I feel that Lisa will be able
to manage herself well at this juncture, I believe
it would be counterproductive to force termination
of therapy before Lisa recognizes her readiness.
Thus the goals for the psychotherapy will be to
work towards helping Lisa reach better resolutions
to the issues of separation and loss. This will
allow her a greater role in determining how the
therapy will end.
                                    — Psychiatrist

When and where to move me from one place to the next had always been someone else's decision, until now. I was almost eighteen and desperately searching for a way out of foster limbo. I wanted all those years of exhausting myself in the attempts to be understood, perhaps even loved, to be behind me. The more than a dozen schools and churches I had attended lingered now in my subconscious like pop-ups. Images of the many beds in dark unforgiving rooms I had slept in had melted into one continuous loop repeating the nasty night terrors of my childhood. Static electricity clinging to my clothing sparked memories of those spontaneous trips I never asked to take, carrying only pathetic plastic black garbage sacks of balled-up clothes sitting on strange porches as I waited for another stranger's door to open. The countless introductions to new faces whose eyes I only remember because of how they watched my every fosterling move were now buried under every step I took. The only word association I could make with *foster parent* was *evil* and the word *hell* was forever paired in my mind with *foster home*. I wanted to be done with all that.

The Parkers had done everything they could possibly do to make me feel like their daughter again. Their dream of re-rescuing me as a teenager, in much the same way they did in 1970 from Junior Village was now past the realm of possible. I could no longer be the helpless, gullible foster child they had loved. The happy toddler named Lisa who once believed she was their beloved daughter had vanished somewhere along the rocky trail of broken placements. I knew my belief in "things getting better" had been a child's fantasy. I had never been as stable as I had been as a child with the Parkers. But those positive feelings had long ago been lost in the mists of time.

There were many unexamined reasons why I wanted to leave a home as good as the Parkers' this second time around. But the strongest reason was that I was tired of having to answer Mama Parker's distrustful questions when I rang the doorbell late at night to be let in. "Where were you? What were you doing?" Her apparent lack of trust in me made it hard to buy into their whole family togetherness idea. My room and board was being provided with FLOC paying the bill. I never asked for anything extra like clothes, recreational money or even bus fare. Basically, I was taking care of myself but tried hard not to throw the family's decency back in their faces by saying that. As far as I was concerned, I could only truly trust myself and occasionally, Dr. Cornell .

My sessions with him continued once a week after school, but the new meeting place was in a townhouse in the Eastern Market section of Capitol Hill about a mile away from the house. Because my one-hour therapy sessions took place an hour after school, I'd hop on the subway near my school. His small office was a quiet and much more comfortable, safe place in which to open up with conversations I would have been hesitant to approach back at the Parker household. One subject we'd often touch on but veer away from as soon as I'd catch an attitude and stop talking all together was about the hypocrisy I felt I was dealing with at home. The "love with no trust" theme was among my favorite topics to argue each week. I would adopt an I'm-talking-ghetto-today accent and start with, "I don't trust them, because they don't even trust me enough to give me a key to let myself in the house. It's all fake and I can't stand people faking on me all the time." He'd smile slightly and then quickly find his serious doctor face again. I loved when that happened. My hidden agenda for our therapy sessions was to catch him off guard and force him to break his stoic doctor expression and reveal his extremely handsome Smokey Robinson smile.

I asked him outright. "I'll be eighteen soon — legally grown. Doesn't that mean I can get out of foster care all together and no longer be a ward of the court?" As usual, his technique was to get me to figure out the answer on my own. But on this topic I was easily frustrated and responded to his lack of an answer by saying, "Well, when do I get to stop coming here and wasting my time?" But I never stayed mad and realized that getting myself out of foster care now, was something I would have to work out for myself.

Mark had been in the Independent Living Program (ILP) for several years. I had been visiting him regularly and saw what a good time he seemed to be having there and envied the relationships he had forged with the counselors and residents. I saw that he didn't have to walk around pretending to have parents or that he was related to people he had just met and who didn't have much of an interest in him. His relationships with his roommates, counselors and neighboring residents were nothing fake or made up. If he got along with a person, that was great. If not, that was fine too. He didn't have to sit down at the dinner table to eat with them. And, best of all, he had a key to a place he called his apartment. He shared the place with three other guys and they each had a key. In my eyes, Mark had it going on. So I got up the nerve to ask him, "Mark, do you think they would let me move in here?"

Mark answered quickly, "Yeah, all I got to do is ask Doc. I can take you to meet him right now if you want to." I couldn't believe how simple this seemed and said, "For real?"

"Me and Doc are cool," he said. "I've been here longer than most of the residents. And everybody is starting to leave now because they are turning 21. Come on, follow me, he's in the counselor's office on the other side." I followed Mark as he walked through the narrow hallway with his familiar pimp swagger.

"S'up y'all, I'll be back in a few minutes so don't leave me," Mark said easily as we weaved through a group of guys.

"Come on Lisa, this is the office." Mark dropped two solid knocks on the office door and a stern military-sounding voice from the other side answered, "Come on in!" I hesitated a minute, because the voice sounded a bit fierce to me. But Mark moved quickly into the office saying, "Hey, Doc Man, how you doin'?" The stranger in the office shook hands with Mark in soul brother fashion. Then he said, "How are you, Mr. Ponder?" Mark introduced us saying, "Dr. Jones, this is Lisa. And to me he said, "Lisa, he's the one you need to talk to." Mark went straight to telling him that I was interested in moving into ILP while I extended my hand to Dr. Jones. He smiled kindly and asked why I wanted to move there and I answered a bit too forcefully, "Because I'm sick of being a foster child!" Then I caught myself and came up with an answer I thought he might prefer to hear, "Also, I'm almost eighteen and I think it's about time that I learn to take care of myself."

Dr. Jones was James Jones of the Jones and Associates Independent Living Program. He was Director and founder of the organization and had worked with hundreds of teenagers over the years and could tell right away which of my two answers was the real one. He said, "We can talk more about it, Lisa, but before you can enter the program, your brother has to be out of it. Mark, you're about to turn 21 aren't you?"

"Yeah, in August," Mark replied.

Jones turned to me and said, "Well, as soon as he's gone, you can move in, okay? But first we'll have a meeting with the people in charge of you now."

I asked nervously, "My foster parents?"

"No, your social workers and whoever else we have to talk to. The people who can help clear you from foster care."

Relieved, I shook Dr. Jones's hand again, smiled and backed out into the narrow hallway. Mark said, "Thanks, Doc," and I told Mark how grateful I was for his help.

I moved into ILP on a weekend. It was a smooth transition because, unlike my past placements, I was in charge. There was a bittersweet taste to it, though, because I didn't want to hurt the Parkers. But once moved in, I didn't look back. By then, I was eighteen and a senior in Eastern High School. I was to share the only first floor apartment on the girls' side of the complex. It had two bedrooms with two beds in each. Many of the residents already there had begun to age out and the first person I shared a bedroom with was a twenty-year-old woman named JoJo who would be leaving in a few months. JoJo was really nice to me because she and my brother were good friends. She was far more streetwise than I was so she looked out for me. JoJo had a hard exterior and a tough face although she had a big gap-tooth smile most of the time. I could see that people somehow knew not to mess with her or there would be a hell of a fight.

I was happy in this place, despite the fact that some of the other residents found it difficult to live there. Many of them had not been in a foster situation and were not adjusting well to the system. At that time, there was a huge crack and PCP epidemic going on in the city and drugs had hit DC really hard. Some of the kids had parents who were caught up in that and they had to move into ILP, a safer, more stable situation which, nevertheless, seemed too institutional to them. For me, living in the place was like having freedom and my own apartment.

After a month or so, JoJo was emancipated and left the program. I knew I was going to miss her but took it in stride because throughout my life I had become quite used to people leaving. The new girls who came into the suite were nothing like JoJo and I could tell right away that, like me, they had been a part of the Child and Family Service system. It was easy to see that this environment was far freer than what they were accustomed to and it was interesting to watch them start to adjust in order to fit in. This was their first real taste of freedom and they didn't know quite how to act. But like the rest of us, it didn't take long for them to learn the ILP code which was to be followed by the residents in the dwelling and went something like this:

- Mind your own business;
- Keep your hands off other peoples' shit;
- If you've seen something you weren't supposed to, you never saw it;
- Respect the personal space of others. In other words, don't step on someone's new kicks or mess up another person's clothing;
- Don't start no he says/she says shit;
- Don't fuck around and get fucked up. Translation: don't start a fight you can't finish.

Everyone learned the code of ILP either by example or the hard way; it was all up to the individual.

Joi and May ended up sharing the room behind mine in the suite. The decision that they would share a room was a good one. They were both heavy smokers and the day they arrived, I asked them to close their bedroom door and open all the windows when they lit up inside the apartment. Back in the 80's the smoking restrictions hadn't yet begun and it wasn't considered rude to pull out a square and smoke it in the presence of nonsmokers without asking how they felt about it. Both girls were going to turn twenty in a few months. Not only was I the youngest in the suite, but at 5'7" and 115 pounds, I was considerably smaller than both of them.

Joi had old-fashioned ways and some might say she even had an old soul or had been on earth before because of the way she carried herself. Her stout build was like that of a farm worker, but she also had missile-like Dolly Parton breasts. She prided herself on the skills she had acquired from a cosmetology school but it was never clear if she was certified. To make extra money, she was usually found in the living room, giving one of the residents a press and curl or clipping someone's unruly ends. Every client she served seemed to leave with the same hairstyle as her own so I figured it must have been the one she mastered while back in that school. Joi wore her hair in an eight-inch high snatch-back that was curled under in the back just off her neckline. She made the finishing touches on each of her clients with two dabs of dark brown hair gel to lay the edges down and then wielded two tall aerosol spray cans — one with oil sheen and the other with extra hold Aqua Net hair spray — to fix the hairdo so well that a tornado could not budge it out of place. The fumes from these cans filled the entire room long after the hairdo was finished.

Joi dressed very plainly, but the way she wore her eye makeup wasn't at all plain or understated. She'd line her eyes all the way around with thick black liner and then layer on electric blue eye shadow, generously smudging it over the entire eyelid. Her thick red rouge and lipstick were less dramatic but still quite bold. Factoring all that together with her bossy mothering ways, you had a real character on your hands in Joi. I liked her because she was always herself, no matter what anyone else thought of her. I figured her persona had been developed over years of having to take care of herself and possibly others. We both attended Eastern High School and were even in some of the same classes. If I missed a day for whatever reason she was sure to confront me about my whereabouts while at the same time handing me the homework assignment she made her business to collect from the teacher for me. I took her mothering with a grain of salt because I knew she couldn't help it and really meant well. I really appreciated her caring about me so when she handed me my assignment I would say, "Good looking out, Joi. Thanks."

But there were times when she went too far in trying to find out why I missed school and I had to tone that down. With one hand on my hip and rolling my neck dramatically I would get her straight right then and there, saying; "Joi! First of all, you better chill with all that bossiness. It's none of your business why I wasn't in class today so... mind your business! Thank you but, nobody asked you to get my homework in the first place. I could have gotten it when I went back to class tomorrow. You don't have no children up in here so stop acting like it." Joi would stand there looking at me as if I were crazy and then answer, "Well, I never!" But after a while we'd both dial down our attitudes and be right back to our old selves within fifteen minutes.

Like me, Joi tried to stay away from messiness and the inevitable drama that went on between the other residents. Whenever there were loud arguments in the common area outside of our apartment, Joi would pop her head out the door to see what was going on and then yell something like, "Oh, hell no! Don't be bringing that mess near our apartment! And don't be all in front of our door either! I don't want Dr. Jones thinking we have anything to do with that mess! Shoo, now, Go!" I knew how serious she was but couldn't stop myself from laughing because she sounded like an old grandma scolding neighborhood kids. Nobody ever paid her much attention, not even the people running toward the ruckus to investigate. They'd fly by saying, "Oh, shut yo' ole ass up and go back in your apartment, Joi."

When nineteen-year-old May arrived, we saw right away that she was different. She came in trying to take over and was flamboyant and bullish. But her attempts to set the tone in her favor always backfired. Though she was 5'10" and 275 pounds, she didn't intimidate anybody in the program. She flaunted herself like a light-skinned version of the well-known singers in The Weather Girls and sang "It's raining men" like an anthem whenever she had an audience. She talked loudly most of the time and her voice carried from our apartment all the way to the guys' side of the complex. Regularly, the counselor on duty knocked on our door and demanded she lower her voice. Asking nicely never worked. For May, whether the attention was positive or negative didn't matter a bit.

May was biracial. She had an attractive face but some serious identity issues. It was hard to tell whether it was because she was overweight or because of her mixed race. The way she chain-smoked and frequently got high with marijuana and Malt-Liquor was her way of saying, "I'm just as black as the rest of y'all." To May, fitting in meant she needed to be blacker than everyone so she worked hard at it. I had never met anyone like her; she didn't think her light skin was a badge of honor. She tried to dress blacker and talk with as much of a slanged-up ghetto vernacular as she could. I felt sorry for her sometimes and tried my best to understand and tolerate her.

There were times when the three of us had fun together in our apartment. We'd cook and eat dinner together, play cards and even indulge in some playful joneing. This was the most fun because it would have us all rolling on the floor laughing until one of us — usually May— gave up and left the apartment until the session had died down. But she was often the one to get the whole session started. She would get high and walk into the apartment and start in on Joi, saying, "Joi, I'm going to start calling you either Ronald McDonald or Bozo. Which one do you like better? 'Cause, girl, you look like a mutha-fucking clown with all that makeup on your face! Hahahaha! Don't she, Lisa? Haaaaahahahah!"

We'd all laugh, but joneing was always personal enough to strike a nerve and the embarrassment usually showed on the recipient's face. The longer the session, the harsher and more personal the cut-down. Joi's response to being joned on was always devastating. "I know your fat, funky ass ain't talking… Should I call yo' big ass an elephant or a mo-fuckin' hippopotamus? It really don't matter because you sloth around here eating everything that ain't nailed down. I've never seen an elephant that steals! Hahahahahaa!"

May and Joi constantly bumped heads about May stealing Joi's food and personal items because she had spent all her money on weed or liquor. May was relentless and kept joneing on Joi with remarks like: "That's ok, Joi, at least my titties don't hang down to my ankles as soon as I take my bra off. You have to roll them bad boys up just to fit them in that parachute you call a bra. Don't you? Hahahahaha!"

By then, I would be laughing so hard that tears were streaming down my face. But I knew my turn to be joned on was coming and I had to be ready. May would start: "Lisa, I don't know what you laughing at with you bony ass self. Don't you go outside today because the weatherman said the wind would get up to 10 mile per hour. Shit! We'll have to go pick your skinny ass up in Canada somewhere by the time it's all over. Oh damn! Where did you go? My bad, there you are, you just turned sideways so I couldn't see you. Hahahahaha!"

Joi climbed on this and added her own twist: "Yeah, Lisa, you better watch out for May because she might get some food stuck in her teeth and use your skinny ass as a toothpick. Are you the black Twiggy, or are you Olive Oil? Hahahahaha!"

Then it was my turn. "May, I'm not worried about being blown away, I'm worried about all these earthquakes you cause every time you take a step. Plus you need to brush up on your being-black-skills because right now the only real black part about you is your tarred-up lungs. I've never seen any-body but your greedy self get probation for stealing food. And Joi, it's getting cold outside but you can save money by unfurling your big ass titties and wrapping them around you like a blanket!" If that wasn't enough to offend everyone, I would carry things even further and bang out a Go-Go beat on the table and start rapping about May with Joi joining in;

> Talk about May, talkin' 'bout May,
> She's a big ass, she's a big ass,
> Now break it on down."

That usually brought things to an end. May would ease her way out of the room because she knew we could go on like this forever.

She made a mistake when she ate our food, and that made us jone on her more than usual. I would say, "May, don't eat my food. And when you use the bathtub, clean it after." One day I came into the apartment after spending the night away. A half a box of pancake mix was gone and an entire pack of bacon. I knew May had eaten it, but said, "Who ate my bacon?" Joi an-swered, "Big ass May!" Well, I just had to do something about that! I couldn't let her bully me by stealing my food, even if she was twice my size. So I got in her face about eating my food. She stiffened up and said, "Whatchu gonna do about it?" And I said, "You touch my fucking food again, I'm gonna beat your ass." She said, "So beat my ass right now!"

So we started scrapping. She grabbed me and tried to squeeze the breath out of me. Finally, I had just managed to get her off me by grabbing her soft, curly hair and twisting around enough to begin punching her repeatedly when a counselor came in. When he saw us, he started cracking up laughing. He couldn't believe I was whupping her because I was so much smaller. He started to hold me back from her but when he pulled me back, she hauled off and hit me in the mouth and hurt my front teeth. She hit me solidly, but the scuffle showed her what would happen if she messed with my food or my stuff.

I was assigned to a counselor named Mrs. Clarke. Right away I noticed that she was the best-dressed person there. She became a mother figure to me. I knew I wanted her to represent me if I needed an adult to go to school for me or something. She always had her hair beautifully laid. And she didn't hold back on giving me good advice. One day she said, "Now, Lisa, I want you to go to school. Don't you be over at that Gurruld's house today." Gerald was my boyfriend who later became my husband. Mrs. Clarke had noticed I was spending all my time with him.

At first I wasn't happy about being assigned a counselor because I saw first-hand how those relationships could go south. May was the perfect example of that. She was assigned to Mrs. McCray because she needed some immediate supervision and Mrs. McCray was up to the challenge. She was a woman who had been there since the beginning and had dealt with hard streetwise girls with nothing to lose. Boy, could those two throw down! One typical morning in our apartment when Mrs. McCray attempted to wake May up to go look for a job, May lashed out. With a lit cigarette clinched between her fingers and taking an occasional draw between sentences, she said, "Ah, get the fuck out of my room and go get on somebody else's nerves. I'm up now so get the hell out." Then May walked toward the door as if to escort Mrs. McCray out. That's when she experienced Mrs. McCray's full power. The gentle understanding she had been showing to May suddenly disappeared and Ghetto McCray just laid into her: "Who the hell do you think you're talking to? Gurl, you better get your fat, lazy ass together and get the fuck up out of here and go find a job. You must not know who you're dealing with. You think you're big shit but I have handled girls way tougher than your wanna-be ass. You got fifteen minutes to get yourself together and get the hell up out of here. I will be back!" Then Mrs. McCray strutted her way out of the apartment and didn't look back.

It had always been easy for me to remember all the bad news women to come in and out of my life like Mama Graves, Ms. McLeach, Mama Wooten and others. Of course, there were some wonderful black women who influenced me along the way, like Mama Primas and Grandma, but being assigned to Mrs. Clarke that year changed my attitude about black women in general and even changed my life and the way I thought of myself. She was different from anyone I had ever known.

When Dr. Jones introduced us for the first time, I had been reluctant to even shake Mrs. Clarke's hand. I feared that her niceness in that meeting might be an act so I disconnected and barely made eye contact with her. But after Dr. Jones left she knocked on the door to the apartment and asked to speak to me. She showed me enough respect to ask for my time and if she could enter my space. We sat down in the living room and that's when she talked to me straight up. She made it clear that she didn't have to be there and was working with us because she knew how important it was and enjoyed it. I could tell she wasn't bullshitting me simply by the unfazed way she carried herself, her middle-aged attractiveness, and the beautiful clothes she wore. She also made it clear that she would never curse me out and that I should return the courtesy she was showing me.

She ended this first meeting by saying, "If you need anything from me or just want to talk, my door is always open." And after that, I felt a sense of safety there that I had never felt before. She had my attention from that point on and soon I found myself seeking her out for advice. I learned right away that I could trust her because of the way she spoke to me and the lessons she shared. She made a point of discouraging me from the kind of loose talk that went around the place, revealing private information about a person. The warning was simple and memorable. It was: "Now Lisa, you don't need to be telling everybody your business."

It was clear to me then that all my private business would be safe with her. So I began to open up and talk to her about everything. I wanted her to attend all of my school functions as if she were my mother because I was proud of everything about her. When prom time came around, she took me shopping for a dress. Her idea of a prom dress for me was far different from the sexy tight off-the-shoulder one I had in mind. She told me beforehand: "Lisa, we will go shopping together to pick out the perfect dress for you. Everybody else is getting these tight cheap-looking dresses that leave nothing to the imagination. You are different; you have class. So let's go find you a dress that says classy not hoochie."

At first I was against that whole idea, thinking I would look off-brand and weird in that environment. But once we began looking at dresses I realized that she was right. I wanted to look classy! I wanted to hold on to my youth and relative innocence a bit longer and let it show in my prom picture. So I picked out a long lavender A-line gown that ruffled around the shoulders. A crinoline made the dress flare just enough and my satin shoes were dyed to match. I wore pearls and carried a small clutch and shawl to complete the look. On prom night, Mrs. Clarke greeted me and my date Chris, an ILP resident who was my best male friend. She admired how he looked in his black tux and told me I looked like a black china doll.

Mrs. Clarke made it her business to drop by my high school just to see how I was doing in my classes, made sure I kept my doctors' appointments and kept my ID with me every time I left the house. She helped me lay out a series of tasks to accomplish each week to be organized and prepared. I began to want something from Mrs. Clarke that I hadn't wanted from a woman in a long time; I wanted her to be my mother. She was everything a mother should be. She showed affection in all her talking and doing and often gave me warm hugs for comfort. I realized that I wanted her to be proud of me. One day she told me that she used to volunteer at St. Ann's where I had been taken after my birth. Mrs. Clarke had volunteered there over the years and told me she loved holding the babies and rocking and talking to them. I often thought happily that by some coincidence maybe she had done this to me when I was a newborn in that place.

I knew without a doubt that she cared about me. She would sit down and talk to me and say things like, "You don't need to fight and get into all the foolishness that goes on around here." I was hungry for that kind of guidance. She said, "You are better than that. You don't need to be fighting like you did with May. Where is she going in her life? You are better than that." She laid it down for me. I remember getting defensive and saying, "Well, May got on me. She got in my doggone face!" Mrs. Clarke answered me calmly: "And listen to you. You are going right into that same place. That's not you!"

In my last year of high school, Dr. Jones helped me get into Saint Paul's College, a small historically black college in Virginia and I decided to try it out. But my many moves to new families and different schools had made me restless and woefully unprepared for college. When my friend Ruby, another ILP resident, and I came back to DC for spring break during our freshman year, Mrs. Clarke invited us to be guests in her home instead of going back right away to our apartments at the program. I was so happy with this warm, trusting gesture that I cried. It seemed to me that she had as much trust in me as I had in her. Her beautiful, well-kept house measured right up there with my childhood favorite, the *Brady Bunch* house. I looked around and said to myself, *I want to live just like this. WOW!* Mrs. Clarke and her husband had two cars, a slick-looking orange corvette and a brown Lincoln that was all luxury as she picked us up. She had a pool in her backyard and said she wanted us to be able to hang out for the weekend around the pool and eat home-cooked meals. We met her husband, and all three of her daughters. When I met them, it was if they already knew me because Mrs. Clarke often spoke of me as being one of her girls.

After I finished the one year at Saint Paul's, I signed up for the Navy. This wasn't a surprise to Mrs. Clarke because I had been very active in JROTC at Eastern High School and had joined ROTC in college. To Dr. Jones leaving college was a big mistake on my part. He took my decision as a personal insult and let me know it on no uncertain terms. "That's just a stupid decision," he shouted. You have every opportunity to go to college right here and now and you want to quit! I know what it is, you think you're cute don't you? You have it all figured out in the little mini-skirt you're wearing!"

He was a tough-talking guy. Kind of a bully for sure, but he tried to expose us to cultural things like plays and museums and he clearly had our interest at heart. Many residents asked him for loans which he gladly gave them. But he would thoroughly cuss out a resident if you didn't follow his advice. I had always had a civil relationship with him and didn't ask him for favors. So I was a bit shocked when he spoke to me like that and answered him back in the same tone he used with me: "What does what I have on have to do with anything? Don't talk to me like that because I'm not one of your little flunkies. I have never asked to borrow a dime from you like the other residents have! I have worked hard since I've been here, so don't try the ghetto talk with me. I don't deserve it!"

He was furious at my response and yelled out for Mrs. Clarke, "Clarke! You need to talk to this girl right now. She doesn't know what she's doing. You better talk to her, Clarke!" She said soothingly, "Lisa, you haven't done anything wrong. It's just that Dr. Jones knows how much potential you have and he knows you'll be successful in school."

I softened my tone for her out of respect, but the message was the same. "I know he has a quota to fill but I honestly don't trust it. I'm about to turn twenty-one in a few months and there is no way I want to get kicked to the curb because I've aged out of the system. I would rather take my chances in the service where I'll really be on my own. I just don't want to be a ward of the court anymore, Mrs. Clarke."

I went back to ILP before going into the Navy and there was a new girl living in my suite. She just had 'tude all over the place. One day, I came in and she was talking about me. I couldn't believe it because she didn't even know me. As I walked past her, she jumped up and hit me. When she hit me, Lanita, a girl who was pregnant and only about 5'3", started whaling on that girl. I was completely surprised that Lanita felt that way about me. It was hard to break up that fight because that girl was brand new to the place and had just come off the street where fighting is a form of social interaction.

White people tend to have verbal fights where they exchange comments like, "Yeah, you did" or "No, I didn't." Black people get into gutter language right away so when somebody strikes a nerve you return it with an escalation like: "You bitch, I know you sleepin' with so and so..." It may be a deadly serious argument, but there is a peanut gallery laughing and screaming happily about what's going on.

It wasn't just the verbal sparring and physical fights in ILP. There were some kids who were getting up to some bad stuff. Counterfeiting, for example. They were copying money on Xeroxes and using it for the Metro machines and arcades. I wasn't about to get involved in that stuff. Some of the guys were rumblers. They were hustling and their tough image was more important to them than going to school.

One guy named "House Man" was a go-go guy. I wouldn't walk down the street with a guy like him because he always seemed to be in trouble. You just never knew if someone was out to get him. Mrs. Clark had convinced me that I was a person who was above getting involved in that stuff. I agreed. I was always trying to feel safe in what I was doing. I was cautious and watched my back. I didn't want to get beat down for nothing. If I had a bad vibe about something, I didn't put myself into that situation.

But many of us were close like a family and hung out together, always looking for fun. There was a guy named Billy in ILP; a little scrawny white boy. We embraced him as part of our family and sometimes teased him in a racial way. There was one guy who would be calling "B i l l y" in a high voice. Billy would answer, and the guy would say, "*B i l l y*, there's gonna be a hangin' tonight, and you're invited..." We would laugh our heads off. Billy was so good about it. He just meshed into the environment. He felt comfortable with us. We all joned on him of course, but he was cool with it. He'd go out and smoke a cigarette with the guys. Being all cool.

There was also a deaf guy who went to Gallaudet, a university for the Deaf in DC. I remember him coming out of his apartment one day. He was saying, "Who fuckin' stole my ra-dido? What motha-fucking ass stole my ra-dido?" We were asking ourselves, "Wow! How did he learn those cuss words?" We were rolling on the floor laughing, dying. But he was serious. He was letting us know, "You ain't gonna chump me just 'cuz I'm def!"

Living at ILP did me a lot of good. It allowed me to open up without worrying about being judged or treated unfairly by adults who had no real faith in me in the first place. The worry of being snatched out of school due to some abrupt transition to another foster family no longer worried me and I was free to come and go as I pleased and had the key to my own living quarters. But the best thing about living in the program was meeting Mrs. Clarke. The last thing she said to me before I left for good was, "Lisa, you can do whatever you want to do as long as you have a plan." That is the code I have lived by since that day. To this day, I call Mrs. Clarke my mother. She had a big influence on me at a time when I easily could have made too many mistakes to recover from. She changed my life.

Chapter Seventeen

"Hey Lisa, it's Lynn."

"Hey, what's up?"

"All the kids are joining this dance school down in Virginia. It starts this weekend so I'll be taking Samantha, Chris, Grace, Victor and Gwen. The first class starts at nine. Y'all can follow me out there if you want."

"Well, Tay's only three. Is there a class for her?"

"Girl, I already have that taken care of. She's in. And don't worry about the cost, we got a good price because we have so many kids."

Before I married my first husband in 1989, we had dated for four years during which I learned to love spending time with him and feeling like part of his large, close-knit family. His mother was the queen bee of a clan so deep with females they outnumbered the men seven to one and were the driving force behind all that went on in the family. Having grown up the way I did, I admired the loyalty his family members showed one another. I could see that any outsider who messed with one of them would have to take on all of them. That is why I never really understood why there was such a strong rivalry among the women. I managed to stay out of most of the infighting but when it came to the kids, I got involved by default. At three and five, my Taylor and Jerry were among the youngest of the cousins, but the queen bee made sure they were never overlooked when some new activity was being planned. There was no way any of *her* grandchildren were going to be left out and I was never surprised when I got a phone call telling me what they were signed up for next.

Those women kept the shit stirred up all the time, good or bad. This time, they had me schlepping my kids to dance lessons in a shopping center in Alexandria, Virginia every Saturday morning when I could have found the same thing much closer to our home in Takoma Park, Maryland. Situations like this usually started when one or two of the sisters-in-law said they were getting involved in something for the kids and the rest of us quickly joined in to prevent being one-upped or misunderstood for not jumping in too. Among us we had fifteen children and that small waiting area at the dance school with its crowd of competitive sisters and sisters-in-law became a big pot of boiling attitude that I wanted to avoid when I could. After living with so many different foster mothers, I had become an expert at steering clear of any hint of female messiness. In this case, my solution was to get my kids settled in their classes and then walk as fast as I could through the cloud of chitter-chatter and out the door trying to stay invisible.

On one of those Saturday mornings, as I waited for the kids to be finished, I wandered bored and aimless around the shopping center and saw a sign in a store window that seemed to shout for my attention: *The Battle of Baltimore Karate Tournament, Sign up Now!* Underneath those words was a picture of a six-foot-tall trophy engraved with the words First Place. I couldn't take my eyes off that trophy. As I stood there, a compact white man with a muscular military bearing opened the door and introduced himself as Sensei Carl. He could see that I was very interested in the trophy and invited me to come into the store. Once over the threshold, I saw an enormous display of trophies and heard the familiar sounds of classes in session. I hadn't thought of being a part of any kind of class, not to mention a karate class. But Carl was a good salesmen and managed to talk me into signing a three-page legal contract, despite my private worry about spending money on myself that Gerald and I simply didn't have.

But I couldn't get rid of the idea of being in a tournament and became intensely focused on winning that six-foot-tall trophy. Soon I was looking forward to Saturday mornings as much as my kids were. I was twenty-seven years old, and up to then the enjoyment of being a young mother had absorbed all my energy and identity. But now I wanted to try something just for me!

After reacquainting myself with the ritual of removing my shoes and bowing when entering and exiting a dojo, fond memories started to return of the time I learned Kung Fu as a teenager. I vividly remembered the horse stance drills in which I had to stand with my legs stretched far apart like sitting on the back of a pony. I remembered how my knees and feet shook after holding that position for many minutes and how sweat poured from the top of my head down the crease of my back as I waited for an instructor to randomly walk by and tap my calves with a yellow plastic bat to see if I would collapse.

Even though the names of the kicks and strikes and blocks of Kung Fu and Karate were different, I began to see that many of the executions were the same. Best of all, my muscle memory and limberness returned as I pushed every muscle to its limit.

After two months of vigorous practice in class and at home, the blisters on the balls of my feet were nearly healed and I was in a Wednesday night sparring class, eagerly absorbing everything I was being taught. I was beginning to feel athletic again, a feeling I had not experienced since I was in the Navy, making my way through boot camp. Each time I landed a clean strike or kick, my confidence skyrocketed. Sparring felt good — natural, in fact. It was as if my body knew automatically what it was supposed to do and when, and I began to anticipate strikes and kicks before they got to me. In time, my reawakened reflexes made each countermove precise and each strike I made landed on point.

But things got harder for me when I started to learn the kata, or forms. One movement was supposed to transition flawlessly into the next but I often got stuck in one position trying to think what came next. So I spent a lot of time looking like a robot and feeling like a fool, but slowly a level of proficiency began to take hold. The sparring nights were a mixture of students in all class levels and a true test for anyone who wanted to move up to a new level, but I kept improving. Finally, I approached Sensei Carl to tell him I was ready to sign up for the *Battle of Baltimore*. When I made my announcement to him, he smiled slightly and showed no surprise, saying simply, "Good, Lisa." I was acting cool, but my heart was pounding: I just knew I was on my way to winning that trophy.

As our World Karate team filed out of the fifteen-passenger van and into the sports arena, we carried ourselves like disciplined soldiers. World Karate's competition uniforms were rather simple — a plain bright white karate gi with the name *World Karate* printed in an arch design on the back with two genderless fighters placed under the logo — compared to the many far more elaborate ones being worn by other karate schools. Our duffle bags were ash-black and our sparring gear red or blue and decorated with the school crest. I felt proud to be a part of such an unassuming yet very disciplined team.

It was time for me to prove to myself and others that I deserved to be there. All the competitors' names were in and matches set up. Instead of weight classes, individual sparring matches were set by age, gender and belt color: I was a yellow belt and would compete in that division. An hour before start time the place was already filling up with spectators and buzzing with activity. There was a festive vibe to the atmosphere and it seemed to send waves of energy through the room as large demo teams paraded down long walkways to the center stage in front of the trophy stand. Individual weapons artists found small pockets of space along the sidelines and in closed-off door-ways to practice their routines. Advanced competitors soared through the air landing their perfect practice kicks on targets held by their coaches as they waited on deck to compete next. Children as young as six breezed through advanced kata looking like little *Power Rangers* and shouting *Kiai*! at the precise right moment. I was stunned. It seemed that every person there had brought their A game. I began to wilt a bit and nervously asked myself, *Damn! I don't know, man. What the hell am I doing here? Wow! Look at that kid kick like it's nothing to it! I shouldn't even be here.*

Seated in front of the small-designated area where I would soon be sparring, I watched in awe as the blur of activities flashed by my eyes. I felt the tears welling up and beads of sweat forming across my forehead and rolling down my face. I stared blankly into the enormous space of that room thinking hard about how I could escape this ordeal. Soon, I tried to rid myself of the negative thoughts by beginning to stretch and warm up, and then began throwing strikes slowly as if practicing Tai Chi. Alternating from the back to the front foot, I slowly placed a series of wavering kicks forward, extending them as far as I could. I tried hard to look as experienced as all the other competitors but I didn't even have an execution plan for my match. Suddenly I heard my name being called along with several others. We were to report to the nearby judges' table. As others darted past me, I seemed to be moving in slow motion. I tried to move faster and fake some confidence, but the whole effort seemed futile and I could only manage a lethargic stride. I was to spar against a black woman who easily outweighed me by twenty pounds. Other than that, we looked about the same age and height.

The first few fights ended quickly, way faster than I'd imagined. My turn was coming soon and all my teammates were in other sections of the room, leaving no hope of having anyone there to support me through the match. When the ref summoned my opponent and me into the center of the roped-off area, I took a deep breath, sucked in my stomach, and walked forward, shaking all over. We bowed to one another and got the signal to fight. Right away I saw that she had done this many times before. She seemed really sharp. Her style and technique were well-rehearsed and on point, and when she landed her first roundhouse kick against me, I knew for sure she wasn't playing around. The ref called, "Stop! Point!" Just like that, the first point belonged to her.

After a brief pause, the ref called out, "Fight!"

We began again in our starting stances. I tried to get inside with a strike, but she delivered a stiff front snap kick. It only grazed my stomach, but it still counted. "Stop! Point!"

She needed only three more points to win, but we had been sparring for less than a minute! I felt myself going negative and muttered, *Man...*

Losing badly, I began to hear a nameless ghostly voice from the past taunting me, "Move, Lisa, move yo dumb ass!"

The trophy I had trained so hard for was slipping away and it was my own fault! I was angry, and somehow that flash of anger cleared my head and I started to understand what I needed to do to win. *Can't let her hit me. If she can't touch me she won't get a point. Gotta move!*

In class I had focused more on what I was going to do to my opponent instead of what could happen to me. But this match was the real deal. I needed to stop standing around waiting for her to come to me. I had to be first and I had to be smart. I started to bounce now and got my legs working. I began circling around her. This time as she leaned in predictably, I shuffled to the side and caused her to lose balance. Then I hit her clean with a light back fist to the side of her headgear. "Stop! Point!"

This time the point was mine. I began chanting to myself, *If you want to touch me, you gotta find me...*

I was setting a new pace now and it was working. She went for another of her hard roundhouse kicks, then, just like on Wednesday nights back at the school, I spotted it, moved quickly and countered. Seeing where her blocks were weakest, I landed a devastating hook kick flush to the right side of her chin.

"Stop! Point!" My second point.

No time to celebrate. Within seconds, we were back at it. I saw that any movement would be the game changer, so I speeded up the pace some more and got into a rhythmic groove. She was staring at me with a laser-like glare. We were both determined to get a third point and stalked each other looking for an opening. Flatfooted, she suddenly pivoted in the center as I stayed on my toes, bouncing and dancing around. I knew I had the longer reach and slammed into her nose with my straight right arm and, just below her head-gear. "Stop!" The ref warned me to ease up or be disqualified. Despite the warning, the ref awarded me the point.

3 - 2 my favor.

I saw my opponent seethe with anger as blood trickled from her nose and I stayed focused on my new method of using quick lateral movements and throwing off her timing. The new round began and my opponent struck me clean to the face.

"Stop! Point!" Her point. 3 - 3.

Clearly she was out to avenge the bloody nose. I smiled in her face to piss her off some more. Now we were back face-to-face.

The ref called, "Fight!" and almost before the word was fully out of her mouth, I sprang forward and delivered a flurry of strikes straight to my opponent's head. She turned her back on me to avoid the blows.

"Stop! Point!" The point was mine. 4 - 3.

I felt tired and a little worried. Not wanting to make the fight harder than it had to be, I was determined to end it. This time, instead of standing toe-to-toe in the middle when the ref waved us in, I bounced on my toes despite my fatigue. She couldn't get to me and began throwing kicks and punches that were missing me by a mile. I smiled, seeing how frustrated and tired she was getting. I was tired, but not frustrated, and that gave me the advantage. I surprised her by landing a left blow to the center of her forehead and sprang back quickly before she could counter. Her open-faced headgear gave me a clear target to her nose but I avoided the possible disqualification of drawing more blood.

"Stop! Point!" The match was mine.

The ref instructed us to bow to each other. I smiled through the exhaustion. Then we parted ways, but the ref motioned us both back into the middle of the ring and raising my arm, proclaimed me the winner of the match. Unbelievable! I had done it. I filled my lungs with air and exhaled in relief. The trophy was mine. *No more dumbass Lisa.*

November 9, 1996 was fight night at our house and everyone we invited was arriving well before the nine o'clock start time of the bout. Rita and Ronnie had caught a ride with Uncle-boy and my husband Gerald returned from the liquor store with beer, rum, and Coke. As I finished up with the kids' bath time and put them to bed, I could hear the excited commotion down in the living room. Our guests were already getting tipsy with a combination of the effects of hastily-consumed alcohol and the anticipation of another Mike Tyson knockout fight. I heard snippets of bantering back and forth between swigs of alcohol about the question of the night: was Tyson going to treat Evander Holyfield the way he had his previous opponents? In our minds, something about Holyfield's nickname, "The Real Deal" gave him a better chance of being able to stand up to Tyson. It seemed like maybe we'd get our money's worth this time because there was little to no chance that a win would happen in the first round, unless one of Tyson's big bolos landed right on target. We had been equally excited and pissed off by Tyson's previous first round knockouts and had grown tired of spending $60 for Pay-Per-View for a dud preliminary bout followed by Tyson's dropping some hopeless bama in two minutes. But we all had high hopes that somehow this night would be different.

As I settled into an empty spot on the couch, photographs of two women fighters suddenly flashed onto the TV screen. I grabbed the remote and turned the volume way up to drown out the noisy chatter in the room. The announcer stepped to the center of the ring and announced that 5'4 1/2" Christy Martin and a total unknown black girl named Bethany Payne were to be the undercard for the Tyson-Holyfield fight! Don King had set up the first televised women's televised bout! And it would be seen by over 1.3 million Pay-Per-View fans gathered in living rooms waiting to see what sort of damage Mike Tyson was going to inflict on his opponent that night.

"What the hell? Is this for real?" I asked no one in particular as I watched the screen, wrestling with a blast of sheer disbelief.

Rita giggled and slurred through her rum and Coke buzz. "I guess it is.

They right there on the TV. Are your eyes working?" Uncle-Boy joined in on his way to the fridge, "Well I'll be damned! Don King got women fightin'. Now I done seen it all. I got to get me another beer! Ha-Ha-Ha!"

"Yeah! Don King'll do anything for a dollar. Even set up catfights." Ronnie added.

I got to see this girl fight, M-a-a-a-n! I can't believe this shit! Don King is a trip!" I had jumped up off the couch and was dancing nervously in place as the fighters took their corners. Fixated on the screen, I wished I was one of those girls. Everyone knew Don King had a habit of screwing his fighters over money, but at that moment I desperately wanted to be in his stable anyway. Everyone in that room but me was buzzed with alcohol, but you would have thought I was as high as Cooty Brown as I pointed to the screen and blurted out whatever came to my mind. I needed to be where those women were. I told myself it's what I'd needed for a very long time — ever since the days when I tried to show Mark I could fight like Ali. Watching Christy Martin slaughter a clueless, poorly-trained Brittany Payne in one easy round, I found an open space between the arm of the couch and the staircase and began doing my best Ali moves, throwing an absurd number of random punch combinations and thinking hard. *Man, people think I'm weak because I'm skinny but, they ain't never been hit by me before. Just like I surprised them at the Battle of Baltimore and, all those other tournaments, I'm going to surprise them with this too. Y'all better stop sleeping on my skills. Yeah, I wish I could get Kelly McLeach's big bouncy ass into a boxing ring. I would punish her and her ho-ass daughter for what they did to me. Ooowa! I never did get my lick back on them!. Ha-a-a-a-a.*

I strung out a fake laugh as I filed through memories of my past as fast as my hands and feet were moving, stringing together a mixture of the karate techniques I learned at World Karate along with all the sweet Ali moves I remembered from back in the day. Rita was laughing openly at me: "Gurlll, you sure you ain't had none of this rum?"

"Naaw. I don't drink."

Then Ronnie added as he threw back the last gulp of his drink, "You must have been sucking on one of those funny cigarettes — that wacky weed!"

Never taking my eyes off the TV, I continued to bounce and move, announcing to anyone who wanted to listen: "Nope. I have a natural high. I don't need none-a-dat!" I was whipped into hyper mode by now. "Karate ain't enough. Forget about all that point sparring and shit. I want to put on the gloves and beat a bitch down. I ain't little no more."

Now I was seeing Lovey Lomax and the mean-ass foster mothers who tried to ruin my life. Those old bitches always knew they were doing me wrong. *Come on Lovey! Hit my brother again and watch me drop this brick on your head.* I threw three consecutive right-looping punches into the air, imagining Lovey's droopy-dog face standing in front of me while I motioned for her to come meet my balled-up fist. *Swing your belt now… and watch me hang you with it!* I laughed as I imagined a new rant. *They took advantage of me because I ain't have nowhere to go. But now…*

I couldn't stop myself and was going off for real now. Then I saw Christy Martin daze Bethany Payne with an assault of deadly blows, and I fell out laughing.

"Yeah! Just like that! That's what I'm talking about." I yelled at the top of my lungs while jumping up and down raising my hands over my head like a winner.

Gerald started to look worried and tried to pull me down to the sofa next to him. "You need to calm yo ass down! Come over here and sit down, woman!" He downed the rest of his beer and opened another one.

"Okay, Okay. My bad," I told him. "All jokes aside, Gerald. I am serious. Dead serious." Breathing heavily, I wiped the sweat from my forehead and chest. Moving closer to him, I waited for his response.

"Okay, then do it! Go ahead. Box!" he said, trying to end the conversation.

"For real though, Gerald, you think I can do it?" I asked, losing some of the bravado.

"Hell yeah! Try it!" He snickered in a half-paying-attention way. By then, Christy Martin had TKO'd the pathetic Bethany Payne in one round and the underdog Ivander Holyfield had badly beaten Iron Mike Tyson.

Uncle-Boy lowered his voice and warned Gerald, "That girl is crazy, man." Gerald wasn't taking me very seriously, but he didn't appreciate Uncle-Boy's opinion. I said back to him, "And you drunk, so shut up!"

After everyone left, exhausted from the excitement of the two fights and from the long-buried emotions it brought out, I told Gerald, "You think I'm playing but I'm gonna start looking for a gym tomorrow, just watch."

The New Year was approaching and the novelty of dance school had worn off for the kids along with my interest in karate. The only thing on my mind was finding some way to get into a boxing gym. But after combing the Yellow Pages and calling the few numbers that were listed, I didn't get a single return call. I was beginning to wonder if none of the gyms I called were willing to let a woman into their territory.

Then one day I was telling everybody I talked to how determined I was about getting into boxing. The usual comment was, "Yeah, you go on ahead and let somebody beat up in your face! Why you wanna be getting hit all in your face?

Smiling to my face, other people would say, "I believe you can do it. Go for it!" and then turn the next second mumbling under their breath, "She gonna get her little ass fucked up and I'm gonna laugh. Who do she think she is?"

Some reminded me, in case I had forgotten, that I was a mother and asked me what my husband thought about it. But by far the most popular comment was, "I told you she ain't wrapped too tight."

None of those comments ever bothered me. I knew I was around people who looked at life through a pinhole and trying to change their attitude would be a waste of my breath. I knew that some so-called friends and family reveled in each other's failures and never wanted to risk trying anything new or different themselves.

One evening when I took the kids to visit their great-grandmother Foster, Gina was there. She was my husband's cousin and a real beauty; a poised runway model who never once looked down her nose at anyone. She was the last person I thought would understand my wanting to be a boxer. But, she got it. She overlooked all the nay-saying and narrow-mindedness and looked outside the box when I demonstrated the Martin-Payne fight with exaggerated moves and play-by-play commentary. I'll never forget what she said.

"Lisa, you know what? Me and my boyfriend Tyrone watched it at his friend's house. Tyrone follows all the fights and he boxes too." I got really quiet then and hung on every word she said as if missing one would cost me my life. Then the questions tumbled out of my mouth, hard to follow. "For real, Gina? Can I go to his gym with him? Do you think he'll let me go with him? Where does he work out? Do you think he would take me?" Gina didn't laugh at me. "I don't know the answers, Lisa. But he'll be here soon and you can ask him yourself. Can you wait about thirty minutes?"

"Oh hell, yes!!!"

"Well, gurl, Tyrone won't mind talking to you at all." Gina said.

I fell all over myself saying, "Oh Gina, thank you, thank you, thank you, thank you, thank you..."

I had only met Tyrone one other time and now I would be asking him for something that I knew could be life-changing for me. For the half hour I sat in Grandma Foster's living room waiting for Tyrone to arrive, I imagined what life would be like as a boxer.

Boxing ain't gonna be nothing like karate. I'll have to fight hard and no-body is gonna stop the match when they see a little blood. I'll have to be quick and throw a lot of punches all at once.

I pictured myself in full gear standing in front of a faceless opponent. *Damn! I know I can take a punch but can I take a lot of punches? What am I getting myself into? I ain't never been knocked out and I don't want to be. Do people die a little bit when they get knocked out? Will it even hurt? Shoot! I ain't getting knocked out. That's embarrassing!* I laughed to myself and then, to push aside the doubt and the questions I said out loud almost like a prayer, "*I just got to do this! I know I'll be good and it's what I'm s'posed to do so that's what I'm going to tell Tyrone when I see him.*"

Little flashes of familiar doubt kept returning but while I sat there imagining, questioning and worrying, a trace of new courage slipped through my nostrils in the form of long, calming streams of warm air. The steady non-rhythmic shaking of nervous energy generating from my right foot slowed as my personal bargaining slowed down to nothing. Suddenly all the doubt and worry ended and I accepted my decision to box with every piece of my being.

That day when I met Tyrone was one of the most important days of my life. His offer of help changed, redefined and saved my life from that moment on. Boxing had been a part of my life for so many years and now I knew why. That little foster girl inside me with a whole bunch of unreachable ideas and dreams was determined to reveal all those things about herself she always knew. Ready to prove that she was a person, not a piece of trash to be tossed about in the street blowing around, landing and sticking for a few moments only to detach and fly again. She wanted to realize her dream to be normal with a range of feelings; happy, mad — even sorry. She wanted to be a girl who could be hurt and bleed just like everybody else, not just to be just a lost girl without a mother and a father whose feelings don't exist. To be a girl who imagined she would be beautiful like girls know they are going to be when they grow up and then can demand attention and respect. To be a girl who is no longer invisible or overlooked while standing in the corner — an unwanted foster. Having those unreachable, unspoken ideas had always gotten that little girl in trouble with people who didn't care enough to understand. There was so much she had never been able to say. She knew her eyes always revealed her thoughts, but that had often led to misinterpretation, resentment, even ha-tred. She never quite had the words to express her innermost thoughts and make them understood by those who should have cared. Maybe boxing would help her say everything she had never been able to express, and in doing so, make her feel a whole lot better about herself.

When I heard voices coming from the back end of the house and realized it was Gina letting Tyrone in, I sat up straight on the couch and put on my best interview face. As I saw their shadows rounding the corner, my nerves would-n't let me stay that way so I jumped up to greet Tyrone. We stood almost at eye level and it was evident by his trim, sculpted physique that he did some kind of working out and was in good shape. A good-looking and clean-cut young man; you would never have thought he boxed. It seemed like a pair of white shorts, a polo shirt and a tennis racket would have suited him better than a pair of red satin trunks and boxing gloves. He was well-groomed down to his fresh manicure and his clothes were a perfect fit. To me, he was the embodiment of metrosexual — a term which was making its way around at the time. His face showed no signs of violence and neither did his demeanor or personality. He walked and talked with a natural confidence.

"Tyrone, this is my cousin Lisa, you know, Gerald's wife? And, Lisa, this is my boyfriend Tyrone." Between the short walk from the back door to the living room Gina must have filled him in on all my overheated boxing aspirations because right away he let me know that he would help me get started.

I unleashed my conspiracy theory on him; "I have called every listed box-ing gym in the phone book and left lots of messages but nobody will call me back. I know what's up. Nobody wants to have anything to do with a female who says she wants to box." Tyrone stayed cool in spite of my tirade and replied, "You're probably right but, don't worry about it, I'll take you where I go. Gene, the gym manager ain't gonna mind and you can train with me."

I was almost shouting now. "For real! When? I mean where and what time?" A ball of nervous energy bubbled into my throat and I started laughing. I couldn't believe he had really invited me to train with him! I had thought I would have to beg and call and beg some more just to convince him that I was serious. He simply said, "Be ready at 4:00 tomorrow and I'll pick you up. The gym is down on W street not too far from Howard University." I immediately got a mental picture of the place. "Oh! Over there by that YMCA?" I asked.

"Yeah! The Y is in the next block at 13th and W. Midtown, the gym we're going to is on 14th and W." He explained.

"You mean Anthony Bowen YMCA?"

"Yeah, that's it," he said.

"Dag! When I was a kid, I used to go the summer camp there and that was where I first put on a pair of gloves. I know exactly where it is. OK, I'll be ready. And I promise not to let you down, Tyrone."

I was so happy. Gina had told me the truth and had delivered Tyrone to me. My life was going to change. No doubt about it.

Chapter Eighteen

Once I saw the Martin vs Payne boxing match, I was on a mission to become a boxer. When Tyrone picked me up to take me to Midtown Gym, I was all eagerness and resolve. Not knowing what the facilities were like, I wore sweatpants with spandex workout shorts under them. My plan was to take off the sweats at the gym. But when I went into that gym, I didn't want to touch anything or take off any of my clothes and have to put them down somewhere. The place was filthy and smelled like cat piss from front to back. The only thing that could help that smell was a packet of Cush Incense which Gene had opened and stuck between the crevasses of the brick wall. It should have overwhelmed the cat piss, but it didn't come close. Now I could smell the Cush AND the cat piss. Gene was sitting behind the front desk when Tyrone introduced us. He acted like he assumed I was Tyrone's woman.

I wasn't looking to impress anyone but Tyrone. As I saw it, he was my ticket to boxing, so I concentrated on him and did everything he told me to do. He said, "Lisa, you don't have to be perfect. Whatever I do, you do it too." So if he did fifty jumping jacks, I did them too. Twenty pushups? I did twenty. I am a good mimic, so I mimicked Tyrone's moves exactly and Gene started noticing my ability. After a while, Tyrone and I started meeting at the gym regularly.

I had put my stock in Tyrone, and he was really nice to me and generous with his time. Also, he never once tried to come on to me, and I loved that about him. He was a gentleman! But after a while, his schedule at work changed to a night schedule and he couldn't come to the gym anymore. He reassured me that I would do fine without him and said to just keep going on my own, adding that Gene would be there to help me. By then, I had become excited by and a bit addicted to boxing and was willing to continue without Tyrone's help. The trouble was that I had to adjust from being told specifically what to do in detail by Tyrone, to Gene's very limited instructions.

Whereas Tyrone had provided in-depth descriptions of what should be done and why, Gene would give general instructions I didn't wholly understand like, "Com'on, man, com'on! Move! Change your pattern! Move that feet right there!" Soon, as I started to spar and then have bouts with other fighters, I realized that although I was doing everything I thought Gene was telling me to do, I was still getting busted in the ring. I would get hit in the eye every single time, or I was getting caught in the body continuously. I watched fights by Gene's other fighters and noticed they were having the same problems I was.

I decided that I had to try to teach myself, because it seemed that all I was learning from Gene was the jab. He couldn't teach me the combinations, the technical footwork, and the moves I needed to win. I was throwing great jabs but getting off balance and leaving myself open because of my poor footwork. Soon, I got the idea of buying videotapes of all the great fighters in action and studying and learning from them. I got tapes of Sugar Ray Robinson, Max Schmeling, Archie Moore, Sugar Ray Leonard, Marvin Hagler, Bob Foster, and, of course, the great Ali. I watched them obsessively and focused on their footwork and dancing.

I had been seeing women come out of the ring with split lips and chunks out of their faces and didn't want to be getting hit in the face constantly and getting all messed-up. When you get hit in the face with leather and the person who hits you twists her hand when she hits you, the glove twists the skin and damages it. When you punch with a pop, then a twist, it's just physics that you will do some damage to your opponent.

Boxing — the Sweet Science — is all about Leverage, Power, Speed and Balance. It is a skilled craft that involves strategy and forethought — much like a chess match. When you have been training hard and boxing regularly, you honestly begin to feel invincible like a superhero. You walk around with your body feeling hard and tight and are no longer in fear of being hurt by others. You begin to find you have admirers — people who don't even know you. They say nice things to you; they show support. They approach you and say things like, "Girl, you a beast. I saw you hittin' the bag, I saw you fightin' over there at Midtown." You listen to what they say and feel flattered. But some people who have known you in your life whisper about you and say mean things to bring you back down to their level. You tell yourself you are in shape — lean and mean — but they don't want to see that. Some feel better if you have no prospects.

The thing I first loved about boxing was that it enabled me to be more social and talk easily to people. I wasn't stuck in my house now. But unfortunately, since I was doing something I loved outside the house, I started realizing things I wasn't happy about in my marriage. It was the fighting — the organized chaos — that was making me happy. I tried to include my husband Gerald in my new life and asked him to be my manager. But he was reluctant. Eventually, it was clear why. He just didn't have what it took. When you are managing a fighter, you have to be able to stand up to promoters, to be confident about your business. You have to speak clearly. Your fighter cannot be effective with a raggedy corner. You are the manager, and you are responsible for a tight, well-run corner. I was happy when Gene said he was willing to be my manager.

I think he had always known I wasn't going to stay with him as my manager but often tried to manipulate me into staying. Over time, I could see that he was building a defense against my leaving. I cared a lot about Gene, no doubt about it. But I saw his limitations as a manager. For one thing, the gym was a mess and that seemed to me to be a reflection of his disorganized management style. After about nine months of working out at the gym, I couldn't stand it anymore and decided that we needed to clean up the whole place. I bought a couple of gallons of Lysol, a few deck brushes and some other cleaning equipment. I remembered all the high quality cleaning I had to do when I was an enlisted person in the Navy and told the guys, "Okay, everything comes outta here!" That meant all those disgusting sofas they had dragged in there from the alleys and had been using for years. And I threw away all those dust and sweat-hardened shirts and shorts that had been hanging on rusty nails on the wall for more years than anyone could remember. The men had not minded just changing their clothes right out there in front of everybody, but I had to change in a little tiny, filthy bathroom with the toilet that shook when you sat on it. All that had to change. So I even built a dressing room in a far corner of the gym. This required a skill set that I didn't really have but I was pleased with the result, even though there wasn't a single straight corner in it when I finished. To this day, the door is still hung crookedly.

Right in the midst of my cleaning and renovation of the gym, Fat Cat, the gym cat, went missing. Alarmed, the little neighborhood kids who loved him kept coming in and asking, "Where Fat Cat?" They were used to stopping in to watch him and always shouted joyfully, "Look what Fat Cat doing!" even when he wasn't doing much at all. Pretty soon, the smell of decomposing flesh overtook the smell of Cush and Lysol. It turned out that Fat Cat had crawled behind the wall — probably chasing one of the huge rats that came in and out regularly — and died. The smell hung around for about two weeks until Bryce crawled back there and came out with Fat Cat's corpse laid out on a dustpan.

There was a guy named Buddy who always hung around the gym. He had a short arm with a little hand on the end. He had a limp, too, and his teeth and head were misshapen and he drooled. Nevertheless, he was hardworking and had a regular job provided by some city program. Buddy would come in and say, "Gene, whachu doing, Gene? Loan me a dolla fo' a soda, Gene!" Gene would mess with him and say in a fake mean voice, "Get the fuck on outta here!" Buddy would start whining playfully, "Com'on, Gene, give me a dolla!" And Gene would finally give him a dollar and Buddy would be sipping on a soda soon after. Buddy always looked over at me and said to the guys hanging around, "That my sista there. Don' nobody fuck wid her. She my sista!" Then he'd look at my sparring partners and say, "Hey, my sista fucked you ass up yestidday, din' she?"

People outside the gym took advantage of Buddy. I had heard that in the past, the drug boys would get him to hold their drugs for them so they wouldn't be caught for possession if the cops moved in on them. Buddy dropped in at the gym a lot where no one used him. After I got to know him, he and I were cool and we started joneing on Gene together. I was a Redskins fan and so was Buddy. Gene was for Dallas so we would be all over him about that. I didn't like the way buddy drooled, but he was so sweet and loving towards me, I would give him a hug now and then. And he always felt he was protecting me.

One day, Gene came in and said to me, "Let's go up to New York and see Izzy." I was thrilled. Izzy was a boxing equipment dealer. Gene bought boxing equipment for the gym from him. But on this trip, he set me up with all this nice boxing gear; sweats, gloves, shorts and tops. The only part I didn't like was that Gene chose black and gold as my fighting colors for my boxing trunks and top. I knew I wouldn't want those to be my permanent colors, but still I was grateful to Gene for all he was doing for me. Nevertheless, after that first shopping trip, I made a point of choosing all my own colors and styles for myself.

My first amateur fight was in Plainfield, NJ, three months after I had started at Gene's gym. One of his friends was putting on a show there and Gene was taking two of his male fighters, Bryce and Blue, along with me to fight. We had no idea who would show up. As Bryce drove Gene's battered old station wagon up the highway, Gene sat regally in the front passenger seat, doused in his favorite African oil, wearing his African garb and a kufi hat in a matching pattern, and holding his decorative wooden cane between his legs. Blue was stretched out in the way-way back alongside the equipment bags and I sat by the window in the back seat fantasizing about the scene we were about to enter and worrying obsessively: *What if I lose or go out there and forget everything I know? Can't let myself get knocked down. I know this girl will come at me hard. Will I get a black eye? I need to punch and move the whole time. Oh god, all I have is the jab and my movement. No other punches. But I can't lose. People I know in DC will gossip if I do. Can't lose…*

At the Plainfield, NJ Police Athletic League, I ended up fighting a girl named Roxanne. We were fighting at 125 pounds although I weighed only 115. Up until that time, I had only sparred in the gym with Blue and a girl who just walked into the gym one day. At the time, I had no clue about what to do in the ring, and right away that girl clocked me with an overhand right. It was like getting hit from behind with a pole. I had never felt anything like that before, and, believe me, I never wanted to get hit like that again. Instantly, the wild side of me came out, and that sparring match had turned into something like a street brawl with both of us just trying to survive. Gene had never bothered to tell me how to hold up my hands for protection in a fight, and I was completely open to her. The guys watching the sparring match told me I should come out of the ring, but I was determined to keep going.

Later, when I told Tyrone about that incident, he couldn't believe Gene had put me in a fight like that. But the experience made me realize that boxing is not nice. It's for real. The goal of sparring is not to hurt the other fighter. But the other girl hadn't read that memo! She had come in there to have a very violent fight. From that day on, when I was sparring with someone I didn't already know or trust, it was ON! I was not going to be caught in a brawl like that again.

The fight with Roxanne was an amateur bout, but to me it was a really big deal. She was a small girl, really Irish-looking. It made me laugh that she had that old-fashioned Irish high-fisted stance going for her. My goal was to hit her and keep moving to avoid being hit. Right from the start, she had been using these precise, painful roundhouse punches to keep coming at me steadily. I wasn't thinking about how hard I was going to hit her, only how fast. I was jabbing and moving, and moving and jabbing while she kept moving forward, stalking me. The ring was a lot bigger than the ring back at Midtown, so I had plenty of room to move. I didn't really know about keeping my guard up, but after watching all those videos of the champions, I knew how to dance around the ring. I just danced on my toes nonstop. In the process, I began to realize that moving like that in a large ring was wearing me out too fast. But suddenly, I dropped her! It was beautiful — amazing! She came after me, boom, boom, boom, and then she missed and I instinctively hit her POP, POP, and I saw her lights go out and watched her drop like a stone. The way she hit the ground made her twist her ankle. Turns out, she broke the ankle and sprained her wrist. So the fight was over, just like that. It was a shock to me. I had been watching those roundhouse punches coming at me and I could see everything else she was throwing my way. All that time I was thinking, "Oh, I'm okay, I'm okay," but I was working on pure fear. When she dropped, the ref told me sharply to get away from her. That is the rule, because it keeps the fighter from being able to hit someone when they are down. But I was green then, and I had wanted to see if she was okay and stepped closer to her which I shouldn't have done.

Gene's knowledge of boxing was all street knowledge although he himself had been a boxer. When he was training me, that wasn't a good thing for me. He just didn't have much to teach me, and I was hungry to learn everything I could. One time I was going to fight someone and Gene saw my husband enter the venue to watch. Instantly, Gene said jealously, "Oh, he's here? I'm leaving!" So he left me alone to fight without a corner to back me up.

Looking back on that, I think he was afraid for me to fight in front of Gerald because he didn't have enough faith in his ability to train me. But he never said that. He said things like, "Stop asking questions!" And, "I can't explain why, you just have to do what I tell you to do." Gene didn't know how to turn down a fight either. My first professional fight was against Downtown Leona Brown. She was a national champ with some 20 fights under her belt. That girl was some pug! And the fight was in her home base where she had a rowdy bunch of fans.

I knew that Gene just wasn't a manager who could watch out for my welfare above all. He couldn't; he just wasn't up to turning down fights. Nor was he the kind of manager who turned up well-prepared to take care of his fighters. As a boxer, one of the most gratifying feelings you can have when entering the ring is confidence that your corner is tight. From the day you learn a basic stance, until the time you are able to put together three or four-piece punch combinations, all eyes will be on you and your corner team. Whether you are an amateur or a pro, the relief of having a proficient, knowledgeable, and pre-pared corner can be the difference between winning and losing. But while Gene was my manager, all I had was a raggedy-ass corner. This led to one embar-rassing situation after another which proved his lack of preparedness. Because I cared deeply about him, I tried to keep believing in his ability to help me win a championship. He would regularly make promises to me in an attempt to stave off my inevitable departure and say things like, "All those niggas I trained in here just up and left me. Those nuffin'-ass trainers came in and stole them out so they could turn 'em pro. That's why I don't let nobody come in here no more. That okay wif me, 'cause none of 'em never got nowhere."

Hearing Gene talk like that made my own abandonment issues from the past resurface and I tried to reassure him by saying things like, "Don't worry about that stuff Gene. I can't wait to get out there and represent you. I won't leave you like that. I'm thankful to have a trainer like you because I know you really care about me and that's the most important thing in the fight game."

I know Gene gave me all he had. In fact, he gave me so much attention that many of the other boxers who had been with him for years before I came got frustrated and simply stopped coming to the gym. Gene didn't seem to care about that. In fact, he started putting people out of his gym if they showed any attitude about the situation. I had three fights under Gene: one loss, one draw and one win. When I moved on, he was hurt and talked about me with bitterness in his tone. I know that was the hurt talking, because we still have a relationship and I know Gene is proud of me and of the time we worked together to make me a champion.

Chapter Nineteen

TOO FIERCE FOSTER VS. DOWNTOWN LEONA BROWN

New York welcomes Too Fierce Foster! That week before we went to New York, I endlessly imagined those words blinking in bright lights over Times Square. My head was filled with dazzling images of my upcoming pro debut. Gene and I would be walking through the front door of a posh five-star hotel after being welcomed by two doormen in uniform coats and high hats. We'd report to the front desk and Gene would announce our arrival. The wide-eyed desk clerk would hand him a large envelope with FOSTER printed on it. Inside were keys to two of the finest rooms in the hotel, a detailed itinerary of events for the next two days with weigh-in information and a press conference schedule and best of all, a fight night program with *Too Fierce Foster* in bold type. The only thing Gene and I would have to worry about was getting down to the lobby in time to meet the limo that would whisk us away to a packed arena.

In my mind, the venue would be like Madison Square Garden; huge, smoky and completely sold out. For my entrance, the hyped-up, half-drunk fans would be filling the room with positive energy. The music would grow louder with my entrance while fight highlights played on the Jumbotron above the spotlighted ring.

Thinking of such an exciting atmosphere gave me goose bumps down my sweaty back, as I pounded the heavy bag with both hands. While I trained in those days ahead of my debut, those thoughts fueled my moving parts while my boxing arsenal remained barely equipped. I did all I could with my basic artillery, but there was the gnawing realization that it wasn't going to be enough. I trained an hour longer each day to further sculpt my physique to where I thought it should be for the center ring. My hard work in the gym was definitely paying off and I felt this was the opportunity I needed to turn pro quickly. Hypersensitivity about my advanced age of 29 and the looming five-year goal I had set for winning a world title had motivated me to speed things up and cut short my amateur experience. The Nationals had given me a window into the world of women's boxing and I knew I would see some of those girls again. But going pro meant graduating out of the headgear and I was eager to try.

Gene sat in his chair, rocked back, and began. "I know when a fighter is ready to turn pro and you're ready. I had a lot of fighters turn pro in my gym, but when I got them out there in good fightin' shape, some slimy ass vulture would come along and take them right from up under me. I know you're ready to turn pro but I hope you ain't like that." Gene shook his head and I could see worry deeply imbedded within the lines of his forehead. He had begun this insecure talk the moment I signed on the dotted lines of that first fight contract. I was so excited about all that we had accomplished up to that point and I couldn't imagine my career without him.

"Man, Gene, please stop talking like that. I don't plan on going anywhere. I trust that you know what you're doing and it sucks that all your fighters left you. I'm not like that. I trust you. I'm going to do my job and train hard, and let you do your job." And that's exactly what I did. I let him handle everything and didn't ask any questions so I could prove my faith in him. I felt his pain and could easily relate to similar abandonment issues. As expected, tension and anxiety built as fight day approached and then, when Gene gave me what he considered more good news about my pro debut, an alarm went off inside me.

"With all my connections and all the people who know me, I was able to get Bryce on the same card as you. Now, both of you'll have your pro debuts at the same time!" Gene stuck his chest out with pride while I tried to conceal the what-the-hell reaction on my face and pressed my lips together to prevent any unscripted words from flying out of my mouth. From that minute on, I restrained the negative feelings welling up inside of me by blocking out anything not pertaining to honing my boxing skills. I began to develop a whole new kind of focus and stuck to survival mode.

When the three of us arrived by train in New York on the morning before the day of the fight, I was feeling high on life and ready for the biggest bout of my life. But it quickly dawned on me that my perception of how my pro debut would play out might not be realistic. For one thing, Gene had assured us he knew his way around New York and that Izzy, one of his oldest fight buddies still lived there. But before we transferred all our gear to a subway, Gene seemed lost and had to call an official fight contact for directions. He lamely assured us, "I knew how to get there, I just wanted to make sure," but that reassurance only made me worry.

When we arrived at our hotel, I couldn't believe my eyes. My five-star hotel had turned into a pumpkin; at best, a run-down looking one-and-a-half-star place. *Keep your mouth shut! Don't say anything!* I kept repeating to myself. I didn't understand what Bryce and Gene were so happy about. But as the minutes passed by slowly, I realized more and more that the two of them were without any expectations whatsoever. They were living in the moment and embraced comfortably whatever was set before them. They picked up our room keys and entered their shared room with great delight while I retreated to mine wondering, *What more will go wrong?* Before shutting his door, Gene announced happily, "We have to go to the weigh-in real soon so don't be too long."

Inside my dingy room, I sat frozen in a stiff-backed chair and lay my forehead on the rickety desk. I was feeling exposed and vulnerable, a feeling I was all too familiar with from my youth. So far, nothing about turning pro seemed professional. With Gene in charge, things seemed even more amateurish than the amateurs. It dawned on me that Gene was resurrecting his coaching career as much as Bryce and I were starting our professional lives. Gene hadn't had a good amateur, let alone a contending professional, since many years before I had ever walked through the Midtown doors and this was his rebirth as a successful coach.

The three knocks on my room door signaled that it was time for us to get started. I consciously checked my attitude and my facial expression in the mirror before I left the room. I didn't want to be the downer on the trip. So, when we arrived at a city hall-type complex to meet with the fight doctor and have the official weigh-in, I perked up and tried to block out all negative thoughts. We submitted all the prefight physical forms that we brought with us. They included a complete EEG and EKG exams as well as an HIV test from both of us along with a requirement for me to take an EPT Pregnancy test, which I passed. Bryce, on the other hand, didn't get through all his paper work so easily. There was a concern about the results of the EEG. The officials wanted to examine his amateur passbook. It seemed they were afraid that he had taken too many hits to the head and were going to pull him from the card.

An official loudly addressed Bryce, saying, "Wait a minute. How many amateur fights have you had and how many times have you been knocked out?" Before I could hear Bryce's answer, I heard my name ring out, "Lisa Foster!" With that, I was called into another room where both Leona Brown and I — the only females on the card — completed our physicals and eye exams and then stepped on the scale; both weighed in at 118½ pounds. Unlike the scene I had imagined, there was no press conference and not even some trash talking. It was all business. Several other boxers periodically drifted in and out as they were cleared through the process. But Gene and Bryce were still dealing with Bryce's paperwork. I waited patiently. They finally appeared from behind a closed office door on the other side of the room. I could tell by Bryce's big, toothy smile that he was being allowed to fight after all. Gene gloated a little and took the credit for himself for making it all work out. I didn't even have to ask what happened because the two explained to me how they had changed Bryce's Amateur pass book from 0 wins 10 Losses and 9 KO's to 10 wins by placing a one in front of the zero and left the rest the same. I guess 9 KO's out of 20 fights didn't look so bad to the boxing commission. What bothered me the most was that Gene was okay with this. *A damn disaster just waiting to happen,* I told myself. Then, *Not my problem, so shut up!*

By the time we made it back to the hotel, the sun had disappeared and I was hungry and mentally worn out. Despite the one and a half stars I had generously given our hotel, the small gym at the very end of the first floor hallway was a sight for sore eyes. It had two treadmills, a stepper machine, mats, random pieces of an equipment line, and most importantly, a wall mirror. After eating and working out I felt that I had accomplished something worthwhile and was ready to go back to my room.

Being alone gave me time to think. I thought back to the time when I first saw women boxing on TV. The one thing I noticed about the sport that seemed consistent and something that I didn't want to fall victim to was the lopsidedness of the matches. Most of the professional female fights I had watched were very similar to the Christy Martin vs Bethany Payne match where one well-trained athlete takes advantage of a clearly inexperienced under-skilled opponent. I promised myself that I wasn't going to be on the short end of that stick. But to be honest, that's just the way my fate had been planned. Coming to New York and fighting in Brown's backyard for my pro debut wasn't the smartest move, but I hadn't known that. I was just a naïve boxer who went to the gym and thought only about the next time I would get in the ring. Brown's greater experience and amateur career had proven good for her in the Women's Nationals where she took home the silver medal. She had won her pro debut and was in the perfect position to win mine.

I'm going to have to fight hard tomorrow. I know they think I came all the way here to just go down for this girl, but they have another think coming to them. I am not some clown in a circus act for everyone's amusement. I'm not some Bethany Payne character, I'm a real boxer and tomorrow I'm going to let them see that.

Now I was getting jittery, and my nerves began to get the better of me as I lay there in my room. The usual sweats and ticks finally launched into a full out panic attack that lasted for at least 10 minutes but felt much longer. Eventually, a feeling of calm came over me and it was over. I called home and spoke to Gerald and my children and afterwards it felt as if the panic attack had never even happened.

Waking up the next day, I felt rejuvenated and positive. All my troubles had faded away within the dreams of a good night's sleep. I took one last look at my boxing attire hanging on the closet door: black satin boxing trunks, a black sports bra, a black robe trimmed in yellow-gold ribbon, black Pony boxing boots with yellow-gold laces and the white pony logo on the side, and yellow-gold socks just long enough to be seen folded once at the top of the boots. Everything was brand new; straight out of the packaging. Knowing I would be looking good was a huge boost.

It was a brand new day for the guys too. They were already full from the continental breakfast being served in the dining area near the lobby. I wasn't hungry, just tuned-up and ready to go.

"You got to eat something before we go so you might as well sit on down," Gene said kindly. It was going to be a good day and I no longer felt that overwhelming urgency I had been feeling yesterday. So I sat down and took my time eating a bowl of cereal and nursed a cup of coffee. Gene made a few phone calls to find out where to go and what time to get to the boxing venue at Yonkers Raceway. Doing my best not to get too deep into Gene's conversation I listened only for any bit of information about the night's events. I didn't want anything to go wrong and didn't want to be late. Gene was saying into the phone, "Okay-Okay-Okay-Okay." Those were the only words coming from his mouth and he wasn't writing anything down. Oh my God! I hope he knows where to go, I thought, trying to swallow my coffee.

We arrived at the venue two hours before the event. I hopped out of the cab as soon as it came to a stop and proudly carried my own garment bag. There in the middle of a large room was the boxing ring with bleacher-style seating all around. The only people there were the workers but the place was already brightly lit and the chatter of business filled the room. It was nothing like I had imagined it would look but by then I had come to terms with the grandiose vision I had once had. Soon other boxers started to arrive and the seats began to fill. One of the officials, dressed in what looked like referee attire, handed Gene an official program. That's when we found out that Bryce would be fighting the first bout.

I felt a surge of excitement when Gene said, "Bryce, you fighting first. You need to start getting ready now." It was an hour before the show would begin and I could see some of the boxers all dressed and ready to go. The energy in the room was rising steadily as the seats filled. Suddenly, I heard Gene say, "Aw, man, Bryce, we forgot the damn gauze and tape!"

"What you mean Gene?" Bryce asked, looking stricken. Gene's voice was sounding a bit panicked, "We need to go out here and find a drug store or something so I can wrap yo' hands up, man."

As for me, all those insecure, worried feelings from yesterday began to surge back, now ten times worse.

"You have to go and do what?" I blurted out.

"We just going to go find a drug store somewhere around here and buy gauze and tape so I can wrap yo' and Bryce's hands." Gene was trying to seem calm. He and Bryce then speed-walked out the door of the complex to canvas the streets for a source of hand-wraps. Tears welled up in my eyes. My unspoken fears were now very real and I screamed inside, *This is not the way this shit is supposed to go!*

One of the officials walked over and asked me where my trainer and the other boxer were. I told them I didn't know. Time was ticking away and Gene and Bryce were nowhere in sight.

I decided, *Forget this mess, I'm going to get dressed and I'll just see them when they get back.* By then, most of the boxers in the dressing room were dressed and wrapped. I sat in one of the folding chairs with my eyes closed and my legs stretched all the way forward. I rested both hands on my lap and cleared my mind and just thought about boxing. I pictured myself back at the gym. I was hitting the heavy bag hard, jumping the rope as fast as I could and shadow boxing. I slowed my breathing and removed myself from the lonely space I was in.

"Lisa! Lisa!" Gene got my attention. "Here's gauze and tape I'm going to wrap your hands with. I also got some water and Vaseline. I'll be right back after I finish wrapping Bryce's hands. We got to hurry up and get out there 'cause he's up first. He'll be all right if he just do what I tell him."

I walked over to the door, grabbed the plastic drugstore bag from his hands and said in the calmest voice I had. "Okay, Gene." I walked back over to my place in the chair and congratulated myself that I had successfully calmed myself down.

I could hear the crowd excitement building up and getting louder. The announcer introduced the boxers in the first match. I got up and watched from the sidelines where no one could see me. The bell rang twice and Bryce started boxing. He was doing a good job moving around the ring and throwing punches the same way he did at home in the gym. Halfway through the round, the crowd got excited. They must have seen it coming. That timed punch combination that sent Bryce hurling off the ropes and onto the canvas sent a thundering crash through the room. The crowd was on its feet. A fight night couldn't have started out any better for those fans. They had just witnessed a first round KO between two big cruiserweights in the first fight of the night, and their hometown boy won!

Bryce's knockout gave me a jolt. My mind was racing, *I hope he's ok, I hope he's ok, I hope he's ok.* I went back to the dressing room and waited for Gene. Bryce was with the doctor when Gene walked into the room to wrap my hands. Gene was talking fast, "Man, Bryce got knocked out again. I tell him to do one thing and he does another. He just don't know how to listen."

I just shook my head and sat quietly while Gene wrapped my hands. I tried to focus on the bag drills running through my head. I thought about my kids and what I would say to them if they were ever faced with a challenge as big as the one I was about to face.

I still have time. I don't even have to go out there, was the thought that slowly seeped into my mind when the official walked to the dressing room, checked my hand-wraps, initialed them while he gave me instructions, and told Gene to be out in five minutes. But there wasn't any time left to back out. This was it. I was about to fight in my pro debut. As soon as I put on my first pair of professional boxing gloves, things got real. I could feel my knuckles through the front of that 8oz. glove. Compared to the 14 and 16 ounce ones I had been training in, I felt that my hands could move like lighting in these. Having missed a warmup while watching Bryce, in that last five minutes before my fight, I stood in the middle of the floor in my robe and shadow boxed trying my best to work up a sweat.

"Come on, man!" Gene said as he grabbed his coach's bucket and began walking out the door toward the ring. I followed, keeping my eyes forward, resisting the urge to look back. Hyper-focused, I could see everything around me without even moving my head and I sensed a strange new calmness surging through me. I remembered the Nationals in Augusta, when Brown came into the ring as a confident aggressor. I knew she would be confident of getting a knockout from me. I breathed in deeply through my mouth and out my nose to further calm my nerves. H-u-u-u-u-u-u-mm - W-h-h-h-h-h-h-h, H-u-u-u-u-u-u-mm -W-h-h-h-h-h-h-h … Walking at Gene's pace, I was still dry and cold, but inside the gloves, the palms of my hands were getting sweaty.

The music played loudly as Brown entered the ring and the crowd erupted. I stood still in my corner while Brown bounced around the ring with both arms raised above her head as cocky as ever. She was letting me and anyone who didn't know it that New York was her house and I was just a visitor there. A crowd of butterflies fluttered in the pit of my stomach but I consciously remained expressionless. I tightened my fist within the confines of those new 8oz. gloves and could feel my knuckles stretch the gauze and tape through to the inner lining of the padding. My teeth clamped down onto my mouthpiece as soon as the bell sounded. Immediately, Brown came rushing toward me and landed a cross on the front of my gloves.

I pushed my arms forward and back-peddled my way around the ring moving just in time to miss the overhand, which would have surely taken me out if I got caught by it. That fight had gone from zero-to-sixty within five seconds of the bell. I knew I was off balance and in full defense mode. Running on pure adrenalin, I let my legs carry me, circling from left to right, nose flaring and eyes locked. Brown's bull-like attack had thrown me off guard and when she connected with a flurry of looping punches, I could feel her knuckles land solidly through those thin gloves. It was a new kind of contact for me; like getting hit with bare knuckles.

"Damn! What the hell?" I mouthed frantically through a mouthful of plastic mouth guard. All her punches were landing and I was gassed out from my constant retreat. Worse, I didn't know how to get settled to set up a punch.

The first two minutes were quickly over and I was back in my corner sitting on the stool. Gene wiped my sweat with a towel and squeezed a squirt of water into my mouth.

"Spit!" He ordered. Then he instructed, "You got to move your damn head and get out of the way. Do what you do in the gym, Okay?"

"Okay," I answered and stood back up while he pulled the stool from under me. But inside I was shouting, *What should I do? What should I do?* I just couldn't put my thoughts, punches or anything else together.

The bell rang again, and once again, Brown charged forward swinging nonstop.

The crowd produced a wave of white noise and the volume turned up sharply when she hit me with a hard shot to the top of my temple. I dropped to the canvas instantly.

"1-2-3…" I tuned in the referee's counting and propped myself up on one knee.

Oh hell no! Not today! Get up Lisa! I was barking inside like a platoon leader at a timid recruit.

I caught a glimpse of Brown standing in her corner confident and arrogant. I knew she was certain I wouldn't recover. But I got up and was ready to keep going. The referee asked me if I was okay and wiped both my gloves on the front of his shirt.

"Yes" I said through the mouth guard, stretching my eyes as if just waking up.

The referee called, "Box!" And Brown charged at me, full speed. This time, survival mode overrode my skill level and I landed two one-two combinations straight into the center of her face, instantly stopping her in her tracks. The bell sounded and once again the round was over.

Back in the corner Gene wiped my face with the towel, squirted the water into my mouth and said, "You did good. Now you know what to do. She's short and ain't got no business hitting you like that. Don't let her touch you. Keep that feet moving!"

When I got off the stool this time, I pictured myself back at the gym and remembered what Rock, an old former champ who used to hang around the gym, told me when he learned I would be having my pro debut. He said, "Lisa, just remember one thing if you don't remember nothing else. The jab will set you free." Then he smiled and said it again while he snapped out four or five sharp snapping jabs to let me see that he still had it.

The third round bell sounded and I got to the center of the ring quickly this time. *The jab will set you free — The jab will set you free — The jab will set you free...* I repeated while jabbing nonstop one after another, moving around the ring while I did so. And those jabs were landing! Now I was moving her back. I could see that her 4 foot 11 inch body couldn't get past my long reach.

We were deep into the third round and I was finally getting the hang of it. I was a pro now! I was fighting with 8oz. gloves and no headgear and it felt great. The butterflies had completely left my stomach and now I felt at home in the ring. As my hands got quicker and my confidence grew, I dug way deep down and pulled out a hard right-cross with pinpoint accuracy right down the pike. Brown tumbled down. It happened so fast I was stunned and stood frozen in my tracks until the referee commanded me to a neutral corner. Then he began to count. Soon Brown was back up and then we were back in our corners.

Gene was excited. "That's what I'm talking about! That's what you 'sposed to do! Good! Now go back in there and do it again!"

I was breathing heavily but felt my second wind. I could hear Gene still talking but I couldn't block out my own thoughts. *She's mad now. I'm going to have to really fight her now. The jab will set you free — The jab will set you free...* I went back to my mantra and took a deep breath. *Two more minutes.*

For the first time I felt I could actually win. Brown's level of confidence had tapered down to caution. I had some catching up to do and knew it. Understanding that I was still in her house and needed a knockout to win, I went back into that last round as if the fight had just begun.

25-26-27-28-29... I was counting my punches from start to finish, forcing myself not to stop until the bell rang. Now I was hyper-focused and relentless and when the bell finally rang, I was relieved. Proud to be still standing although Brown won the unanimous decision.

Chapter Twenty

"Fuck this shit! I'm out!" Gene and I had been going back and forth arguing for twenty minutes, and this was my final pronouncement. "Go on then! Leave! See if the fuck I care!" Gene shouted over his shoulder as he sat in his coach's chair facing the ring and refused to look at me as I walked out the door.

As I escaped from Midtown, still pissed, into the five o'clock chaos of 14th street, I swore I would stick to my guns this time; no matter how I felt or what Gene might try to say, I was never going back to let him manage me. Months before, I had promised myself that I would break free the next time we bumped heads. I had never been able to shake off the way he deserted me at my fight against Rose Johnson in Glen Bernie, MD because he was annoyed when my husband showed up. And although I won against Mary Shaida in Atlantic City with Gene as my manager, I felt that I couldn't trust him anymore.

I had planned the leaving part, but had no clue where I would go next. So I started attending just about all the amateur and pro fights in the DC area, met plenty of trainers, learned where all the gyms were, and believed that since I had a fight record now, I could take my pick. Women's boxing was on the rise by then and there had already been two Women's National Championships. Female boxers were the new normal, and hungry boxing trainers had begun looking at women as potential moneymakers. While still training with Gene, I had occasionally trained and sparred in some other gyms, and found encouragement when coaches, trainers and onlookers often complimented my performance and saw potential in me, always adding, "with the right trainer," as a cheap shot at Gene. In those days I always thanked them for the encouragement, but stayed to myself silently demonstrating my loyalty to Gene.

But now Gene and I were done, and I knew I had to find a new camp and take control of my own boxing career. Reminding myself not to repeat old mistakes, I told myself; *From now on, everything is business. I'm gonna let-um-know right off that I ain't tryin' to be nobody's friend. I don't have time for all those fake-ass liars who can't do half the shit they talk about doing for me. Shoot! I'm the one taking the ass whippins' anyway. If I want things to happen for me, I gotta be the one makin'um happen.*

Despite the tough words, the pain of parting from Gene and Midtown Gym would account for a serious ache in my heart for a long time. I knew the way I dealt with that pain could help me in my relentless pursuit of success. And so, the day after I left Gene, I showed up at the Charles Mooney Academy of Boxing dressed and ready to work out. The gym was an old elementary school in the DC suburban community of Rockville, Maryland. The word around town was that he had acquired two or three new girls in his stable who were serious about fighting, and I wanted to check that out. I had only met Mooney once in Glen Bernie when I fought his girl Rose Johnson, and I wasn't sure he'd even remember me.

Many trainers have a tendency to size up potential clients by testing how knowledgeable they are about boxing and then dropping a load on them with a list of meaningless credentials. Many are fast-talking hangers-on trying to pull a buck out of the air and not caring about anything but creating a position for themselves. I've seen it a million times; guys loitering around different gyms, observing real training sessions as they pick up a few boxing terms and then grabbing some poor piece of new meat coming in off the street and trying to demonstrate expertise as a "trainer." The real messed-up part happens when the piece of new meat gets chewed up and spat out. Trainers like this can go on in the business for years, never being more than mediocre at best, but never being exposed as phonies either.

Charles Mooney wasn't that kind of trainer. He knew boxing but never came across as a Mr. Know-it-all. I admired the way he asked other trainers for advice when he wasn't sure about something. Mooney was hitting his fifties but managed to stay in extraordinary shape by participating in the training sessions he gave in the gym. Although he won a silver medal boxing in the bantam weight division in the 1976 Olympics in Montreal, his face showed no obvious signs of past battles and he remained a nice-looking man. Mooney ran his gym like a boot camp. He had learned a set of strategies during 22 years of military service and they were now embedded in his DNA.

When I walked through the door that first day, Mooney looked up from sweeping the ring and showed no surprise. He simply said; "How ya doin', have a seat." I watched him climb out of the ring, as spry as a twenty-year-old.

"Lisa, right? Go ahead and sit down. What's up?"

"I'm looking for a new gym."

"What happened? You not with Gene anymore"?

"Naw, I'm not at Midtown anymore and since I don't live that far from here I figured I'd check you out," I explained, trying to seem casual.

"Oh, Okay." Mooney looked at me and paused awhile. It seemed that he already knew more about what had happened between Gene and me than I was willing to reveal. But without further questions, he reached into a file folder and pulled out a short application and a printed price list. The printed instruction, PAY THE MANAGEMENT BEFORE YOU TRAIN – NO EXCEPTIONS, left no question about Mooney's management style. After reading and signing the agreement, I dug into the deep inner pocket of my gym bag, pulled out two rumpled and grimy twenty-dollar bills and placed them in his outstretched hand. Gene hadn't required this kind of fiscal compliance, but I welcomed Mooney's policy; after all, this time I wasn't there to make friends. Mooney was all business and now I, too, was going to be. He sold everything in his gym from hand-wraps to extra gym time and made no bones about letting everyone know that he wasn't in the business of giving loans or freebies.

Mooney then pointed to a small room in the back of the gym and gave me the option to change there or down at the end of the former elementary school hallway in what had once been a girls' room. After Midtown, I wasn't used to the luxury of such privacy and answered quickly while pulling off my sweatpants, "I'm okay right here. All I have to do is take off my sweats. I've got my workout clothes on underneath."

Compared to Midtown Gym and many of the other gyms I had visited, Mooney's place was state-of-the art. Mainly, it was clean and organized. The space consisted of what had been two connecting school classrooms. On opposite walls where blackboards had once hung, seven-foot high mirrors were mounted along the entire length of each wall. The open space in front of them was perfect for jumping rope, stretching, warm-up exercises and shadowboxing. Beyond that space, six black heavy bags of different weights wrapped at the top and middle with silver duct tape hung from exposed steel beams in the ceiling. And in front of the heavy bags, two double-end-bags were suspended between thick black rubber bungee cords which were attached to D rings on the ceiling beam and on the exposed part of the tiled floor. Three differently-sized speed bags were mounted on the back wall on platforms with professional built-in swivels. These were surrounded by omnipresent motivational wall posters which seemed to shout Mooney's favorite mottos: NEVER GIVE UP and BLOOD – SWEAT – TEARS. In case those didn't send a strong enough message, there were full-body fight photographs of legends like Sugar Ray Robinson, Joe Louis "The Brown Bomber," and Muhammad Ali.

At the center of the gym floor was the biggest attraction of all; a 20'X20' regulation-size boxing ring enclosed by red, white and blue ropes with corner pads and what seemed to me to be a brand-new red canvas cover accented with a black skirt enclosing the lower half of the ring and hanging down to the floor. I was excited about being for the first time in a gym with a real professional boxing ring. It seemed to me that sparring in it would be more like being in a real bout, and would certainly be easier than sparring in the small phone booth-sized ring back at Midtown.

It surprised me that after being away from Midtown for about three weeks I was experiencing the same lost feelings I always felt when leaving a foster home and going to the next. My disagreement with Gene had driven me to leave all the friends I had acquired at the gym in those short nineteen months and I felt the loss in an acutely painful way. When I felt myself becoming sad and thinking too much about my Midtown 'family', I soon realized that I could convert that growing depression into some powerful aggression and bite down even harder while I was training. Within a few weeks, the longing for Midtown began to fade into the background as I felt myself becoming stronger, faster and more confident as a fighter.

U-u-s-s-s-s, "U-u-s-s-s-s, U-u-s-s-s-s-s-s-s… While shadowboxing, I felt with each powerful punch the exhaled streams of air between my tongue and teeth as my lungs emptied with my three-piece combinations. *H-h-h-u-u-u-, H-h-h-u-u-u- H-h-h-u-u-u*... The sounds bursting from my abdomen combined with the pounding of leather-on-leather as my gloves smashed into the slick leather bag while I imagined hitting the faces of the abusers of my youth. One face would disappear like blown dust as another reappeared just in time for me to land the next combo.

W-h-h-i-s-s-p, W-h-h-i-s-s-p, W-h-h-i-s-s-p... As I skipped rope, that sound blazed over my head, then under my feet while my hands remained steady with tension; this intense effort built up such heat that I soon felt like a lion jumping through a ring of fire. I worked nonstop until the sad thoughts of loss and lost time stopped. Then I'd go home, relaxed and blessedly satisfied by the day's efforts.

During normal business hours, the gym was full to capacity with local, middle class, mostly white customers who were eager to get a boxing workout. They paid their money to go through the motions of boxing and avoided having to learn actual technique. For them, it was exciting just to be in a gym where real pros trained and fought on a regular basis. They admired Coach Mooney and knew he had trained the middleweight three-time WBA World Champion, William Joppy, right there in that gym.

Mooney was usually occupied giving mitt work and special attention to his male pros who had upcoming fight dates on the horizon. The female boxers were seldom there during normal gym hours. I had only seen Rose once or twice when she stopped in to observe what was going on and, I assumed, to make sure she wasn't missing out on anything. After Rose's disappointing performance against me in Glen Bernie and Mooney's recent discovery of Keena, a former Olympian with a lot of potential, it seemed that Mooney had put Rose on the back burner.

After a month at Mooney's, I began to notice that Keena was Mooney's favorite. She was an attractive young lady in her mid-twenties who was often on her way out of the gym after training sessions with Mooney just when I was arriving. We spoke to each other in passing but never made an effort to be friendly. She had long thick hair, strikingly deep defined features and a Middle Eastern accent. I noticed that we were about the same weight and both in excellent fight shape. I had heard Mooney describe her to potential new gym clients as "a former Olympian with an extensive background in the martial arts." I told myself that she must be his new ace in the hole. I hadn't received nor asked for any special attention from Coach Mooney since I had been there, but Assistant Coach Diaz — whose 18-year-old son was on a winning streak on the local boxing circuit — often gave me pointers and fixes while he watched me shadowboxing or hitting the heavy-bag. "You need to step into it when jou throwing jou yab," he'd offer while showing me a slow motion example to clarify any confusion caused by his heavy Spanish accent. He was precise in his teaching methods and stood there watching until he could see that I understood before he walked away.

I had grown content with training two to three unsupervised hours every day except Sundays. However, right when the routine began to get a little monotonous and lonely, Coach Mooney yelled out to me as I was at the door to leave. "Lisa, hold up for a minute. Can you be here at 4:00 o'clock tomorrow to spar with Keena? You ain't scared, are you? Ha ha ha!" I was surprised by his request, but composed myself and answered nonchalantly, "Ahh-alright."

"Okay, don't be late! Keena trains early," he called over his shoulder as he walked back over to the young amateur kid he was running drills with on the mitts.

I hadn't sparred since leaving Midtown, but the next day I showed up a half hour early to warm up and shake out the butterflies that had been fluttering in my stomach since yesterday. When I arrived, Coach Mooney and Keena were already in the ring working the mitts. I could tell by their sweat-soaked attire that they had been training for at least an hour. It was just as I had thought; this was not to be an equally beneficial sparring session. Apparently, I was being brought in as a human punching bag for Keena. I knew this was the way things worked at other gyms, where a "B Rated" fighter would be brought in to spar with the expected hopeful to prepare them for their grand entry into their Pro status. But I hadn't expected this to happen here, or to me.

Shocked at my promptness, Mooney stopped in his tracks as soon as I pushed the door open and blurted out, "Hey!" You're early, why ya here so early? I said 4:00."

I smiled and answered, "Hi! I know. I figured I'd take at least fifteen minutes to stretch and warm up before getting in the ring."

Mooney had already turned back to Keena and picked up her training where he had left off. I could tell by the tightness in his face that he didn't appreciate my early arrival. Maybe he didn't want me to catch a glimpse of Keena's awesome skills. This thought pushed my button, and I muttered to myself, *Oooh, It's like that — alright. Then this is how it's gonna be.*

No doubt about it, I felt disrespected. Not by Keena but by Coach Mooney. I guessed she was worth more to him than I was because I wasn't paying him daily personal training money nor had I been to the Olympics, a bond he and Keena had in common.

The butterflies were completely gone by the end of my warm-up. I had coasted through twenty minutes of jumping rope instead of shadowboxing. I didn't want either of them to see me throw a single punch, pump one head fake or slide out of one pocket. I was steaming by now, and psyching myself up: *I ain't nobody's damn sparring partner and by the time this is over they'll wish they never asked me. Oh Hell No! That's not me!* I was thinking about how Gene used to complain about guys leaving his gym only to become sparring partners in somebody else's. And how they were used as stepping-stones for other fighters and never made it past a few local club fights where they would be used as opponents to pad somebody else's record.

"Alright, you ready, Lisa?" Mooney called over to me as I was changing into my white Pony boxing boots. Despite feeling white hot angry, I managed to answer calmly, "Yeah, I'm just putting on my boots."

Then I thought to myself, *I ain't rushing. Fuck that, I'm gonna make 'em wait.*

I took my time undoing and retying both boxing boots. Then I pulled out my long golden yellow Mexican-style hand-wraps and slowly wrapped each hand as if this was an art project. Coach Diaz had arrived by then and walked toward me to ask if I needed help putting on my gloves. Focused, calm and very serious, I gave him both gloves and he loosened the laces on each. One-by-one he firmly pushed them onto my hands until they felt comfortable.

"Do me a favor, Diaz," Coach Mooney said in his buddy voice. "Turn that bell to three-minute rounds with thirty seconds' rest." Normally, rounds for women last two minutes with one minute allotted for rest between them. I knew right away that Mooney had been training Keena at the three-minute rounds level in order to build up her wind and to pace herself throughout the rounds. But it didn't faze me in the least because I had just left Midtown where Gene had us in his 12'X14' foot ring sparring for four and five minutes at a time with thirty second rest intervals. Sometimes Gene even forgot about the bell all together.

There were many advantages to sparring in the regulation-size ring at Mooney's, but the one that made me most confident was the fact that I would be able to move around as much as I wanted and needed to. I would get on my bike and she would have to find me if she wanted to get off her shots. I knew Keena must have some major karate skills to make it to the Olympics twice. And from what I had heard, she had been doing martial arts and kick-boxing since she was a kid. I realized that thinking about Keena and what she could possibly do to me had started up some of those old butterflies again. I didn't want to prove Gene right or let myself down so I just relaxed and thought, *She's flesh and blood just like me. I'll show Mooney that I ain't no-body's sparring partner. I'm not gonna let them play with me...not gonna get in a dog fight with her... probably that's what they want me to do. Gonna make her box me ...yeah, that's my fight.*

By now it was 4:15 and we were both in our corners; Mooney in Keena's and Diaz in mine. I noticed that for Mooney's benefit Coach Diaz downplayed working my corner. But I trusted him and figured there was a good reason. He had been friendly to me from the day I arrived and showed me respect — even admiration — for my boxing skills. Almost every day he'd come close and watch me working. It seemed like he was waiting for an opportunity to help me by correcting my mistakes or perhaps showing me something new.

"Okay, next bell, work!" Coach Mooney demanded in his all-business coach voice. Shining with Vaseline smeared generously over her face, head-gear, and gloves, Keena bounced around in her corner with her hands up in ready position waiting intently for the bell to ring. Mooney seemed relaxed and confident as he rubbed her shoulders and whispered last minute instruc-tions into her ear.

Ding-Ding! The bell sounded and we both stepped to the center of the ring. I leaned forward and extended my right glove for a sportsmanlike shake but Keena ignored the gesture. That did it. My mind was made up: *I'm going to take her out.*

I immediately drove a stiff hard jab to the top of her forehead and saw her head snap back. She was stunned by my quick action. Her loose bounce disappeared and her posture went from a low and guarded boxing stance to a stiffened chin-up stance as if we were about to begin point sparring. She had no technique! I began relentlessly delivering waves of double and triple jabs to Keena's chest, throat and nose. She was on the retreat and moving around the ring desperately trying to get away from my jab. But I kept forging forward using only the jab. Things weren't going the way Coach Mooney wanted them to go, so he began to scream loudly from the corner, giving urgent commands to his Olympian: "*KEENA!* Go over top of her jab with a hard cross! It ain't nothing but a jab, counter it and get out of the way. Do it now! Now!"

But Mooney wasn't feeling the hits she was feeling. I was delivering every jab with pop and power. I wasn't thinking about anything but landing each one solidly and began counting as I delivered them. By the end of the first round, dark drips of Keena's blood were spattered over Mooney's beautiful new red canvas. I stood in the corner for the thirty-second break while Coach Diaz excitedly wiped my face. He made quick work of removing my mouthpiece and squeezing water into my mouth. I swished it around and then spat into the bucket he held. Then I turned back toward the middle of the ring.

Diaz's final words to me were, "Ok — this time mix it up a little more." I nodded yes and rushed back into the center of the ring at a fraction of the first bell chime; Di — !

Keena was looking more confident and better adjusted now and charged forward, throwing a barrage of out-of-sync punches. Her plan to neutralize my success in the first round went out the window when I planted myself in the center of the ring and started cranking that same jab into her face over and over and over.

I remembered Diaz's last words and began to add the right hand, throwing the one-two punch in the same fashion I had thrown the jab in the first round. My gloves were doing all the talking while sweat poured down, sliding off the Vaseline on my face. But I hadn't been thinking of controlling the pace, and soon began to feel tired and worn down. Luckily, before I knew it, the bell rang. Exhausted, I leaned on the rope as Coach Diaz began to prepare me for the next round. Then unexpectedly, Coach Mooney sounded off, "Okay, that's it! We're done for the day." I glanced over and saw him taking out Keena's mouthpiece and removing her headgear. It was a relief; I was glad the fight was over and felt certain Keena was too. Coach Diaz was not only amazed but amused and told me I had "demolished Keena." Before I left the gym that day, I knew he was quietly spreading word of my victory by giving his son and the other pros a play-by-play of what had occurred in the ring. He seemed as proud of me as if I were his fighter, and he expressed his belief that I would be a champion someday. I was happy that word would go out that I had not been willing to be Keena's punching bag. However, I was not at all proud of my overall performance. She hadn't landed a single solid shot on me but I still felt beat down physically. As much as I tried to play it off, that tired feeling exposed my vulnerability. One round more, and she might have beat me just on pure stamina.

After the sparring session, I grabbed my things and left quickly. Physically and mentally exhausted, I drove home slowly, going over and over the day's events in my mind: *What's wrong with me? Only two rounds and I could barely last. Can't be getting tired like that! What if I had to go another round? Awww- man, I probably woulda died. Why did I let Mooney make me so mad? Wonder if he's pissed at me for treating his girl like that. How will he act tomorrow? Maybe I shouldn't even go back. Damn! I'm not gonna crawl back to Midtown. Na-a-w... if I go back I'll be stuck there forever. I hate boring ass running but I need to start a running program tomorrow. No more jumping rope longer as a way to avoid running. No way around it. Gotta start running tomorrow!*

I showed up ready to train the next day, but I had run two miles that morning. After that fight with Keena, training at Mooney's would never be the same. In the coming days, I saw that I was being recognized as a proven threat, even in Mooney's eyes. But more importantly, I knew I was adopting a new attitude which would suit me much better than the one that caused me to fight so viciously. I didn't like the person I was that day in the ring. Keena had paid the price for all the anger and resentment I had built up about Gene and boxing in general, and for all the negative mindset I harbored from my past. I knew I had become an angry person, and that was not what I wanted. Things in boxing hadn't been going the way I thought they should and as a result, I directed a lot of resentment and anger toward women like Rose and Keena. I had assumed that they were getting all the breaks that life could hand them while I was getting nothing.

In boxing, you burn more energy when you are emotional. In my case, hotheaded. I knew that was part of the reason I burned out so quickly while fighting Keena. I wanted to see blood and was running on pure anger without thinking. I had come into boxing a positive and enthusiastic learner. Out of pure kindness Tyrone had helped me get started, and I had been excited and grateful. I liked that old Lisa a lot better than the angry, resentful me who was in the ring with Keena. I wanted to rediscover the old, positive me.

After the Keena sparring match, I was being treated as a professional at the gym and Coach Mooney began to give me the same attention he gave his male pros. I imagined that he seemed to understand why I had put up such a fight against Keena and respected me for that. And to my surprise, Keena warmed up to me after our fight and we became friendly teammates. Along with the personal sessions she received from Mooney, she added a few days of regular gym time to her schedule so we could train together. We were never to spar against one another again. Things were starting to feel just how I had imagined they would.

I was thrilled when Coach Mooney started working with me on the focus mitts. His attention to this part of my development reminded me of the night back in Glen Bernie at Michael's Eighth Avenue when I got a taste of the focus mitts while working with Doc, Reggie Green's trainer. Before that, I had only briefly used focus mitts at Midtown, when a trainer named Greg introduced them to me. When Gene saw Greg and me, he had flown into one of his jealous fits, shouting: "Stop! Stop right now! Lisa get out of the ring and go do something else. I ain't ask you to do that, Greg. Don't mess with her no more, either! All y'all niggas try to do is come in here and mess with my fighters. Leave her alone. Next thing I know, you be tryin' to take her outta here. You think I'm stupid, don't you? You crazy. Just stay away from her!"

For some reason, Gene prided himself on being able to train his fighters without the use of the mitts, but I always felt at a real disadvantage without them. Gene was very good at giving his fighters the right kind of emotional attention, but when it came to actually working with them physically, those days had long gone for him.

After I worked with Coach Mooney for a few months on the mitts, underwent sparring sessions with the guys, and had many of my bad habits corrected, I was given a big opportunity. Coach Mooney came to me and said: "Lisa, I got a call from the promoter yesterday to see if I had any females ready to take a fight. I said yes. Do you want to take it? It's in two weeks — you think you can be ready by then? Or are you scared?"

I wanted him to call right away to make sure the chance didn't get away. "Yeah, of course I'll take it. In Vegas, too? Yes, call them and tell them I said yes!" I was so excited that I didn't even bother to ask what the money would be. After all, money wasn't my goal, getting the fight was! I was going to realize my dream of boxing like those women I had seen on TV only two years ago!

Mooney was all about business and reached into his file drawer to pull out his management contract which outlined his fight fees. I signed it immediately and then Mooney made the return call to Vegas. For the next two weeks, the training got tougher. I stepped up my roadwork to three miles a day and tacked on another hour for strength training. Grueling sparring sessions continued until two days before we left for Las Vegas. I had been going toe-to-toe with the guys, giving just as good as I had been getting.

But one of those sparring sessions got heated after one of the guys — I didn't even know his name — couldn't handle receiving what I was putting out, mainly because it happened in front of a small audience of men. Embarrassed from a combination I landed that gave him a lump over his left eye and deep red bruise underneath, he came after me with a vengeance and gave me a hard shot square in the nose. I dropped to the canvas briefly, then quickly recovered. But that finished what would be the last round before the trip. His punch had broken my nose.

Along with the broken nose came unaccustomed sinus pressure and constant headaches which I hoped would go away before the fight. I didn't want anything to interfere with Vegas. There was no way I wanted this amazing opportunity to pass me by, so I ignored the new problems and went on with the business of ordering new boxing attire and preparing for the trip.

The early morning five-hour nonstop flight from DC to Las Vegas was uncomfortable and I only drifted in and out of sleep. This was a worry because I hadn't gotten much sleep the previous two nights because the nostrils of my busted nose had to take turns switching from one side to the other — one draining, the other stuffing up and vice versa. The swelling wasn't that noticeable from the outside, but the pressure on the inside made my head feel inflated and tight; a big, red hot air balloon! Not feeling well made me think of Gene. He would have noticed and taken care of me in his own little overly-protective way. It was the first time I was traveling to a fight without him and my feelings were definitely mixed. Coach Mooney was professional, organized and never out of the loop with fight protocol. He had taken care of everything. Alex — the male pro scheduled to fight a ten-rounder on the same card as me — felt as I did that there was nothing to worry about under Mooney's management. Everything went smooth as silk and I knew my corner would be tight at fight time. All I had to do was focus on the fight. The only thing Mooney completely missed — or chose to overlook — was my newly acquired nasal twang and watering eyes from the broken nose.

Despite the reassuring sense that everything was under control, I missed the comfort Gene brought with him despite the sloppiness of everything else he touched. We used to joke around, jone on each other, and talk about everything under the sun. The loneliness I felt without Gene was real. Occasionally Coach Mooney or Alex would turn in their seats and ask politely if I was all right. I would nod yes, but really, things were just okay.

Chapter Twenty-One

I had a string of coaches during my career. Not as many coaches as foster mothers, but I was churning through them pretty fast before I retired from the ring. I had already learned from my foster experience that I had to be in charge of my own life and not rely on a paid stranger to nurture and protect me. And then, as an aspiring world champion, I had to learn that I was probably not going to find a coach that would always have my best interest at heart. As with the foster situation, I learned pretty quickly that I needed to depend on myself above all. But, still, I was always hopefully looking for coaches who had my back and could keep me safe.

Keeping a boxer safe means a lot of things. Like finding opponents who aren't twice your boxer's size, and carrying around a reputation for being vicious and underhanded. Or teaching your boxers everything you know to protect themselves in the ring. Gene was not the best coach for teaching me how to box so I could protect myself. But he was the best for nurturing me because he really cared about me as a person. But because of his limitations as my trainer, I had to leave him if I wanted to be a winner in the boxing world. But I never stopped missing the closeness we had.

Coach Hinton was number three in a string of coaches along my way to a title. He got me into the Ada Velez four-rounder in July of 2001. Trouble was, the fight was in her hometown and in her gym; two things that should have raised a warning flag long before the bell summoned us into the center of the ring to fight. I was still naïve then and didn't know how to protect myself from bad decisions, so I depended on my coach to handle my arrangements. Velez was fighting out of a training center in Davie, Florida and that should have been enough to get Coach Hinton to think twice about signing me up for this four-rounder. Fighters from that gym were known for head-butting tactics aimed at cutting up an opponent's face. I had learned enough up to that point that no bout, especially a four-rounder, was worth getting my face all cut up. So it was my mistake that I didn't refuse the fight when Hinton first told me about it. I guess part of the learning curve for me was that sometimes I had to see or experience something to understand how it was a problem.

I started learning fast when I walked into the dressing room with all the other visiting contenders and got a look at all the cuts, gashes, blood soaked ice packs and towels on the faces of fighters brought in to fight at this gym. This — along with that brand-new letter L on their fight stats — seemed like a good reason to avoid fighting here. When I was offered a pair of still warm and newly bloodied gloves to fight in, Coach Hinton accepted them as if they were a brand-spanking-new pair, but I refused to touch them. The officials reluctantly gave in and brought me a dry, unbloodied pair to lose in. By then I had figured out that this was a crazy situation. I had eagerly agreed to the fight on only a week's notice and without knowing anything about unstop-pable Velez. But I was in shape and ecstatic about finally fighting again after eight whole months. I thought I had asked all the right questions and knew that having a bout only one day after my arrival probably was not a good idea. I also knew the venue was in Ada's hometown, but I looked at the bright side of it all. I even agreed — as I always had — to the chicken feed purse of $500 with 1/3 to Coach Hinton. For me, it seemed that a bout like this would help me get closer to the title. When doubts arose, I reminded myself once again of what an old trainer once said to me, "If winning a world title was easy, everybody would have one."

Among the many lessons I learned that day was that sometimes boxing goes beyond fighting the person in front of you. I was up against Ada, her corner, the referee, my own corner and the little red devil sitting on my shoulder called Lisa's Ego, that kept whispering in my ear: *butt her back, get mad, knee her in the ass, just go the hell off and bring the streets into the ring, show her you ain't no punk bitch!*

At the end of the first round I went back to my corner and said right out to Coach Hinton, "This girl has tied me up and butted me four times in a row. Can you say something to the referee? He's ignoring me when I signal him about that!" Hinton didn't react, so I continued, "I know he sees what's going on. I feel like I'm being hit in the face with fastballs after she butts me and every time it happens I get woozy. *It's a dirty fight*, so please say something when it happens again!"

"I know, I got it. You just box that girl and don't worry about the referee!" Coach Hinton's answer was enough to encourage me to try to pull myself together for the next round. I knew I was down one round. When the bell rang, I moved right in and popped out my first two jabs. But Velez was unfazed and rushed in head-down, holding, pushing, and pulling me in close like an animal trapping its prey and setting it up for the kill. As I frantically tried to pull away from her grip, three more head butts like the ones in the first round crashed into my temple, forehead, and brow.

Tears streamed from the corners of my eyes, not because I was crying, but because the butting was taking a toll on my head. From my corner Coach Hinton was screaming, "Get out of there! Get her off you! What are you doing?" I was trying to snatch my arms loose from her vise-like holding technique, and was pulling so hard that it felt like I would rip my arms from their sockets. By now I knew for sure there would be no help coming from my corner or anywhere else. The referee never called a break in the fighting or gave a warning, or acknowledged my signs that I needed help. So instead of trying to get help, I jerked around quickly and managed to set myself free. With my back to Velez and the referee, I waved good-bye and casually walked to my corner. Hinton leaped onto the steps and with clinched teeth growled, "What the fuck do you think you are doing"?

"I'm done," I said with as straight a face as I could muster, trying not to show anger, pain or sadness. Then I stood in the corner, hands on the top rope. Everything in me wanted to climb through the ropes and out of the ring, freeing myself from further involvement in this fiasco. Instead, I reminded myself that this kind of thing comes with the sport I had chosen to dedicate myself to. So, as the crowd roared for Velez as the winner, I held my head up and smiled, shook her hand and then turned back to the audience flashing my best defiant smile. I was taking care of myself now.

As I stepped out of the ring and walked down the three steps to the gymnasium floor, Coach Hinton was yelling at me: "I can't believe this shit! You gonna just quit? You are a quitter now! Yes, you are a quitter!"

As he shouted, I kept my head up and walked past him calmly saying, "I wouldn't have had to stop fighting if my coach had protected me from being in a fight like this." I walked to the dressing room with my right hand on what were now two large raised lumps forming over my right eye, praying that they would not open up and bleed, leaving scars. I was proud of myself that I had refused to resort to dirty tactics like Velez's in an attempt to prove I could make it to the end of a bout that I had absolutely no chance of winning.

The way I carried myself as a professional seemed to discourage shady characters from approaching me. This was a skill I had developed during my foster childhood and I had honed it to a fine art. However, there were still those out there so loaded with the gift of gab that they could smooth talk their way into my trust without raising a red flag. That's what happened when I met Brian, after I'd made the decision to take personal control of my career. Of course, it was a controversial decision on my part, and I received messages from promoters indicating that they didn't want to negotiate or even talk with me directly. Promoters claim that boxers who put themselves too high on a pedestal this way are too difficult to deal with. The truth was, it was in their interest to deal with a hungry opportunity-seeking trainer or a shiftless manager eager to make a side deal. Business could be handled much more cheaply and more swiftly with these people speaking for their fighter.

Brian was a middle-aged, plain-looking white man with an amazing telephone voice. When I met him, he had just moved from North Carolina and landed a job as a national radio news anchor based in DC. He was intrigued with me because I was a female running her own boxing gym and working as a personal trainer at a high-end social club while in hot pursuit of becoming a world champion boxer. I was instantly drawn to his voice and felt he would be a perfect mouthpiece for me when it came to speaking by phone to promoters. Though at the time Brian knew nothing about the business of boxing, I wanted to use his voice to get what I needed.

When promoters called my gym inquiring about my availability to fight, I handed Brian the phone and listened to their conversations on the speaker. That way I could tell him what I would accept and the deal could be made or refused accordingly. It worked just as I had imagined it would. The promoter would explain his offer to Brian and I'd know right away what was being left off the table, and then I could ask all necessary follow-up questions through Brian, my new professional-sounding white male voice. By paying close attention to what other fighters got in previous match ups, I had learned to ask for the same deals and amenities my opponents were getting. This system worked well when we set up a bout with a tough Philly slugger, Lakeysha "The Total Package" Williams at the Big Kahuna resort in Wilmington, Delaware.

I had been training and sparring for a month in my own facility with World Champion Boxer Mark "Too Sharpe" Johnson under the tutelage of his father Hamm. That crew had a bite-down, gritty, get-it-while-you-can way of training, which I enjoyed and adjusted to immediately out of sheer ambition. For them the arrangement was all about having a place to privately train Mark, using Black, their mitt-man; Reddz, their sparring partner; and Too Sharp's brother James who did a little of everything including sparring. I hoped the arrangement would give me an opportunity to be around and get experience from a coach and boxer who had already made it to world championship status. I badly wanted their experience to rub off on me. I was still hearing Mrs. Clark's advice from the Independent Living days: "Lisa, you've got to be around the people you most want to be like if you want to be successful." And I saw myself becoming a successful world champion.

The arrangement was a good fit all the way to the fight with Lakeysha Williams. Hamm Johnson and Tyrone worked in my corner and Mark "Too Sharp" Johnson and his whole entourage were there in my opponent's backyard to cheer me to victory. It was the closest to a hometown reception I would ever get in an away venue.

After my successful fight against Lakeysha, I began to trust Brian even more and we became friends. I had seen how he worked tirelessly to secure the contract for what would become the title fight of my lifetime. I was walking on air, thinking; *finally things are coming together*. Even a well-known local promoter named Barrington "Bo" Scott took interest in me when he heard from a friend that I would be boxing for a world title.

Bo was a big, charismatic pretty boy who strutted right into my gym and told me without any doubt what he could do for me; "Lisa, you have been right here in our city and no one has ever heard of you, not even me, and I know *everybody*. You are the real deal and people should know who you are. I can help you!"

I didn't know what to think. Bo saw me perk up and continued; "I just want to be a part of helping you get your name out there. And now that I've seen you work out and checked out that fight footage of you, I know you're going to be a champion." In a matter of a few months, through Bo, I had a small entourage which included Yvonne, who took on some personal relations and management; Mike, a young talented photographer and graphic designer who laid out everything from tees to banners; and Bo himself who had connections with everyone from the Mayor of DC to Professional World Champion Boxer Jacqui "Sista" Frazier-Lyde who came on board and supported me. I was in full training mode and for once I felt good because I didn't have to think about anything but boxing. My business was running smoothly and things felt natural.

Reddz, Too Sharp's sparring partner, even got bit by the Too Fierce bug. He had grown tired of just being a sparring partner and asked me if he could stick around my gym helping with the inner-workings at Too Fierce Boxing & Fitness. I felt that God was providing me with all the people I needed in my life at just the right moment.

But eventually, Hamm and the Johnson crew moved on and I was once again without a trainer. I had been sparring and training with Reddz and Mark for an entire month so I felt I knew Reddz well enough. He had an eight-year-old daughter who he picked up from school on most days and brought to the gym with him. I watched him with her and thought; *I like seeing a young black brother taking full responsibility for his daughter.* I asked Reddz to be my trainer and once again, I had a complete team including Brian, my trusted manager, which brings us back to the championship fight with Kathy "Shake 'em Down" Williams, a tough police officer from Thunder Bay, Canada who was a real shoo-in for the title. This is the fight in which I won the title and the belt I had always wanted.

Because I had three months to train, I had time to review Kathy's tapes and was able to get physically and mentally ready to fight her. I had a team in place, and I was able to go to the venue several days before the fight and get comfortable. I had no jitters and didn't get sick the night before. I was so well prepared that I had my nerves under control. I didn't fear getting hurt by Kathy, even though she had far more experience, and I knew I was ready. I was the underdog, but the bout was in my country and she is from Canada, which gave me an advantage. She was the previous titleholder and needed to regain the title by winning this bout. The odds were 13 to 1 against me. Not to be undersold is the fact that I was a black fighter taking on a white woman in the Deep South. None of that bothered me.

The night of the bout, the fight doctor came into the dressing room looking for me. I was sitting around in my sweats, relaxing after a workout and he came in and asked for me in a thick Southern accent. I raised my hand saying, "I'm over here." He looked all surprised and said, "Oh my god, you look like an ice skater! You don't look like a fighter. You sure you want to get into this fight?" I laughed, but Reddz started grumbling, "Whatsamatta witchu? She IS a fighter!" I guess I looked too demure to be believable. It was an all-female card that night and everyone was considered good. Kathy seemed to be well-known to the crowd. I suspect that her rather tough look made them assume she would beat me.

I was focused that night, and when we all piled into the limo to go to the venue, I was so quiet the guys were asking me if I was okay. That worried me a bit because I had never felt this relaxed going into a fight. I wondered if feeling calm was a bad sign. But there is something about the walk to the ring that never fails to get the adrenalin going. When you walk up those steps and climb through the ropes, for that moment it is like your first fight all over again! And that is how I felt.

I knew that the crowd thought Kathy would kill me in the fight. They had good reason. I had watched her tapes and knew she could hurt people. But I told myself that she couldn't touch me with my jab going right. My whole fight strategy was to keep that jab working all the time and to throw flurries while working her with the jab. If it was a double jab, I wanted to finish off with a right cross and a hook.

That really worked in the first round. Kathy came out fast, straight to me. She was trying to go through all her fancy moves, suck me in and then rush me, letting me know that she was going to win the title again in one round. But I was not having it. I sucked her in while she was trying to get me up against the ropes and put me away. I let her come to me and backed off, using only light jabs, letting her dominate, and when she got me to the ropes, I threw a combination and then a lead right hand. She ran right into it and went down just like that. After she got dropped so quickly and with such a hard punch, she just seemed to unravel.

In the second round, Kathy was slower and very reluctant to come in as quickly as she did in the first. I was taking over the aggressor role, but taking my time and just trying to concentrate on making good hard shots. I knew what a solid puncher Kathy could be and was trying hard not to get hit. She wasn't big, but she had a lot of leverage. She and I were very well matched in that way.

Third round, I was dead tired and thinking that I was going to crump. I knew Reddz would be all over me in the corner but I also knew that if I could hold on, I would get warmed up and get that important second wind. Somehow I was able to psych myself up and by the fourth round I did have my second wind. Now that I was warmed up, it was all about me using my legs right and throwing the punches properly. I began to step it up and put the press on Kathy. I couldn't really see out of my left eye because I had caught a tough punch in practice a day before the fight and that eye had filled up with floaters and messed up my vision. But that punch had taught me to keep my left hand up during the whole fight, something that I often had not remembered to do! In the fifth round I kept up the barrage, looking for ways to wear down the Canadian.

After several more rounds, I wasn't even tired. I had trained well and was very fit. Before the fight I had had a dream that I was going to knock Kathy out in the 6th round. During that round, I started rushing to get the KO I had imagined, but she wasn't going down and was moving around the ring trying to keep out of my way, so I couldn't knock her out. By now Kathy had a big nosebleed which wouldn't stop and her eye and nose looked like chicken liver.

When my dream prediction didn't happen, I slowed down a bit and coasted, taking more time in the next two rounds. Then in the 9th round, she was trying to jab and get into me with her right hand. Now I was hitting her body more and noticed she was slowing down. I thought about my dream and said to myself, OH, that wasn't a 6, it was a 9! I'm gonna knock her out in the ninth! I hit her a couple of times and she started back peddling. I was going forward and hit her hard with a jab, then followed that with a solid right. I followed that with two solid hooks and Kathy went down hard. The ref gave her the count and saw that she was finished. The championship fight was over, the cherished belt mine!

Kathy was a real boxer and I liked that. Up to that time, I often had to fight brawlers. But Kathy was a boxer, quick and slick. I enjoyed being evenly matched with her and was extremely proud to have beaten her for the championship. Later, when I got back to DC, Lamont Peterson's trainer, Barry Hunter, looked at my tapes and said, "Lisa, you fought the perfect fight."

After the championship fight with Kathy, things suddenly changed. Brian began to see himself as he thought everyone else saw him; the great brain behind the success of Lisa "Too Fierce" Foster's rising career. He started to freelance as my promoter without bothering to tell me what he was doing. After I signed the contract to go against Kathy Williams for the IFBA Junior Featherweight title, he had secretly worked out an arrangement with the promoters of Daisy "The Lady" Lang of Germany in what would be a shot at two of her title belts. To a person who knows little about the business of boxing, this might sound as if Brian had presented me with the opportunity of a lifetime. But he knew that this deal was not going to fly well with me because he waited until less than a month away from the event to tell me about the contract he had signed on my behalf. Although I was still in good shape after having only taken a few weeks off training after winning the title, I was completely unprepared for a trip abroad. First of all, I didn't have a passport. Then, I didn't have a trainer. Reddz was furious at Brian and said he wouldn't have anything do with 'The Germany Fight,' advising me not to accept it either. Not only had Brian betrayed my trust, he had just negotiated the worst deal of my boxing career. I would have to apply for an emergency passport right away and pray it would get to me in time. And I would have a mere three weeks to physically and mentally prepare for another 10-round championship bout against a champion I had never seen and without any help from Reddz. I knew how easily a boxer could be at the top of the world one minute and blacklisted the very next and I was worried this could happen to me.

On September 14, 2002, I sat alone onboard an international flight heading to Hamburg, Germany. Physically I was sculpted and strong but, somewhere within myself I had neatly packed away all traces of my surging emotions. Reclined fully, the moderately comfortable economy seat provided me just enough comfort to safely close my eyes and think. I had not been out of the country since my days in the Navy. This time it wouldn't be a six-month cruise, it was an overnight flight to Europe. I hadn't seen nor heard from Brian for a week before the trip although I had tried to reach him. I would be lying if I said I didn't feel abandoned and betrayed. Those were not good emotions for a fighter about to enter the ring for a championship. I told myself I would have to get over it. I was my sole representation for this fight. At least this time I knew what I didn't know.

At least I had with me a new boxing outfit in khaki with red trim which I had designed myself. Oddly, that made me feel some small measure of control. I smiled at the thought that I had brought a matching corner man's jacket with me but had no idea who could be my corner man. At least my corner won't look raggedy, I thought. I tried to focus on some of the things that were going right. The promotion company in Germany was a class act when it came to hosting me and made sure there was a driver waiting for me at the airport. The expression on his face registered shock that I was alone but he quickly moved to carry my things and usher me to the car. It must have been hard for him to imagine that a fighter had arrived in the country on her own, soon to go ten rounds. I had tried to settle my nerves during the drive, but as soon as I arrived at the hotel, the fight promoter met me with an hour-by-hour schedule of events that I was expected to attend. I was exhausted after the long flight and felt overwhelmed at learning that in less than three hours, I would have to step on the scale for the official weigh-in. As it turned out, this took place in a big factory warehouse where the German workers gathered around to cheer loudly for their hometown favorite.

For the first time in my career I weighed in at six pounds overweight! I chalked this up to drinking too much water and juice in an attempt to stay hydrated on the flight. Whatever the cause, I forced myself to remain calm and focused on trying to lose the six pounds quickly. I started jumping rope, taking short walking breaks in an area where boxers were working with their trainers and managers. As I walked around, I heard a group speaking English. I saw it was a group of black men, and my heart started to pound. I knew the trainer! I had trained with him for several weeks at the Sugar Ray Leonard Gym alongside Coach Hinton. He was Pepe Correa. I walked over to him, not even caring if I seemed overly excited and happy to see him.

Pepe answered my greeting, "Hey girl! What are you doing all the way over here in Germany?" We both laughed.

"The same thing y'all doing over here." I joked. "I'm fighting in the co-main event."

"Oh yeah? Well, we're the main event! You fight right before us." Pepe answered back.

Pepe introduced his fighter along with the rest of the guys within the group, "Oh, by the way guys, this is Lisa "Too Fierce" Foster and this sister right here can *fight!*"

I asked Pepe if could I speak to him in private. He excused himself and we walked the rest of the way around the room. "Pepe, there's a long story to how I ended up over here so I'm not even going to go there. The important thing is, I need a corner man for my fight. I'll pay you what you want if you will work my corner for me."

"Lisa, don't worry about a thing. I got your back. I know your style and I know you can fight. I'll be happy to work your corner. It's perfect because you go on right before my guy so I will be out there anyway."

I felt instant relief as he ended the conversation with, "Okay Lisa, see you at the show! Everything is going to be all right."

"Thank you God," I mouthed as I went back to the task of shedding the pounds. Now I was jumping harder and faster and with more enthusiasm to get rid of that unwanted weight.

Later, when I stepped back on the scale the second time and the weight master announced, "Foster weighs in at 8.7 stone," I held my breath until everyone in the warehouse began to applaud. I was exactly 122 pounds and the fight was officially on. Now I could go back to the hotel and get some rest.

Brian suddenly showed up in Germany, and although our relationship was badly strained, I was glad to have someone with me finally and we kept up the appearance of being fighter and manager, although that deal was shattered. Before the fight, we were driven to the venue together, and although it was quite early, I saw that the place was already filling up with Daisy's German fans. Oddly, I felt the pressure begin to release and I started to focus on the fight ahead of me. I had seen Daisy twice, once for the weigh-in and once for the press conference, and I knew at least what she looked like. But I hadn't seen any fight footage and had no idea what kind of fighter she was.

When it was time to enter the arena, I walked out of the dressing room into the smoke-filled venue accompanied by music the Germans had selected for me. It was kind of a soft American rock number, but I went with it, jogging slowly in time to the music. Daisy's entrance was to a more hardcore rock and roll music which seemed to me kind of like music from *Mad Max*. Pepe was hyped up and started working to get me hyped too. He was enthusiastic because he had seen me spar before and erroneously thought I had been in Germany long enough to be rested and comfortable. He gave me a pep talk in the language of a motivational speaker. I responded eagerly because I knew that he was experienced and capable, having worked with big name fighters. I was psyched, but still, there was that jet-lagged, tired feeling that wouldn't go away.

Pepe wanted me to use my speed to the best advantage and before the first round bell sounded, gave me my instructions. "I want you to go in there and feel her out. Be first. Stay out of her range using your long jabs," he said.

Daisy and I touched gloves and moved into our starting positions. The floor of the ring felt strangely bouncy to me and made my legs feel kind of rubbery. I liked that at first because it went perfectly with my style of boxing; staying on my bike and moving all the time. I was jabbing and moving and managed to stay out of danger. In fact, I don't remember getting hit once during that round. When the bell rang and I returned to my corner, Pepe was extra excited. "You're doing good! I want you to keep that jab in her face! Back her up. Don't rush! You'll see it." Then he wiped my face and shoulders. I was already up off my stool and waiting to get back in the ring when the bell sounded. I was feeling good, mainly because I felt well taken care of.

In the second round, Daisy was moving better, causing me to have to go after her even harder than before. The room was oddly silent and I could hear every word Pepe yelled out to me. "Double up that jab, drop that right hand right down the pike!" I doubled up the jab and then even tripled it a few times. But I was waiting for the exact moment I could get a piece of her with my right hand, the power side. I was going too hard and fast and knew that if I missed her completely it would drain me of some of that much-needed energy. Then I heard Pepe shout, "NOW, Lisa, NOW! Just try it!" I felt I wasn't in the right position but went for it anyway. My glove landed right on the bridge of her nose. "There you go, Lisa! Do it again! Do it again! This time I followed it with a left hook. The crowd sighed in disappointment. They didn't have any reason to cheer for their girl. The round was over.

My legs felt heavy in the third round. The bouncy floor was taking its toll. I needed to slow down and cut off the ring. I needed the six pounds back and about a week's worth of sleep. I should have gotten my second wind by now.

During the next three rounds, Daisy started to land some punches because I was still feeling worn out. The fact that she was finally landing some punches woke up the German audience which had been so oddly silent up until then. They began to cheer her every move, and after each round they clapped politely. By the end of the sixth round, I was determined to get through the tiredness and ignored the voice inside me that was telling me I could lose this fight.

Coming into the seventh round, I started to feel more energized, and Pepe was encouraging me, helping me feel more lively. He told me, "Lisa, you have six more minutes to fight. YOU GOT THIS!" That helped me be more positive about what was left of the fight. Thinking in minutes was a better way to think than in rounds. He told me I had won half of the fight already. But I knew that because we were in Germany, Daisy's hometown, the only way I could win was with a knockout. A decision would go her way no matter what. Pepe said, "You can tell that you are winning when the crowd is this quiet." I told him, "I can't even feel it when she hits me!" He replied, "There's nothing in her punches. But you betta believe she's feeling yours!" I knew I could beat her in the US no matter what, but I understood what the situation was.

In the last three rounds, I stayed with my basics and moved Daisy around. The crowd stayed pretty quiet throughout. Daisy was ramping up her performance, but at the end of the fight, her face was all busted up. Her nose looked broken and she was holding an icepack over one eye.

Before the winner was to be announced, Pepe told me, "If they don't steal it from you, you got this one!" When the announcer called Daisy the winner and she was handed the two championship belts, it seemed to me that she was jumping around and cheering out of sheer surprise. I could tell that she knew she had lost. We hugged and she was handed the microphone. In the US, both fighters are interviewed, but this was not the case in Germany. The crowd cheered wildly for Daisy, but once out of the ring, I felt really good about myself. Later, the officials and promoters in Germany were very complimentary and said they'd like me to fight again there. I was pleased about that and knew that my being a good sport had helped. In the long run, this was one of my favorite fights, along with the championship I won against Kathy Williams. That fight in Germany had tested my ability to be independent and self-sufficient. It wasn't easy to go there alone without a corner or a manager. I thought, *if I did that, I can do anything.*

Chapter Twenty-Two

It was a week before Thanksgiving 2014. I had made the first of what would be several trips to our Florida home, joining my husband Neil who had taken the auto train a few weeks earlier to deliver the car and open the house for the season. The temperature had just begun to drop below freezing in DC and I was happy to be getting off the plane into the 70-degree weather of southwest Florida. I was relaxed and without the anxiety I had in the past of worrying about my children back in DC. My son Gerald had graduated from Norwich University the previous winter and my daughter Taylor was doing well in her third year at Temple University in Philadelphia.

This trip was to be only two weeks long so I decided not to play any competitive golf or tennis this time. I was going to just relax and lounge on the patio next to the shimmering Florida waters. This would be precious me time before the holidays kicked in and I would return to DC. I always insisted on going back for the holidays and spending time with family and friends.

One afternoon my cell phone buzzed and without looking at the caller ID I reached down and picked it up.

"Hello?"

"Ahhhhh-Lisa?" I knew immediately it was my birth mother.

"Yes, it's Lisa, what's up?" I drained down to a dull monotone. It wasn't just the voice on the phone that gave her away, it was that annoying way she always had of skipping the hello and starting right in with that "Ahhhhh-Lisa" thing.

She got right down to business. "Oh, okay, I want to come over to your house for Thanksgiving dinner."

Damn! Here we go with this again, I thought as I gazed toward the water, feeling annoyed. Not knowing quite what to say, I repeated her request in order to buy time.

"Oh, okay, you want to come to my house for Thanksgiving dinner."

After a short pause, came the reply, "Yes."

"Alright, you are welcome to come," I exhaled, a bit surprised at my response.

Then, without dropping a beat, she said, "Can you pick me up?"

"I felt my attitude going south and told her with a hint of sarcasm, "No, I won't be able to pick you up because I will be busy cooking and receiving visitors."

After a very long pause, she answered, "Okay."

"But if you need a ride to my house you can take a taxi and I will pay for it," I offered, trying to remove the irritation from my voice.

"I don't take taxies," she replied gracelessly.

"If you don't want to take a taxi by yourself maybe you can get one with Anthony or Winston."

Here it was again, that superior tone, "No, I said I don't take taxies."

"Okay then," I replied without emotion, and on that note, she hung up.

It was unusual for me to get a call from her asking for such a major thing as an invitation to Thanksgiving dinner, but it wasn't all that unusual for her to call randomly to ask for things. I was often blindsided by those calls in the past and surprised by how much they upset and angered me. They often left me walking around the house talking to myself, trying to make sense of her actions. This day was no exception.

What kind of shit was that? She didn't even say hello. Just started talking. Just went right into her side of the conversation. And what the hell is that, "Ahhhhh, Lisa" shit? Doesn't she know how to say hello like an adult? Damn, I can't understand her to save my life. Then she's got the nerve to ask me for something like we've been talking every day and are even friendly!

It had always been clear to me that she called only when she wanted a ride somewhere or wanted me to buy her something. And I knew she felt she was entitled to make demands because she was The Mother. Once, she asked me to start sending her $100 a month and I agreed to do it. But one month she called and told me the money was late! At the time, I thought: *Throughout my entire life that woman never even gave me a birthday card and now she's telling me I'm late with her gift money!* That was the day I stopped allowing her to manipulate her way into getting privileges from me that I did not feel she deserved. And I no longer took phone calls from her when I saw her name show up on caller ID. But she was wily. When she realized that I had stopped answering, she began blocking her number. One day I picked up and there it was again; her voice on the other end saying, "A-h-h-h-h-h, Lisa? "Can you take me to the store?" I asked her why she called on a blocked number. Like everything else in her life, she denied any knowledge of her intentions saying, "Oh, I didn't know it was blocked." I congratulated myself when I let this pass, telling myself, *Good, I didn't let her get to me this time.*

Later I asked Jeff, "Does she call you and ask for stuff without even acknowledging your existence?" Knowing my sensitivity about the whole subject, Jeff just kept quiet and continued to listen in his understanding way, while I continued my rant. "I can't stand that! She won't even say hello or ask me how I'm doing. What the hell is that all about? I stopped bothering to answer her calls so she decided to block her number. And you know what Jeff? When I don't answer she doesn't leave a message Now, that's some deviant shit."

Thanksgiving dinner was ready two hours later than I had planned and Winston and Mark were no-shows, but Anthony came on time and an unexpected highlight was the arrival of Metisse and her daughter Tiffany. I hadn't seen Metisse for months but we comfortably got into our usual habit of reminiscing about the good times we always had together. Neil was happy because there was turkey in the oven and stopped by the kitchen regularly to see how he could help. Taylor had my back and was helping with food prep and cleanup while Jerry was happy in front of the TV flipping between football games.

More people were arriving as the pies went into the oven, and Metisse's mom, Sandra, and her son Christopher came just as we were close to sitting down. Aunt Sandra and I had gotten very close over the past twelve years and I had never forgotten the love and acceptance she showed Jeff and me when we were kids. Christopher was twenty-one now and he and Taylor began talking and catching up on news of mutual friends. Moments later Jeff and his wife Renee arrived with our birth mother. Aunt Sandra let them in while Taylor was bringing the food out, and I could hear Jeff announcing himself in the loud playful way he always did. Then he proceeded to announce the two people who were with him. I guess I wasn't surprised that Doretha had enlisted him to be her transportation service. But nothing could ruin my good feelings about having so many people together in the house again on this important holiday.

Normally, we would say a prayer together before the food was served, but this year Doretha had her own idea. Grabbing the center of attention, she casually reached into her purse, pulled out her Bible, and aimed it at me without saying a word. I tried hard to keep from rolling my eyes, and then she announced, "I want you to read this," while pointing her finger toward an open page. I didn't reach out to take the book, and she again motioned to the open page and repeated, "I want you to read this." I smiled my most gracious smile and asked Jeff to read it in my place. At one time Jeff had contemplated becoming a minister and was well-versed in the scriptures. He gladly read the preselected scripture in his most pastoral voice. I knew that although Doretha had lost this round, she had no intention of giving up. She was on a mission of some kind.

Jeff began the table conversation by recalling a situation that had recently happened to him. Everyone listened intently as they ate and he quoted someone's comment which included the word *FUCK*. The story wasn't nearly as exciting as what happened next. As soon as that word left my brother's mouth, our birth mother — sitting right next to him — dropped her fork loudly and jerked away from the table as if Jeff's words were a bolt of lightning striking the plate in front of her. We had never seen her so animated. Jeff was clueless because he had been concentrating on telling the story, and the whole thing played like an overdramatized scene from a bad play. Everyone at the table burst into laughter, especially me. I teased Jeff, "This time it was you who said the curse word that broke the camel's back." In the past, Doretha had made a point of calling me out for cursing in her presence. Her customary retort for my cursing was, "You act just like your father."

Caught off guard, Jeff nevertheless rolled with the general laughter. But Doretha sat motionless in her seat with her face scrunched up as if she had eaten something disgusting. I looked over at Jerry and Taylor, amused that they were for the first time witnessing their grandmother's manipulative antics. She continued to sit frozen with this expression for at least three more minutes before continuing to eat.

By the time everyone had finished first and second helpings followed by plenty of dessert, an hour had passed. One-by-one, all the males except Chris excused themselves into the other room either to talk or watch TV. Chris and Taylor stayed seated at the table and Doretha sat on the other side of Renee separated by the empty chair where Jeff had sat. There was a moment of silence when no one said a word. Then Doretha took the opportunity to leap into the silence.

"L-i-i-s-s-a." She drawled. Surprised, I quickly looked her way and answered, "Yes?"

She repeated my name once more as if to assure herself that she had not only my attention but Renee's, Aunt Sandra's, Taylor's and Christopher's as well.

"L-i-i-s-s-a," she repeated for the third time. I sat forward to show I was listening. Then she began motioning with her hands while talking as if she were trying to pull a sentence out of her head. She struggled to get out these words, "Lisa, you don't …you don't… you don't…"

Watching her, I thought: *What the hell is this all about? She never says anything meaningful to me privately so what is she desperately trying to ask me here at the dinner table in front of people? Must be a damn set-up.* Finally, I just jumped in and said, "I don't what? … like you?

"Yes!" she exclaimed as if I had gotten a test question right. Then she repeated the question without the stammering. "You don't like me, do you?

I felt the adrenaline kick in as I thought: *No, she is NOT sitting at my damn dinner table trying to start some shit! She's trying to get a rise out of me by catching me off guard with this inappropriate stuff and trying to make points with her audience. Hell, I should be asking her that question. I'm not gonna do it though.*

"You want to know if I like you? I can honestly say that I don't dislike you," was my reply.

She set her mouth to say what came next and chimed in before I finished my sentence, "That doctor was right. When I came back to DC from Ohio, I went to a psychiatrist to talk about you and he told me that you were not going to talk to me. He said that the boys would, but because you are a girl you wouldn't like me. I went to him after I went to that place to see you and you didn't want to talk to me. He was right because you never do like Jeffrey does."

"No, I don't do like Jeffery does because I'm Lisa." I knew she was talking about the time she dropped in on me at Independent Living and demanded to see me. When she showed up unannounced I told Mrs. Clarke I didn't feel like talking to her. After all, it had been more than four years since I had even heard from her. And suddenly she wanted to claim her rights as my mother. No way! But Mrs. Clarke told me not to be impolite that way, and out of respect for her, I agreed to talk to my birth mother for a half hour.

Doretha just kept talking. She said my four brothers still liked her and didn't have any problems with her. My thoughts were racing now: *Bullshit! That's what you think! And believe me, there's no way in the world that I would give you a chance to treat me the way you've treated them in the past.*

Taylor, Christopher and Renee uncomfortably began clearing the table and tidying up the kitchen. Doretha had a smile on her face now and I sensed that she was enjoying the moment. She liked seeing me squirming around her provocative words. I guess she figured she was proving to the others that I wasn't as nice as they thought.

I began to speak slowly. "No, I don't dislike you. I just don't like or agree with the way you handled your responsibilities as a mother. As a mother of two children myself, I don't understand how you didn't do everything you could to keep your children. I would have fought for my children until the bitter end. And I would have done whatever I needed to do to make sure my children knew that I loved them and was constantly trying to get them back. I asked you for your side of the story at least four times over the years. I wanted you to tell me why you felt you had to give us up. I wanted to know why we were in foster care while you were still alive, still in DC. I wanted to know what happened to our family. I have heard so many stories about this, but never your side of it. Your answer — even when I was almost thirty— was always, 'Lisa, you're too young to understand.' That's when I told myself forget it, that I would never ask you again. And I haven't."

She never blinked an eye as she counterpunched, "Well I had five children and I don't remember you asking me that."

"Now that's what I mean," I said. "It wouldn't matter how many children I had, I would have fought to the bitter end with everything I had to get every one of them back." I refrained from continuing with what I was thinking: *Bullshit! You can remember going to see a psychiatrist when I was nineteen years old but you don't remember me ever asking you that same question all those times. And you claim to be an Ordained Minister. Child, please!*

The pleasure I had heard in her voice when she thought she was in control of the conversation had faded. She looked at Aunt Sandra who had never left my side at the table and suddenly said, "Oh, I remember you. You're her friend's mother. I remember you."

"Yes, I'm Metisse's mother. I've known Lisa since she was 12 years old. She and Jeffrey used to come to my house almost every day. She even stayed with us for a while."

Thank goodness, Aunt Sandra had lowered the tension by joining the conversation. I was feeling much better now and, laughing, added, "We used to come over and play video games and eat up all your snacks."

At forty-six years old, I watched the stranger who gave birth to me sitting on the other side of my dinner table and saw something I had never before understood. For all those years I had been trying to put together a puzzle but now I saw there were so many missing pieces that there could never be any logical picture. The hopeful blinders that I had been wearing since my youth — the ones that made me think that there might be some reasonable explanation for why our mother had rejected my brothers and me — were now torn away and the truth was being revealed. She herself probably had no idea. She just didn't get the whole motherhood thing.

Foolishly she had thrust herself into the spotlight at my table thinking she could manipulate everyone into feeling sorry for her. How odd it was that she thought that confronting me in this manner would somehow bring me into line. That she could say these things in front of an audience who were near and dear to me and somehow get them on her side. She wanted to tame me into submission. She didn't understand anything. She had quit being a mother long ago but had no clue how earthshattering that was for her children. Apparently it wasn't earthshattering for her.

The woman my brothers referred to as "our mother" thought that she could somehow convince me that she wore the title "Mother" with some understanding of its actual meaning. She gave birth to me, but that is all. She would never know me as more than the name she had given me or the generic title "daughter." She was not even slightly interested in me or what my life had been after her decision to give me up into the care of strangers. She had no clue that eventually I might have come to care about her in some way if only she had taken me into her confidence and shared with me some of the truth of her story, in the process revealing even some minute level of emotion or pain she herself might have felt. Her attempt to explain her actions with the words, "I had five" said a lot about her. We were five objects that she could give away, forget about and then revisit once or twice a year or whenever there was something she wanted or whenever she thought she should remind us that SHE was our mother. When we five were in foster care, she understood it was her obligation to show up to court, and somehow that morphed into her feeling that she was entitled to continue exerting control over us. She came to court, didn't she? Fulfilled her obligation. That meant she was our mother. We were hers whenever she wanted to visit.

History has taught me that slave women whose children were torn from their arms by their masters fought to near death, were brutally whipped, and often risked death to catch a mere glimpse of their lost offspring. Those slave women possessed powerful, loving attachments to their children long after they themselves had been taken away to become slaves. Those mothers dearly loved their children despite the distance and yearned to let them know they had a living mother who wanted to know them, to touch them, to be in their presence.

I saw that the woman across the table was only looking for a spot in center stage, bathed in the spotlight of a tragedy she did not, could not feel. Was there no remorse, no acknowledgement of poor judgment, no mental illness? Whatever happened, it was someone else's fault, maybe even her children's. Had we disappointed her in some way? That saintly finger of hers always pointed in every direction but her own. It aimed toward our father, our foster parents, the social workers, the psychiatrists, our lawyers, her lawyers, the judge, the schools — oh, there were plenty of others for her to blame. After all, she had done everything she could, hadn't she?

As a child, I wanted to know about her. I asked myself in what way was she sick? Had she completed high school? Had she ever worked and had she ever had an occupational skill? Did she love her husband? Why was being an ordained minister on a piece of paper more important to her than taking care of her five children? Her self-absorbed saintly persona had always made me sick to my stomach.

Some people have said to me, "Lisa, you have to respect your mother for giving birth to you."

To those people I have said, "Who wants to be born without a caring mother? It's like being born in a petri dish."

Some people have even told me that I was lucky my life was so hard because it made me who I am today. Now that is some strange logic. Should I be grateful for getting physically, sexually and mentally abused and neglected because these things made me the woman I am today? The fact is, I am a true exception to the rule. Most people who have these experiences *and* a living, breathing mother who *could* have loved and taken care of them do not turn out very well. People who say these things, those defenders of the woman across from me — who I resemble physically in such an eerie way — have not experienced the miracle of motherhood themselves. If they had, they might not feel the way they do.

I got up from the dinner table that evening feeling a new energy. What started out to be a bad situation ended better than I could have imagined. Somehow a weight had been lifted off me. I guess I needed that conversation despite how and where it happened. I hugged everyone goodbye *including* our birth mother. When I hugged my sister-in-law Renee, she leaned to my ear and whispered, "You did very well, Lisa."

Relieved that I didn't come off too messed up I whispered my thanks for her understanding. Aunt Sandra was next. She said, "I'll talk to you soon Lisa and I just want you to know that I thought you handled that whole situation very well. I'm proud of you." After everyone had made their exit and the door closed, Taylor stood next to me and said, "You did good, Mom." Those words from a daughter to her mother were the greatest prize of all.

Epilogue

For many years I tried to avoid even thinking about my past. I marched forward trying my best to evolve into a completely different person and chose not to feel sorry for myself. Writing this book has forced me to explore my past. I thought I was okay but now realize I wasn't, at least not when I started writing the book. When I turned twenty and was no longer a ward of the court, I felt I now owned myself. I joined the Navy, got married and had children. But, underneath the white uniform, the wedding dress, and the boxing gear I was still the same person. I didn't like her. I thought she was weak because she didn't speak up for herself or fight when it counted. I wanted to believe that God would eventually allow me to wake up one day as someone different, someone better.

Writing this book has taken me on a difficult emotional journey. There were moments when I doubted I could finish it because the memories became so vivid, so present and terrifying that I was reliving the moments, smelling the smells, tasting the air, unable to escape the past. Eventually I'd have to stop writing and thinking about the book. Several times I needed a reset. Friends and family frequently asked if I had finished my book. "Oh, I'm still working on it." I told them with forced cheer. But for real, I was going through some serious changes. I would cry, shake, throw up and find myself wanting to seek out and confront those people, including my birth mother, who had hurt my brothers and me. I confess that I wanted vengeance.

The cathartic tears never scared me during this journey. I had learned through many years of therapy that they were important to the process of healing. As much as I hated mentally having to revisit the likes of Mama Graves, Mama Wooten, Lovey Lomax and Ms. McLeach and the rest, the process helped free me from their psychological bondage. I no longer experience the dull ache in my stomach that turns into a lump in my throat and rises into fury at the top of my skull. Experiencing that pain always incited feelings of disorganized violence quite unlike the organized violence of boxing. Going through this writing process has freed me more than my formal emancipation from the foster system did. I hope it has been the ultimate release.

While I know that there have been many people who have gone through foster care unscathed and become productive, grounded citizens, I also know that there are far more who have not. And I am all too aware that there are people who make generalizations about former fosters like, "Oh, she is a whore, he is a drug addict, she is gay, she is psycho, he is a thief, they went to jail, they are dumb… because they were in foster care." When people call me the exception to the rule because I have become a person they think of as normal and upstanding, I think to myself how hard it has been for me to become — by any means necessary — what they now see as an exception to the foster child norm.

My by-any-means-necessary attitude was all about survival. There are normal people like me who happened to have been foster children through no fault of their own, and unfortunately resorted to unsuitable coping mechanisms in order to survive. I want to say to my little sisters and brothers who are still in foster care: *If you are in a good home with a foster parent or parents who genuinely care about you, the best advice I can give you is to stay there as long as you can. Accept their goodness without guilt or regret. If you are able to make it back home to your families, thank God and never forget those people who looked out for you before you got there.*

I want to say to those little sisters and brothers who have been unlucky in their placement and have foster parents who are the problem rather than a solution: *stay calm. There are ways to protect yourself without being afraid. Fear turns into anger, depression, sadness, and all sorts of negativity that is hard to lose. So be brave, be sure to report all acts of violence, and most of all, be Too Fierce.*

Acknowledgements

In the three years it has taken me to recall and compile memories from my childhood and intertwine them with the story of the challenging journey through my boxing career, I have gone through an emotional transformation of the best sort. It has not been easy, and quite frankly, at times it has been devastating. The conjuring up of old pains I swore to never revisit along with those pleasant memories of people and places I have since reacquainted my-self with is what started the healing process of my heart.

The people who somehow emerged as puzzle pieces fitting perfectly into this phase of my life made the dream of writing my story possible. Dr. Matthew Petti, my English Professor from the University of the District of Columba gave me the courage to tell my story in all its raw truth. Matt, your stimulating writing assignments and your encouragement for my efforts led me here. To Tansy Blumer, my editor, I know that if it were not for you I would still be walking around saying, "I really want to write my story." You are so dear to me. You have been my editor, sounding board, therapist, and appreciative audience for whenever I felt the urge to get up to show you a boxing move, the way I rolled my eyes at eight years old or mimicked one of the colorful characters in my gym. You are the real deal, and a real friend. Thank you. To Neil, my wonderful husband who has been by rock solid supporter throughout this trip and has graced me with the ultimate compliment, "Artist", thank you. And to my children Gerald and Taylor, thank you for being so understanding while I was on this journey. Taylor, you and your Stevie impression, "still working on that novel?" helped me laugh at myself. Jerry, your cool, just-get-it-done attitude made me work even harder. You two are all a mother could ask for. Thank you all for having my back.